German Dramatists

OF THE 19TH CENTURY

By

FRIEDRICH WILHELM KAUFMANN

Essay Index Reprint Series

originally published by

LYMANHOUSE

BOOKS FOR LIBRARIES PRESS
FREEPORT, NEW YORK

First Published 1940
Reprinted 1970

INTERNATIONAL STANDARD BOOK NUMBER
0-8369-1578-X

LIBRARY OF CONGRESS CATALOG CARD NUMBER:
72-108641

PRINTED IN THE UNITED STATES OF AMERICA

PREFACE

IT is the chief duty of the teacher of literature to discover for his students and to communicate to them the living values in creative writing. In the opinion of the author of this treatise, the surest approach to these values is through a study of the problems which confronted the writer and his times and which moved him to artistic expression. It is the purpose of this book to search out and to clarify the problems which occupied the minds of the chief German dramatists of the period from 1800 to 1890. A chapter on Ibsen has been added because in his social dramas he is under the influence of the German tradition and because these dramas had a far-reaching influence on the later development of the German drama. Although the several authors are treated individually and in separate chapters, the whole German dramatic production of the nineteenth century may be considered as a single unit, for all of it proceeds from the same idealistic point of view and tends in its development toward a realistic-naturalistic conception. In order to clarify this general trend, there is given a sketch of the philosophical tendencies of the time, with especial emphasis on the changing conception of man.

It may, and probably will, be objected that this book is based on an "academic illusion"—a preconceived theory. It must be admitted, however, that it is humanly impossible to give a systematic presentation of any sort without an underlying philosophy, whether or not the author is aware of it, and that even the apparently most objective and factual presentation is based on a philosophical theory, namely, the empirical. One may accept or reject the existential point of view outlined in the introductory chapter and still admit its value as a working hypothesis. The author's only concern is that literature should be conceived of not as a manufactured product of reason, but as an outgrowth of the artist's serious struggle with the problems which beset him and his time.

This study is not based on a primary acquaintance with existential philosophy; rather, the author's existential views were developed in connection with his literary investigations. The author is, however, greatly indebted for the clarification of his views to Heidegger's *Sein und Zeit*.* It may be of benefit to those with less philosophical training,

iii

however, to begin their reading with the chapters on the individual dramatists and to return to the chapters on philosophy at a later point of their studies.

The book has grown out of courses in German literature given by the author at the German School of Middlebury College, at Smith College, and at Oberlin College. Its appearance is largely due to the encouragement of the author's friend, Ernst Feise, of the Johns Hopkins University, whose generous help and friendly criticism have made the completion of the work possible. For valuable suggestions and criticism the author is also deeply indebted to Professors T. M. Campbell of Northwestern University and Martin Schütze of the University of Chicago, to his Oberlin colleagues, Mrs. A. B. Harroun, Mr. J. W. Kurtz, and Miss Marjorie Lawson, and to Miss Eleanor Oldenbourg.

To the following the author wishes to acknowledge especial indebtedness for their suggestive interpretation of the German drama:

H. A. Korff, *Geist der Goethezeit.* Leipzig. Vol. I, 1927; Vol. II, 1930.

Gerhard Fricke, *Gefühl und Schicksal bei Heinrich v. Kleist.* Berlin, 1929.

Joachim Müller, *Grillparzers Menschenauffassung.* Weimar, 1934.

T. M. Campbell, *Life and Works of Friedrich Hebbel.* Boston, 1918.

Paul Bekker, *Richard Wagner: His Life and His Work.* New York, 1925.

Hermann J. Weigand, *The Modern Ibsen; a Reconsideration.* New York, 1925.

Halvdan Koht, *The Life of Ibsen.* New York, 1931.

F. W. K.

*First published in the *Jahrbuch für Philosophie und phänomenologische Forschung,* 1926. Cf. the article on "The Value of Heidegger's Analysis of Existence" in *Modern Language Notes* XLVIII (1933), pp. 487 ff.

CONTENTS

GERMAN DRAMATISTS
OF THE NINETEENTH CENTURY

CHAPTER I

INTRODUCTION

ROMANTICISTS have sought to explain literature as the product of genius; "true-to-life" critics have conceived it to be an artistic imitation of nature; Freudians have thought of it as regressive or substitute reaction. If for the romanticist and the naturalist it is a mere by-product of life, the psychoanalyst, at least, sees literature in its functional relation to life. In spite of the one-sidedness of the Freudian theory, we can agree with its general assumption that literature, like philosophy and art, is an expression of the "problematic situation"* of human life, and that its function is to attempt a solution for the problems with which man is confronted. For human life is fundamentally problematic: simply because man has the ability to transcend the actual situation of the moment. The animal follows its impulse and tries to appease an instinctive urge at the same moment in which it arises, but man has the power to control the impulses of his instinctive nature and to anticipate the ultimate realization of other aims, comparing them in value with those of the actual impulses. In this comparison he becomes aware of the limitations of his physical nature, of the irresistibility of his instincts, of the restrictions forced upon his activity by his symbolic nature, and, finally, by the inescapable fact of death. Man's particular fate is that these limitations are consciously experienced with ever-recurring anxiety. This is the price he pays for his ability to transcend the actual moment and for the freedom of choice which is thereby essentially his. Within the finite situation in which destiny of birth has placed him, he has a virtually infinite freedom of choice. In the realm of thought and wish, this freedom is absolute, but in the realm of reality, it is subject to man's general and specific limitations. Thus, the infinite potentialities of the realm of thought and wish conflict with the determining circumstances of the

*"Situation" refers to the rootedness of man in a definite historical moment, with its particular economic, sociological, political, and intellectual structure, on the one hand, and its standards and habits of behavior, which influence and determine his decisions, on the other. This situation becomes problematic through the ability of man to detach himself from these determining factors, to examine the trends of his time, and to let his actions be guided by motives which transcend the moment. This problematic situation is called "existential" because it is the essential trait which distinguishes man's existence from that of the animal.

[1]

moment, and it is in this conflict that man realizes his problematic situation.

Man realizes that most of his actions are neither mere reactions to instinctive impulses nor genuine responses to a given situation but are determined by the traditions and conventions of his environment. He seldom takes the trouble to inquire into the real nature of the situation and often is too cowardly to assume the responsibility for a judgment which is contrary to prevailing opinion; he is even more reluctant to face the consequences of an independent action. The average individual, therefore, never gains a deeper insight into the existential situation, because his insight is obstructed by prejudice, by the judgments of others formed under different circumstances and laid down in conventional rules and attitudes for which he himself assumes no responsibility.

The unprejudiced individual tries to experience immediately the situation and to be unbiased in his judgment and his decisions. He is "open" to genuine experience; he is "original" inasmuch as he penetrates the surface of preconceived judgments and decisions to their origin, in spite of all the obstacles erected by former experience between man and men and between man and things.

The real artist and philosopher is original in this sense. He is a man who is able to experience the problematic situation of life, who desires to establish immediate contact with men and things, yet who discovers that he is separated from them by an almost impenetrable maze of conventions and traditions. Art, therefore, even naturalistic art—insofar as it deserves to be called art—is neither mere reproduction of an object of nature, nor a beautiful or effective shaping of an indifferent subject matter, nor mere esthetic play detached from any reality. Even this naturalistic art expresses the experience that reality permits no active and meaningless participation in solving the most urgent problems. It is in the last analysis an expression of the attempt to establish an immediate contact with the peculiar problem confronting man in his particular situation and to find a genuine response to it. Art is the result of a conflict between a stereotyped pattern of life and the self with its desire to penetrate to the essence of existence.

Literature is the author's attempt to reveal and to solve the problem of his particular situation in the medium of language which appeals to emotion and to intellect alike; it is a confession of the conflict between an inherited mass of pre-formed judgments and conventional attitudes, on the one hand, and the independent reaction against this inherited order, on the other. Inasmuch as convention is but a set of decisions, judgments, and attitudes which originated in the past and which have lost their value as an adequate response to a given situation, and inasmuch as the situation of man is subject to constant change and therefore requires a constant reconsideration, literature takes on a temporal aspect. Literature arises out of the actual problem of the moment; this problem is to be solved by a response which is found in the conflict between tradition and convention, on the one hand, and the necessity of doing justice to ever changing circumstances, on the other; it is a conflict between the past and a future in which the immediate contact with situations is yet to be realized. Literature is thus a function of life, a means of finding the proper response to the problematic situation in which every man is placed by reason of his birth, a response to an historical moment which contains rigid norms of the past and hopes for a better and more integrated order in the future.

Great authors have repeatedly recognized and stated this functional significance of their work. When Goethe calls his works fragments of a great confession, he means to say that he has risen above the chaos of meaningless and momentary existence through the revelations of his mistakes; his work is for him the salvation of his personal substance through the pro-duction (*pro-ducere*, bring forth) of a deeper essence, which is not content with passively yielding to impulses affecting only the surface of the ego. Schiller points to the functional significance of literary creation in his essay *Über naive und sentimentalische Dichtung* when he considers the conflict between nature and art—the artificiality of the contemporary stage of civilization—as the cause of *sentimentalische Dichtung*. He feels, with Rousseau, that civilization obstructs the natural relation between man and things. Hebbel, in the preface to *Maria Magdalene*, sees in the drama a decisive factor for the solution of the conflicts of the time: "The function of dramatic art is to help end the worldwide historical process of our times, which does not tend to overthrow the existing political, religious, and moral institutions of humanity, but to give them a better foundation, rather, therefore, to secure them from overthrow."* The expresison "to give . . . a better foundation" *(tiefer begründen)* implies, too, as will later be demonstrated in Hebbel's works, that tradition tends to divorce man from immediate contact with his environment and that a new, deeper, and more vital relation to existence must be found.

It is, therefore, an essential task of literary analysis to study the

*Translated by T. M. Campbell, *Hebbel, Ibsen and the Analytic Exposition*. Heidelberg, 1922, p. 91.

problematic situation to which the artistic product is a response and to interpret the author's work in its relation to the conventionally regulated, undiscriminating, and ambiguous surface attitude of ordinary men. The artist is a man who, because of a higher sensibility or because of extraordinary circumstances of his life, is more exposed to conflicts than the average man. In many cases, he is predestined for this experience by the divergence in the temperaments of his parents. The father often represents a pedantic, conservative, rational type; through his professional activity a certain attitude and view of life may often be imposed upon him. The mother, however, in her home environment, may express herself more freely and be more apt to represent the imaginative, irrational type. Goethe's Xenia:

> Vom Vater hab' ich die Statur,
> Des Lebens ernstes Führen,
> Vom Mütterchen die Frohnatur
> Und Lust zu fabulieren,

is the clearest statement of this influence of inborn or early acquired traits on the artistic disposition. From early childhood on, the artist's life appears as a struggle against the suppression of his own natural relation to things and to men; he fights against the restraint placed upon him in school, in his profession, and through such institutions as the church, marriage, and state autocracy, which he believes have become lifelessly traditional or conventional; thus he strives for a more natural or a more personally responsible reaction to the problems of life.

Since man, however, is not an isolated individual, but essentially a being in an active and reactive relation to his environment, his personal problems reflect the problems of his time. The author, therefore, becomes the "secret partner to the silent brother of all things," and the "point where the energies of the time tend to balance each other,"* or to use Hebbel's words:

> Dem Dichter ist es an- und eingeboren,
> Dasz er sich lange in sich selbst versenkt,
> Und, in das innre Labyrinth verloren,
> Des Äuszeren der Welt erst spät gedenkt;
> Und dennoch hat ihn die Natur erkoren,
> Zu zeigen, wie sich dies mit dem verschränkt,
> Und es in klarem Bilde darzustellen,
> Wie beide sich ergänzen und erhellen.†

---

*Hugo von Hofmannsthal, "Der Dichter und diese Zeit" in *Die prosaischen Schriften* (Berlin, 1907), I, 27.

†Dedication to *Maria Magdalene.*

The author's struggle for a more genuine and essential response to the problematic situation of his time expresses itself in a re-examination of the traditionally accepted views, which disturb the sympathetic relations between men. He becomes the champion of tolerance and humaneness, or of the emancipation of women, or of social justice, or other life issues. In his work he reflects the conflicts of his time and contributes to their solution without, however, making the change of actual circumstances the major object of his work. His relation to life is that of esthetic remoteness; he creatively visualizes the problematic situation, but a relative inability to immediately influence or change this situation may even be considered an important factor in his esthetic expression.

In his preface to *Maria Magdalene*, Hebbel enumerates three types of drama: first, a drama which is "to make clear the existing state of man and the world in relation to the Idea, or to that moral center which conditions everything, and which we must assume in the organization of things, if only for the sake of their self-preservation;"* second, a partial and national drama; and third, an individual and subjective drama. Hebbel himself, however, considers only the first type as first-class literature. From our point of view, we may say that all three aspects are to be found in a drama of high artistic value, the word "national" being taken in the somewhat wider sense as reflecting the specific historical situation. For true literary art, especially in the drama and the novel, is always concerned with the ego and its environment simultaneously, and it always reflects the "existing state of man and the world in relation to the Idea." Any such classification as that made by Hebbel could only take into account the relative emphasis which these aspects receive in the visualization of the complex problem. Accordingly, the differentiation between historical literature and *Zeit-Dichtung*, which is often made, concerns only its external form, and never the inner attitude of the author. Historical literature is essentially literature concerned with problems of the present. These problems are, however, projected into the past, thereby providing a certain remoteness from actuality and producing an effect of more universal validity. This projection makes it easier for the reader or the spectator to free himself from his own prejudices and those of his environment and thus to penetrate the surface of life in the attempt to arrive at the essence of his situation. The historical content is not merely the subject matter, it is itself a symbol for the idea of the work of art. The author selects this or

*Campbell, *op. cit*, p. 86.

[5]

that particular historical event or character because it is especially suitable as an adequate symbol for the problematic situation of his individuality at a particular point in the historical development "of the existing state of man and the world." An interpretation, therefore, which considers only the subject matter and its esthetic presentation is bound to remain superficial and to miss the real intention of the artist.

If we assume that literature in its highest form is the expression of the author's effort to arrive at a solution of his problematic situation, we may expect that his work will show a gradual approach to a solution. Consistency of development, of course, cannot be formulated as a law; the author may well have to make several attempts to solve his problem, but these would be a genuine, sincere expression of his striving. A careful analysis of an author's complete work, however, betrays often enough a certain logic in its development, which may be interpreted as an approach to the solution of the problem. On the whole, it may be said that the development proceeds between two poles, with the conception of life as a more or less blind fate at one end, and as a meaningful order at the other. For literary creation begins as a liberation from an oppressing and suppressing tradition and tends towards a more active and essential relation to the world. From this it follows that the common judgment that one work of an author shows a less satisfactory solution than another is but a truism. A difference between the individual works should rather be taken as a criterion of true art, inasmuch as the gradual approach to a more satisfactory solution reveals the sincerity of the author's striving. For literary interpretation, therefore, a work less perfect esthetically may be more valuable than one of greater perfection, written at a period when the author has reached the solution of his existential problem as far as he is able, and when he writes merely for the sake of writing, instead of from inner compulsion.

Chapter II

THE HERITAGE OF THE EIGHTEENTH CENTURY

HISTORY is a continuity of change; only the impossibility of apprehending the variations in an organic whole forces us to divide the development into periods, and to attribute to each period certain features which are characteristic for this and for no other period. A more detailed analysis, however, reveals that such a classification has to take into account an overlapping of subsequent trends of thought and artistic expression. This is due to the fact that an independent reaction to the problematic situation is always the privilege of a select few, whose opinion only slowly and gradually becomes the opinion of a wider group; that it takes even longer before it reaches the mass of the people, in the deteriorated form of a rigid tradition, which completely lacks the immediacy of first experience. Thus, it is obvious that at any given time we should find, besides the dominant trend of thought, several strata of more or less normalized and petrified thought of preceding periods, which have the double function of stabilizing the life of human society and of causing the reaction which is responsible for the progress of life in all its higher forms. This stratification must be considered in the interpretation of literary works; the more so, since it is not limited to human society as a whole but affects the very core of the individual personality.*

Accordingly, in the Germany of the nineteenth century the intellectual tendencies of the eighteenth century still exerted their influence, and the generation which came to the fore around the year 1800 had to examine their validity and acceptability before it was able to formulate its own expression and view of life. Apart from the Christian religion, it was especially the rationalism of the eighteenth century which, in its popularized form, determined the thinking of the educated classes and was largely responsible for the general attitude towards life of the bourgeoisie. According to the philosophy of the period of Enlightenment, the world is a rationally ordered system. There is nothing senseless and radically unreasonable in it; that which appears to be so, either has a

*This point will be given a more detailed analysis in the discussion of Ibsen's dramatic work.

[7]

hidden meaning or becomes meaningful as an instrument to a higher end. This end can be revealed by a careful analysis of things and events and their relation to other things and events. The particular can be subsumed under a general rule, and through this subordination an increasingly clear understanding is gained of the meaning and value of the particular which, in turn, leads to a better comprehension of the inherent law governing the same particular. In this way, events become calculable and controllable. It is, therefore, the main function of human reason to contribute to the unification of the world view through consistent application of the category of causality.

This rationalism is essentially concerned with life in this world, and accordingly man is the supreme end of the cosmic order. His worldly happiness is the moral aim, and the moral system is mainly a guide to this aim. Virtues are means to a happy existence and to progress toward the perfection of man. Rational enlightenment is a moral duty, because, according to this philosophy, man can be virtuous only if his reasoning is not obscured by emotions.

In its later phase of a more complete detachment from the religious and Christian order, Enlightenment becomes the expression of a superficial worldliness, or a self-complacency and self-sufficiency which merges with bourgeois convention and tradition, and by its commonplace norms tends to inhibit the development of personality. The rationalism of Enlightenment emancipated man from a theological interpretation of life and supplied the means for a systematic conquest of the world. After the analytic and causal principles had been established, and the enthusiasm over the first technical inventions had subsided, and after reason had begun to restrain life, the limitations of rationalism became evident: it failed as an explanation of irrational experience, of emotion, and of imagination.

The reaction against rationalism took the form of scepticism: could reason establish any universally valid truth? Is a rationally organized civilization a desirable development of mankind? Are the intellectual and cultural achievements of human reason values for which irrational values should be sacrificed? In his philosophical essays, Hume attacks the foundations of the rationalistic belief. He questions that there is anything like a human nature unaffected by the conditions of place and time and equipped with a definite and absolutely reliable basic knowledge, both theoretical and practical. He demonstrates that this belief is mere fiction and provides empirical evidence that human nature is in fact very far from being rationally organized, and that it is rather a

THE HERITAGE OF THE EIGHTEENTH CENTURY

chaos of conflicting instincts. Rousseau sees in the rationalist's complacence and contentment with acquired knowledge, as evidenced in the rationally refined conduct of life in his time, merely a deflection of man from his true self. Civilized man surrenders to superficial diversions because he is afraid of himself; he would despair if he realized his inner hollowness. Therefore Rousseau summons man to be himself again and return to his original nature.

Lessing's ideas, too, are deeply rooted in rationalism, but he finally rejects the rationalistic, static conception of the world in favor of a dynamic conception. For him there is no reason in the Enlightenment sense of a hypostatized power which hovers immovable and immutable over an ever changing world. Reason itself is for him immanent in the infinite evolution. His religious struggle is therefore directed against the rationalistic dilution of Christianity, as well as against dogmatic and authoritative belief. His God is no longer transcendent, as he was for Enlightenment thought; he is immanent in the process of the world. Lessing's literary criticism, his fight against Gottsched and against Gottsched's French models is a fight against rationalism in literature, a fight against rules and norms for the liberation of the genius who, through his work, creates his own rules and norms. Thus his main works do not illustrate rules, as one is led to believe by Lessing's own remarks but are the expression of his struggle against the heteronomous forces which restrained him and his contemporaries; his critical and dramatic works were essential factors in the regeneration of the mind through an intimate contact with life.

This critical reaction against rationalism was accompanied by the emotional revolt of the *Sturm-und-Drang* movement. Immediate concrete experience of life is the principal postulate of its adherents. Nature is no longer conceived of as a rationally ordered and essentially computable cosmos, but as a living and creative organism. The irrational faculties of emotion and imagination replace the rational categories. As an active and dynamic being, the adherent of *Sturm-und-Drang* feels himself to be one with nature and God. He is conscious of his role as creator of his poetic productions which make the one claim of being a vital expression of life itself. Action, passion, revolt against political, social, and religious norms and bonds are the characteristic expressions of this new vitality. But since this movement gained its main impetus from the antagonism to reason, its limitations were soon realized. Dynamic life can find its satisfaction only in the exhaustion of its infinite potentialities, which is, of course, impossible for a finite being like man,

[9]

whose infinite desires are restricted by the finiteness of his nature and thus become a source of continual disillusionment. Vitality divorced from reason finally becomes just as futile as reason became hollow in its isolation from irrational and vital experience.

Thus the *Sturm-und-Drang* problem is the problem of life itself, of energy without direction and without aim, unless one conceives of life in its totality as metaphysical energy, moving in a definite direction which is known to man. In any case, the final end of man remains unknown to him, and such a view can thus only temporarily satisfy him; it is really tolerable only for enthusiastic youth with its excessive vital energies. The passionate assertion of unrestrained life in the *Sturm-und-Drang* movement is, therefore, necessarily followed by a new attempt to find a purpose in life and to subordinate the irrational impulse of life to a higher principle. The conception of a chaotic order of life yields again to that of a cosmic order which gives man's existence a meaning by relating it to ideal and absolute values. Such an ethical principle can either be found by further developing the rationalistic view of life in a transcending order, or it can be derived from the monistic and vitalistic views of *Sturm-und-Drang*, so that the ethical principle is conceived as a force inherent in life itself.

The rational solution is attempted in the philosophical and poetic works of Kant and Schiller. Kant in his *Critique of Pure Reason* shares with *Sturm-und-Drang* the doubt in the power of reason to solve all problems of life, and he restricts its domain merely to the world of phenomena. He does not submit the creative mind to the category of causality, but neither does he ascribe to it any absolute validity. Accordingly, experience is not merely an impression on a passive human mind; it is rather the result of a factor outside of the individual consciousness and the active participation of this consciousness in categories and ideas. The empirical data are classified in space and time, and perception is transformed into knowledge proper through the application of the idea of causality. A greater spontaneity is attributed to practical reason. It aims at a complete liberation of man from the causality of instincts and foreign authority, when it is directed against conventional opportunism and rational subordination, but simultaneously also against the dissipation of *Sturm-und-Drang*. The decision with regard to the morality of an action is left to reason, which judges the value of the action by applying the universal principle of the categorical imperative: "Act in conformity with that maxim, and that maxim only, which you can at the same time will to be a universal law." This imperative is merely formal;

[10]

any content is deliberately omitted. The judgment on the merits of the practical case is left entirely to the individual. Through his decision man is to prove his dignity as a reasonable being in accordance with a variation of the categorical imperative: "Act so as to use humanity, whether in your own person or in the person of another, always as an end, never as merely a means." Man shall do his duty not for any personal advantage, but out of respect for himself as a representative of humanity; also in his contact with his fellow men, he shall respect the dignity of personality. To conform to this law as against the debasing tendencies of instinct alone is moral conduct. The realization and preservation of human dignity is for Kant the regulative principle of life. It is free from the rationalistic concern about human happiness, and it furnishes the impulse of life which emancipated itself in the *Sturm-und-Drang* period, with a new orientation towards an ideal aim.

Schiller's dramatic work is the expression of the same twofold endeavor, first to replace an egotistic and opportunistic bourgeois rationalism by a higher ethical principle and then to bring the vitality of *Sturm-und-Drang* under the control of the idea of ethical personality. He opposes to the pressure of his rationalistic environment the *Sturm-und-Drang* postulate of freedom from any authority, and ennobles this freedom in the moral idea of the dignity of human personality. In his first drama, *Die Räuber*, he revolts against the rationalistic regulation of human relations; the criminal's struggle against a rationally ordered society is presented here as the self-defense of a noble character against a demoralized environment. In *Wallenstein*, he continues this fight against rationalism by revealing the depravity of egotistic materialists like Octavio, Buttler, Terzky, and the emperor. At the same time, he subdues in the character of Wallenstein the *Sturm-und-Drang* type of noble criminal, who now fails because he is unable to accept a higher regulative principle for his action. In this way, Wallenstein, too, is involved in the catastrophe, from which neither the wicked nor the good can be saved. The trilogy is a negative vindication of the categorical imperative and its corollary, which demands a respect for the moral personality; a world in which egotism is made a universal law and in which man is considered only as a means for egotistic purposes, is irrevocably doomed. In *Maria Stuart* and even more in *Die Jungfrau von Orleans*, the ideal of the moral personality finds its most positive expression. Moral idealism becomes in these dramas an enthusiastic faith in the moral power of man to realize the highest dignity of man in himself and in mankind. The moral personality appears here in its sublimity, as

[11]

a conqueror of death. Only the egotistic and naturalistic realist, like Talbot, has to face death with despair and fatalism. For the idealist, however, death triumphantly assures the absolute value of the humanitarian principle.

For Kant and Schiller the world is essentially regulated by ideas which transcend the phenomenal world. Their world is dualistically divided into phenomenon and *das Ding an sich* (noumenon), into the realms of causality and teleology, of necessity and freedom, of realism and idealism. Whereas their world view remains under the influence of rationalism, Herder's and Goethe's views are more closely related to *Sturm-und-Drang* vitalism. Herder identifies the infinite world process with God, and the forms of nature are for him the expression of the divine. In a similar way, the divine is immanent in existence for Goethe. There is no dualistic division of the world for him; there is no exclusive antagonism in the cosmic order, which is essentially one; and the opposite extremes are interdependent poles. Nature develops through contraction and expansion. Contraction—concentration on one's own self—is the source of all egotism and evil, expansion and self-effusion, that of all goodness. In man, these two tendencies are combined:

> Genug, wenn nur anerkannt wird, dasz wir uns in einem Zustande befinden, der, wenn er uns auch niederzuziehen und zu drücken scheint, dennoch Gelegenheit gibt, ja zur Pflicht macht, uns zu erheben und die Absichten der Gottheit dadurch zu erfüllen, dasz wir, indem wir von einer Seite uns zu verselbsten genötigt sind, von der andern in regelmäszigen Pulsen uns zu entselbstigen nicht versäumen.*

Accordingly, Goethe's characters are not as sharply contrasted as Schiller's realists and idealists, whose traits would be incompatible if they were combined in the same character. Such characters, as Goethe's Pylades and Orestes, Antonio and Tasso, and even Mephistopheles and Faust, are, in the final analysis, impersonations of two opposite poles of the one *Urphänomen* (original phenomenon) man, and the higher type develops in contact with and in an inevitable antagonism to the lower type. The Evil One in *Faust*, for example, is not radically bad, but a promoter of goodness,

> die Kraft, die stets das Böse will und stets das Gute schafft.

The regulative idea is found in life itself: in the limitation of the species man and in the moral obligation to perfect one's individual potentialities.

*Goethe, *Dichtung und Wahrheit*, Buch 8.

It is because of this fact that Faust rises from an environment imbued with the rationalism and eudæmonism of the Enlightenment period, through a *Sturm-und-Drang* existence in which he tries to experience the whole of life with all its joys and hopes, with all its suffering and disillusionment, with all its guilt and error, to a life of responsibility and higher endeavor; to his very end, however, he is never satisfied. No universal law, such as that of the categorical imperative, leads him. He fulfills only his personal destiny and lives up to the idea of man as the Lord expected him to do when, in the *Prolog im Himmel*, he expresses his confidence in Faust's invincible striving. This idea is repeated again in the words of salvation sung by the angels at the end of the second part:

Wer immer strebend sich bemüht, Den können wir erlösen.

The philosophy of Enlightenment, in spite of all its worldliness, tried to support with rational proof the belief in immortality and in an absolute but personal God. Classical idealism had basically lost this belief and had tried to rescue the idea of the absolute as being the immanent force of nature, as being historical development, inner experience, or practical reason. Religious reverence, however, centers in the idea of humanity, and it is this idea from which all human action derives its meaning. It is the eternal value which, according to Kant's and Schiller's view, has an ideal existence in the statically and rationally conceived realm of noumenon and is at least partially realizable in man. Only in so far as the mere vision of the ideal can be considered as motivating the actions of man, is the idea of humanity dynamic. Goethe's conception of humanity is essentially dynamic and immanent: the idea of man manifests and unfolds itself in the individual man. Whereas the aim and the perfection of man is for Kant and Schiller moral goodness, Goethe finds them more in the realization of the human potentialities inherent in the individual. In every case, however, the classical idealistic order is attainable only by a never ending process of approximation, which can be realized only in an esthetic vision. The idealistic belief is essentially associated with the problematic tension between the highest belief and despair of the possibility of realizing the ideal. The idealistic belief can be saved only by an ever ready consciousness of the highest human values and an unyielding will to fight for their realization. It will influence the conduct only of those whose vision is capable of penetrating beyond the narrow boundaries of everyday reality and whose enthusiasm is great enough to attempt the impossible.

Goethe's conception of an immanent ideality was one way of bridging

[13]

the gap between the abstract realm of the idea and the concreteness of reality. This tendency is continued in the nineteenth century, but the idea gradually loses its universal validity in its transcendent as well as in its immanent form. It becomes a general metaphysical substratum which unfolds itself in concrete reality and guarantees a meaningful development. Reality and ideality, however, become identical, so that the realistic view may simply and almost imperceptibly be substituted for the idealistic view, as soon as any doubt with regard to the meaning and value of humanity arises.

CHAPTER III

THE CULMINATION OF IDEALISM IN THE EARLY NINTEENTH CENTURY

KANT's idealistic system maintains the antithesis between reality and ideality and that of the corresponding categories of necessity and freedom. It resolves this tension only in the domain of esthetics, where the finite can be used as a symbol for the infinite. Otherwise freedom remains a regulative idea, a continuous urge to transcend the realm of conditioned reality. Man strives towards the realization of the ethical idea or—with Goethe—towards the development of all the potentialities inherent in him, without ever being able to approach the ideal.

Romantic philosophy tries to carry the idealistic viewpoint to its logical end. The phenomenon which was for Kant only in part a product of creative reason becomes entirely an act of consciousness.

> Solange man den Gedanken von einem Zusammenhange unserer Erkenntnis mit einem Ding an sich, das, von ihr gänzlich unabhängig Realität haben soll, übrig läszt, wird der Skeptiker immer gewonnenes Spiel haben.

writes Fichte with regard to this problem in a letter addressed to Reinhold, in the year 1794. He removes the last reason for the dependence of consciousness upon an independently existing *Ding an sich*, by deriving all existence out of the activity of consciousness. Reason, which held its dominant position in Kant's system, is now replaced by the spontaneous activity of the mind.

> Das hervorbringende Ich darf ihm [dem Idealisten] weder ein Ding noch ein Sein bedeuten, darf kein 'Bestehendes' und nicht einmal ein 'Tätiges' genannt werden — das alles ist noch zu objektartig und seinem Wesen heterogen — , es ist vielmehr nur ein Tun, ein bestimmtes Handeln. Und der Sinn desjenigen Seins, welches die zusehende Intelligenz als ihr Wesen erfaszt, ist lediglich der dieses 'Handelns' selbst, nicht eines Handelnden hinter ihm.*

Prior to all existence as objective reality, prior to all non-ego, is the ego as pure activity. This ego is the active center out of which the diversity of reality is derived, and in relation to which alone there is any reality. Activity can only be displayed in a world of objects. The active ego,

---

*Cf. Nicolai Hartmann, *Die Philosophie des deutschen Idealismus.* 1. Teil. Berlin, 1923. p. 52 ff.

[15]

therefore, must establish an objective reality. This reality is not known first and then willed, as it still was in Kant's philosophical system, but is first willed, and only then does it become the object of perception and knowledge. The ego next feels itself limited by the object, and from this it derives its task of transmuting the objective non-ego into the ego, of transforming through constant activity a chaotic diversity into an integral whole. The practical ego represents chiefly this last stage of the metaphysical process, the transformation of the non-ego into the ego.

Consequently, freedom is for Fichte not actual freedom from determination by the object, but a challenge to realize this autonomy in the ego, to approach the ideal of pure activity. A deed is not good because it is in harmony with a principle or because it can be made a universal principle, as it is according to Kant's categorical imperative, but it is good as activity; lack of activity, indolent yielding to instincts or to any exterior motivation is immoral. A moral person, therefore, does not act in order to achieve an aim or for the sake of the feeling of happiness which accompanies the achievement. He wills to act for the sake of activity itself, incessantly striving to attain to the ideal of pure activity. In this striving the individual becomes the creator of the moral world order. He also determines the relation between individual and community. The individual who is truly moral in the Fichtean sense does not simply accept the laws of the community; he rather serves them truly by fulfilling the law of his own personality. In its contact with other individuals, the ego finds its essential task in harmonizing its own laws with the claims of others. In mutual recognition, in voluntary limitation of the separate spheres of freedom, originate the community and its laws as an expression of the active and autonomous will of the individuals concerned.

While Kant grew up in the rationalistic atmosphere of the period of Enlightenment, Fichte belongs to the *Sturm-und-Drang* generation. His philosophy, therefore, is not only a consistent evolution of Kant's criticism, especially that of the *Critique of Practical Reason,* but also a reaction of vitality against the rigidity which his generation felt to be inherent in the rationalistic system. This explains the activism which is equally as characteristic of his philoposhy as it is of his life. It also explains why his philosophy shows so much similarity with Goethe's views—the stress on activity, on the development of individual potentialities—in his endeavor not to suppress the subconscious and the irrational, but to assign it to its proper place in a consciously irrational order.

Fichte's system is essentially an ethical idealism. It undervalues nature in order to save the autonomy of the moral personality. Nature is for Fichte almost exclusively the material for the activity of the creative mind; it is a means for an ethical end. In a later form of the *Wissenschaftslehre*, Fichte's ego grows into the absolute mind, in which thinking and the existence of nature become identical; nature is the thought of the absolute Mind. The *pan-theos* is life and reason, the absolute and reasonable will.

While Fichte, in the development of his theories, penetrates deeper into the inner self, past the individual ego, until he discovers the absolute ego, Schelling proceeds in the opposite direction, out of and above the individual ego into the world of objects. The metaphysical principle which he assumes to explain the essence of nature is similar to that of Fichte, namely, a spiritual energy without a substratum, a pure will, which acts, however, in an objective reality outside of the ego. Fichte, in purely idealistic terms, explains nature as a creation of the activity of the ego, whereas Schelling's philosophical system is idealistic only in so far as its basic principle of explanation is mind; it is realistic in so far as he assumes an objectively existing reality. Nature, inorganic as well as organic, is life. In inorganic nature, life has degenerated into petrifaction; in its higher forms it strives towards consciousness. According to Schelling's *Untersuchungen über das Wesen der menschlichen Freiheit* of the year 1809, the evolutionary process is as follows: the origin of all existence is undetermined striving, unconscious will. The object of this will is identical with its subject, and, willing its own self, it creates reason as self-contemplation. The reciprocal relationship of unconscious will and self-contemplation is the cause of the world, which, in consequence of this origin, is divided between instinct and reason, between evil and good. The evolution of the world, however, has as its aim the establishment of the domination of reason in the universal will. The world is thus a progressive realization of intelligence, an evolutionary process of reason, in which the individual being is subordinated to the evolution of the whole and therefore has only transitory significance. The development of the world is the self-development of God.

Fichte had subordinated the world of objects to the mind. The only meaning he could attribute to this world lay in the fact that it furnished a goal for the moral striving of man; existence as such is imperfection and therefore subordinated to the ethical Ought. Consciousness is, except for the later form of the *Wissenschaftslehre*, severed from its existential basis, and the biogenetic order, according to which consciousness represents the last stage in the evolutionary process, is here

[17]

GERMAN DRAMATISTS OF THE NINETEENTH CENTURY

reversed. Schelling restores this order by deriving consciousness from nature, the unconscious mind, and by evolving both, nature and mind, out of the absolute. This absolute is the indifferent and the unknown, which in itself offers no explanation for the evolution of concrete reality.

At this point, Hegel continues and thus brings the idealistic system to its perfection. He ventures to analyze the absolute and to attribute to it those qualities which may explain the evolution of reality in its diversity and in its contradictions. At the same time, he saves the idealistic primacy of mind over matter, which in Schelling's system was threatened by the principle of the identity of nature and mind, without, however, reverting to Fichte's devaluation of nature. According to Hegel, the world is not perfect, but meaningful, for all reality is a manifestation of the absolute mind. This absolute mind, however, has not a static existence before any creation or evolution of this world; it is not the immovable first cause of all evolution, but evolution itself. The universe is the creative evolution of the absolute mind.

In this evolutionary process, every subsequent stage invalidates the preceding one; every stage has a positive value with regard to the preceding one, but is of negative value in comparison to the next following stage. All stages together constitute the evolutionary process. Everything, therefore, is true, valid, and reasonable in its proper place in the evolutionary process, but it becomes false, invalid, and unreasonable in the further evolution of the absolute mind whose unfolding is historical development. Thus, historical development proceeds as thesis and antithesis, each of which is reasonable and becomes unreasonable as the development continues. History, then, as the evolution of the absolute mind, is not reasonable in its final result, as in Schelling's system, but as a whole.

Es hat sich aus der Betrachtung der Weltgeschichte selbst zu ergeben, dasz es vernünftig in ihr zugegangen sei, dasz sie der vernünftige, notwendige Gang des Weltgeistes gewesen, des Geistes, dessen Natur zwar immer eine und dieselbe ist, der aber in dem Weltdasein diese seine eine Natur expliziert.

As a reasonable process, history does not contain any contingency. It cannot be explained causally, as conditioned by "external necessity." It can only be understood teleologically, as progressing towards an aim and an objective finality—the self-comprehension and self-realization of the objective mind. History is the process of self-perfection of the absolute mind. Since this mind is essentially freedom, world history is the progressive evolution of freedom.

Die Orientalen haben nur gewuszt, dasz einer frei, die griechische und römische Welt aber, dasz einige frei sind, ... wir aber wissen, alle Menschen an sich, das heiszt, der Mensch sei frei.

Since every historical phenomenon is the product of the evolutionary process of the absolute mind, the latter manifests itself in the individual as well as in the state. The national spirit—*Volksgeist*—is the objective mind in its historical individualization. The individual and the national spirit are correlative in their existence. Even the most outstanding historical personality is but an exponent of his people and thereby an exponent of the universal mind.

Dies sind die groszen Menschen in der Geschichte, deren eigne partikulare Zwecke das Substantielle enthalten, welches Wille des Weltgeistes ist . . . . die aus sich zu schöpfen scheinen, und deren Taten einen Zustand und Weltverhältnisse hervorgebracht haben, welche nur i h r e Sache und i h r Werk zu sein scheinen.

However optimistic Hegel's system, with its belief in a progressive realization of reason and freedom, may be, it is, at the same time, eminently tragic so far as the individual as well as a people is concerned. Both have value only in the transitional stages of the universe. Their existence becomes void of any meaning as soon as the purpose of the evolutionary stage which they represent is realized. They are even destroyed by the same passions which gave them the heroic energy to fight for the purposes of the absolute mind. Alexander the Great, Caesar, and Napoleon met their fate in consequence of their own ambition, once their mission was fulfilled. Nor do nations have more than a relative significance in the evolutionary process. They tend to develop their essential qualities to the highest perfection, and, arrived at this point, make their contribution to the evolution of the absolute mind, after which they again fall back into insignificance and transfer the leadership to another people whose essential qualities are such as to promote the historical development at this particular stage. The tragic aspect of this transitoriness is alleviated only when the individual (man or people) is conceived as part of the superindividual evolution of the objective mind. The objective mind in eternally seeking self-realization experiences man's errors and sufferings and is in its teleological progress, at least, meaningful in itself.

Hegel completed the idealistic system by interpreting the historical evolution of mankind as an evolution of the absolute mind. At the same time, however, he prepared for the transition to a realistic interpretation,

[19]

for he combines a deep knowledge and consideration of concrete facts with the metaphysical belief in a reasonable evolutionary progress and the final domination of absolute reason. In the last analysis, the degree of idealistic enthusiasm and creative consciousness will decide whether one must emphasize the metaphysical interpretation more than the concrete facts, whether one is to apply the teleological rather than the causal category. The concrete and materialistic tendencies of the nineteenth century favored the concrete and the causal, which, indeed was merely a logical continuation of the development beginning in idealism itself. If we consider, for example, the conception of man—which is most important for our interpretation of literature—we find a distinct tendency to attach less value to individuality. For the early Fichte, man surpasses nature because he possesses consciousness and reason; both involve the faculty and the obligation for autonomous and responsible action. Human individuality, however, loses importance when the universal mind is substituted for individual consciousness by the later Fichte, by Schelling, and by Hegel. The individual becomes merely an integral part of an all-embracing whole, and his former dignity is now attributed to the universal spirit, whose dignity, in turn, is reflected in the individual only in so far as he is, to a prominent degree, an exponent of the evolutionary process, that is, in so far as the universal mind attains to a higher degree of consciousness in him than in other men. From the point of view of individual autonomy and dignity, we may say that these philosophers prepared the way for an increasingly deterministic conception of man and for the decline of idealistic belief.

CHAPTER IV

THE DECLINE OF IDEALISM

FICHTE's activistic philosophy is characterized by its ethical nature; Schelling's and Hegel's idea of a progressive realization of the absolute value in the universe contained an essentially religious belief in the reasonableness of the universe. If Fichte's activism is deprived of its ethical tendency and Schelling's unconscious Will, of its rational goal, there yet remains Schopenhauer's "will to live," a purely vital force, aimless and without reason. This is in essence Schopenhauer's world view as it is exposed in his work *Die Welt als Wille und Vorstellung* (1819). Will is for him (1) the physico-mechanical change in inorganic nature, (2) the susceptibility to stimulation in the vegetative and instinctive life of organic nature, and (3) the motivated action in animals and man. This will is for him *das Ding an sich*, or the fundamental principle of all existence. It is not individual will, but universal will; it is effective in all nature; it is pure will, not a will directed toward any conceivable aim.

Intellect is only secondary to such will-to-live, an instrument whose function is to present objects to the will and thereby to stimulate voluntary activity. On the whole, this relation between will and "idea" prevails with animals and with the great majority of mankind. "What is opposed to our party, to our plans, our wishes and our hopes, we often cannot seize and understand, whereas it is clearly perceptible to everyone else; what is favorable for us, however, attracts our attention even from a distance . . . . Thus our intellect is daily deceived and bribed by the jugglery of our inclination. Only more highly developed men succeed in freeing perception from the service of will and in reaching the plane of disinterested contemplation." Since Schopenhauer deprives the will of direction and aim, he has to assume that it proceeds incessantly and without meaning, without fulfillment or satisfaction. Want and need continuously stimulate its activity, but boredom seizes him who has fulfilled his wish, and he is thus drawn to new and equally disappointing desires. Life is an endless alternation between desire and fulfillment, a process in which the displeasure of willing and striving is always, by far, greater than the enjoyment of the attained object. Life is constant suffering; and this suffering is the greater the higher life rises above the level of the original, non-differentiated stage of instinctive symbiosis. Man, who has developed beyond this stage, can only hope to alleviate and finally deliver himself from the suffering inseparably connected with the "will to live." Since all things are individual entities only as phenomena, although identical in their essense—as integral parts of the universal will—sympathy is the fundamental moral relation between man and his fellow men. To react with sympathy to the suffering of others, to feel their suffering as our own, to mitigate their fate as far as possible, is the highest moral task. The final aim can only be the complete renunciation of the will to live by all living beings. As long as the will does not annihilate itself in a universal suicide, only a relative mitigation is possible in the disinterested contemplation of the arts and the sciences. Since the ethical attitude of sympathy also tends to decrease the amount of suffering, the classical triad of truth, goodness, and beauty represents the highest value in Schopenhauer's system; but these values, too, are essentially forms of resignation to the tragedy of the aimless will-to-live—a conscious attempt to lessen the tension between the blind urge of the instinct and the longing for salvation.

Schopenhauer's system results from disillusionment with idealism and its applicability to practical life. His pessimism cannot conceal the wish that the mind might have the force to master the blind instincts of life. However much he may doubt this mastery, he leaves to mind the capability of achieving at least a theoretical and contemplative separation from the fundamental instinct, and he fosters the hope that mind will finally be strong enough to renounce the will-to-live. This final aim betrays idealistic belief in the victory of reason. On the other hand, his system reinstates life as the necessary prerequisite to the rise and development of mind. Man is, for Schopenhauer, first of all, part of a life context, although this context has still more of a metaphysical than of a concrete, realistic character. In his system, mind retains its power to escape the bonds of reality in the independent realm of contemplation, but the beginning of a naturalistic explanation of man's determination by his environment is undeniable. This is also the reason why Schopenhauer's philosophy reached the climax of its influence in the sixties and seventies, when the materialistic tendencies of the time and the dependence of man upon economic conditions began to be felt.

Schopenhauer's metaphysical principle was the pantheistic will, which sought in the cessation of existence—or Nirvana—the same relief from an antagonistic reality as other idealists had projected into the infinite mind. This final harmony in a divine infinity as the fulfillment of human happiness stands also at the beginning of Ludwig Feuerbach's thinking. As a pupil of Hegel, however, he had inherited his teacher's respect for concrete reality, while at the same time his enthusiasm for idealism declined with the general growth of materialistic tendencies in the nineteenth century. Thus Feuerbach objected to Hegel's abstract system as a falsification of reality. He answers Hegel's dialectic system with a materialism which reverses the relation between life and mind even more radically than Schopenhauer did. He declares sensual existence to be the true reality. He calls spiritual existence an illusion of the sensual individual. Mind is not an immanent principle, but a product of the brain, which has only the secondary function of arranging sense data. Nor can mind arrive at any transcendent truth. Soul, immortality, and God, which Kant retained only as postulates of practical reason, are for Feuerbach only anthropomorphisms of man's wishes. Man's mortality is an undeniable fact, which involves the moral obligation of increasing one's own happiness and that of one's fellowmen. Since man is a sensual being, his happiness and goodness depend upon his external circumstances, and thus the mitigation of social distress is identical with an increase in altruism and therefore in morality. History has moved in this direction, and this fact inspires us with optimism concerning the future development of mankind. Feuerbach makes man even more dependent upon the concrete situation than Schopenhauer did; thought itself becomes a product of this situation, although the mind still retains, to a certain extent, the creative ability of the idealistic period—the power to change the external circumstances of life.

Karl Marx' and Friedrich Engels' materialistic philosophy of history closely follows Hegel's dialectic interpretation. But, with Schopenhauer and Feuerbach, they reverse the relation between matter and mind. In their view, as in Feuerbach's philosophy, thought is dependent upon the material conditions of life. The economic situation and the economic development determine the political life and decisions of the state as well as the development of science and religion. Economic evolution progresses dialectically in three stages: in the first, individual labor creates private property; in the second, the antithesis to the first is the capitalistic system with its separation of labor and property; and in the third, the capitalistic system is superseded by the higher synthesis of a socialization of labor and capital. In this system, too, the romantic-idealistic belief in an immanent idea of development is combined with that of a causal dependence of man upon the material conditions of his existence.

[23]

The scientific theory of evolution is also indebted to romantic idealism. It was Schelling's pupil Oken who began to consider the conceptual gradation of organic life as an historical process. At about the same time Lamarck developed an evolutionary theory (1809), in which inheritance and adjustment appear as the main factors. Charles Darwin added to these factors that of natural selection, and thereby seemed to have eliminated the teleological idea in favor of the mechanico-causal explanation of nature. But even in this theory the idealistic view of an ascent to higher and more valuable forms of nature exerted its influence.

Darwin applied the historical and causal explanation not only to the origin of species, but also to the individual specimen. One of his main arguments is, in fact, based on the phenomenon of atavism; of organs like the appendix, which have an actual function in the lower species but have lost it in the higher stages of development. Friedrich Nietzsche applies this idea of historical stratification to explain the morality of man. According to his opinion, the original instinctive, energetic nature of man was superseded by the morality of the slaves and serfs. They had no other weapon against the persecution and suppression of their masters than that of raising to the dignity of virtues the qualities of the weak, such as sympathy, patience, humility, industry, and the like. In this revaluation they were supported by Jewish and Christian ethics. But Nietzsche opposes to this decadence of man's vital energies his ideal of upper-class morality (*Herrenmoral*), which is to free the fundamental value in life,—the "will to power,"—and to reinstate the aristocratic virtues of the strong individual, namely, strength, courage, pride, severity towards one's self and one's fellow-men, even cunning and brutality. In the last analysis, Nietzsche identifies Christian virtues with the attitude of the middle-class bourgeois who anxiously guards his property rights. But the superman is not afraid to risk everything, because he has the energy and ability to emerge from any misfortune with renewed physical and moral strength and an enriched experience. He thus becomes the prophet of "radiant virtue" *(schenkende Tugend)*, the virtue of the great personality who is imbued with an abundance of life and feeling for cultural values, whose only desire must be to find those who are able and willing to share this wealth, whose only unhappiness is the isolation into which he is forced by the slothfulness of an egotistic and materialistic populace. Nietzsche's philosophy is an idealistically inspired protest against the limitation of personal freedom by the rational materialism of the nineteenth century: against the levelling influence of the machine, the amorphous civilization of the growing cities, the domination of the economic spirit in private and political life. It is this development of civilizaton which Nietzsche branded as intellectualism and slave morality and against which he protested by his idealization of the vital energies, without which he sees all intellectual culture doomed.

The idealistic movement which began in the eighteenth century reached its culmination in the systems of Fichte, Schelling, and Hegel. These philosophers raise the mind to the dignity of the supreme and only principle in the structure and the evolution of the universe. Nature and history become the manifestations of the absolute mind. Their evolution follows the same laws which rule our human thinking; their aim is also the consciousness and the freedom of reason, which has reached its preliminary climax in man. In this idealism, however, develop simultaneously the causes of its decline. Fichte's ethical activism of the creative mind already contains an extraordinarily strong vitalistic quality, which could be made its fundamental principle as soon as the belief in the spontaneity of the mind had been shaken. Schelling's unconscious mind and his identification of nature and mind further strengthen the significance of the vitalistic component, which was only temporarily veiled by the emphasis on the idealistic aim of the evolution of the universe. The same is true for Hegel's metaphysical construction of the historical process and his hypothesis of the reasonableness of any actual evolutionary stage—theories which invited a realistic and causal reinterpretation.

The further fate of idealism until the year 1890 is closely connected with the progress in science and engineering as well as in every other phase of progress, which, on the one hand, is a victory of the human mind over nature, but which, on the other hand, entails an increasing application of the category of causality to explain human nature and behavior. In addition, political disillusionment weakened enthusiasm for the idealistic belief in the freedom and the creative power of man, and the economic revolution with its emphasis on the material side of life seemed hardly reconcilable with the faith in a progressive self-realization of a divine principle. Schopenhauer considers life an irremediably aimless and meaningless agitation, tolerable only in so far as the mind can detach itself in contemplation. For Nietzsche the same principle of life becomes the source of energy for the physical and the intellectual rise of man and thereby helps to save life from degenerating into the shallowness of a materialistic civilization. Although in the philosophical analysis of the problem "man" during the course of the nineteenth cen-

[25]

tury the emphasis shifts from the principle of mind to that of life, the idealistic desire for a higher intellectual development of man remains a determining factor. But belief in an essentially rational structure of the world and in the teleology of absolute reason yields to the conviction that the mind depends on vitality as the human factor.

CHAPTER V

HEINRICH von KLEIST
(1777-1811)

EXCESSIVE authoritarian pressure is liable to stifle all initiative and all spontaneous expression of inner experience; and in the end, it may entirely undermine even the ability of an individual to have any genuine and deep experience. The absence of all constraining pressure may lead to aimless esthetic reverie and to shallow formalistic art, but never to an art which is the expression of a deep and valuable experience. Such experience can be gained only at the price of disappointment and disillusionment, of unfulfilled desires and wishes, and this is the way of the artist who creates works of lasting value.

> Des Herzens Woge schäumte nicht so schön empor und würde Geist,
> wenn nicht der alte stumme Fels, das Schicksal, ihr entgegenstände.
>
> (Hölderlin)

Kleist's life and character were determined by the concurrence of two opposing factors. As the descendant of an old family of Prussian army officers he was subjected to the rigid discipline of his father, whereas his mother fostered in him the emotional and sympathetic reaction to life's problems. Orphaned in his early life, he spent his adolescence from his fourteenth to his twenty-second year under the discipline of the army. Soon afterwards, he accepted a position in the civil service, but he was not able to stand the strain of daily routine for any considerable length of time, nor did he dare to keep his engagement to Wilhelmine von Zenge. After a rather pedantic attempt to educate her for the duties of married life, the engagement was broken, and Kleist tried to find himself in a return to nature a la Rousseau. Soon, however, he was on his way to Paris, whence in 1804 he returned to Berlin, disillusioned by his vain search for a place in life. Again he attempted to settle down as a government official, but the Napoleonic occupation of Germany disturbed his mind and he was arrested on a mysterious journey to Berlin and taken to France as a political prisoner. After his return, in miserable isolation, he turned to the creation of his dramas and his novels, but he never had the satisfaction of seeing any of his works* produced. Despairing of

*Goethe's production of *Der zerbrochene Krug* on the Weimar stage was a discouraging failure.

[27]

himself and of the destiny of his oppressed fatherland, he freed himself from the intolerable burden of an unsettled life by suicide. His work is thus the reflection of an existence tragically torn between authority and flight to freedom, between self-discipline and passion, between ambition and despair. This extreme dynamic tension is reflected in the characters of Kleist's dramas, whose fate depends on the excesses of passion and devotion, of cruelty and fear. In this respect, he is accordingly a poet of the conflict between rational control and an irrational and creative emotion. In and through his dramatic works he finds the solution of those problems which he fails to resolve in his life.

Kleist was born at a time when Enlightenment rationalism still dominated the thought of the educated classes, and he was imbued with the ideas of Kant's critical idealism. He first believed, as did the philosophers of Enlightenment, in a rational world order, in happiness as the goal of man in this world, in the ability and duty of man to rise to higher levels of perfection through the acquisition of knowledge and through the training of the power of reasoning. For this purpose he devoted himself to the study of mathematics, physics, and philosophy. Even when he resigned from military service, which in itself was a reaction against a rationalized discipline, he motivated his decision by saying, he desired to perfect himself in striving for happiness and virtue. Characteristically enough for this rationalistic age, he conceives of them as identical:

> Ich nenne nämlich Glück nur die vollen und überschwenglichen Genüsse, die . . . im erfreulichen Anschauen der moralischen Schönheit unseres eigenen Wesens liegen.*

He wants to plan his life, to find reliable principles for his actions, for,

> solange ein Mensch noch nicht im Stande ist, sich selbst einen Lebensplan zu bilden, solange ist und bleibt er unmündig . . . Das hohe Ziel, dem er (der Mensch mit seinem Lebensplan) entgegenstrebt, ist das Mobil seiner Gedanken, Empfindungen und Handlungen. Alles, was er denkt, fühlt und will, hat Bezug auf dieses Ziel, alle Kräfte seiner Seele und seines Körpers streben nach diesem gemeinschaftlichen Ziele.†

He fears that without a plan, without a definite goal, he may be torn between conflicting wishes and duties, and be left to the mercy of chance, a puppet of fate.‡ In the motivation of this decision the real problem of Kleist's personality is revealed: he feels an unrestrained

*Letter to Christian Ernst Martin, March 18, 1799.
†Letter to Ulrike von Kleist, May, 1799.
‡Letter to Wihelmine von Zenge, March 22, 1801.

vitality and seeks protection from this urge in the rationalistic principles with which he grew up. Emotionally, he reacts against the domination of reason, yet he does not dare to let himself be guided by his emotions, so great is the conflict between rationalistic tradition and the emerging emotional vitality in him. This conflict reaches its climax when, during the winter of 1800 to 1801, he tries to find support for his wavering world view in Kant's *Critique of Pure Reason.** The criticism of the validity of reason beyond the realm of the phenomenon, and the philosophic reserve with regard to the nature of *das Ding an sich* shake Kleist's entire confidence in human reason, as well as his belief in the progress towards absolute knowledge and truth which had determined the optimistic attitude of his youth. The pure forms of intuition, space and time, with which Kant intended to give absolute validity to the perception and the interpretation of the phenomenal world, are for Kleist proof that our knowledge can be only subjective and deceptive illusion.

> Wir können nicht entscheiden, ob das, was wir Wahrheit nennen, wahrhaft Wahrheit ist, oder ob es nur so scheint. Ist das letzte, so ist die Wahrheit, die wir hier sammeln, nach dem Tode nicht mehr—und alles Bestreben, ein Eigentum sich zu erwerben, das uns auch ins Grab folgt, ist vergeblich . . . †

Nothing but his vitality, the irrational depth of his existence, survives in this intellectual and moral catastrophe, and he suffers from the absence of the goal which had guided him until then. Kleist now begins to feel and resent the traditional domination of reason in the family, society, and the state as an oppressing fate. It becomes for him a dismal power which tends to substitute passive knowledge for active experience, and prejudice, habits, and norms for the natural and sympathetic relations of man. This revolt against a rationalized and standardized attitude towards life is responsible for the beginning of his dramatic art. Rationalism becomes the negative pole, and the search for a new principle becomes the positive meaning of his whole work.

The first drama to express this problem is the tragedy *Die Familie Schroffenstein*. The two branches of the noble house of Schroffenstein are held together by an old agreement of succession. Once in the past,

---

*The traditional view that this conflict was brought about by the reading of Kant's *Critique of Pure Reason* must be dismissed as too rational. It is refuted on the basis of Kleist's letters by Martin Schütze in 'Studies in the Mind of Romanticism," *Modern Philology*, XVI (1918), p. 125.

†Letter to Wilhelmine von Zenge, March 12, 1801.

this agreement may have been the expression of a friendly relation, but as a rationalization of an emotional bond it only leads to catastrophe. For later generations it means nothing but an objective claim, a dead legal form which destroys by its very existence the sympathy out of which it grew. It becomes the cause of distrust, hatred, and open enmity, since every death in one family increases the chances of the other family's reuniting the whole property. When Peter, the young son of count Rupert, dies by accident, two superstitious servants of count Sylvester cut off one of the dead boy's fingers. The servants are arrested and, dying on the rack, one of them pronounces the name of his master. Rationalized prejudice can interpret this word only as a confession that the murder was ordered by the other family. An open feud develops. Jeronimus, a common friend of the two families, is killed while attempting to reconcile their differences, because each one believes him the instrument of the adversary. Finally, the love of the two children, who have met without knowing each other, promises to settle the conflict and fulfill the original meaning of the agreement. But when Rupert finds out about the love of his son Ottokar for his enemy's daughter, he follows the youth to a rendezvous with his beloved in order to kill her. Ottokar, comprehending that her life is menaced, covers her with his overcoat and is killed by his own father, while Sylvester stabs his daughter thinking to avenge the murder of his son. To complete the cruel irony, the blind father of Sylvester is the first one to discover the horrible error.

When Kleist reached the point at which he despaired of the possibility of any true knowledge, he expressed his despair thus:

> Wenn alle Menschen statt der Augen grüne Gläser hätten, so würden sie urteilen müssen, die Gegenstände, welche sie erblicken, sind grün — und nie würden sie entscheiden können, ob ihr Auge ihnen die Dinge zeigt, wie sie sind, oder ob es nicht etwas zu ihnen hinzutut, was nicht ihnen, sondern dem Auge gehört. So ist es mit dem Verstande.*

This is exactly the tragedy of the characters in this drama. All of them, with the exception of the two children, wear the "green spectacles" of reason and would approach reality with preformed judgments and more confidence in the dead letter of the law than in the natural sympathy of the unprejudiced. Rationalism is worse than physical blindness, because it is essentially passive and dependent upon the deceptive data of the senses. Kleist contrasts this disastrous effect of reason with the effect of a sympathetic emotional relation between men, which would have saved

*Letter to Wilhelmine von Zenge, March 22, 1801.

these families from self-destruction. Reason, detached from immediate contact with reality, isolates man in distrust; its triumph is identical with ruin. The tragedy of man, as illustrated and symbolized in the fifth act where the father allows himself to be misled by the overcoat, lies in the fact that whatever is perceived only through the senses is ambiguous, and that all purely abstract reasoning about human relations prevents one from understanding one's fellow-men and thus contributes to the destruction of human values. The dramatic presentation of such a destruction is, however, not only the expression of disillusionment; it also implies the postulate that human relations should be such that human values may survive and be furthered. In Ottokar's heroic sacrifice lies the only possible foundation for a reorganization of human existence, namely, sympathetic and confident response to another personality. This drama, however, does not leave much hope for the realization of such a harmonious order, for it is overshadowed by fear of the suppressing and devastating power of prejudice and abstract reasoning.

In the dramatic fragment *Robert Guiskard, Herzog der Normänner*, the power of the outside world is even more oppressive, and the power of the will to shape and to reorganize this world around a spiritual center is here represented as being less effective than in *Familie Schroffenstein*. Guiskard experiences the intolerable tragedy of a man who feels in himself the urge to live a free, creative life and who encounters one insurmountable obstacle after another in his effort to reach the goal for which he is striving. It is—to use the Fichtean terminology—the tragedy which results when man fulfills his duty to transform the non-ego into the ego. With the unbroken will and clear vision of a born leader, Robert Guiskard is engaged in the siege of Byzantium, the capital of the declining East-Roman Empire, in order to create a Germanic Empire. Convinced that the city will soon be forced to surrender, he refuses to win it by treason. At this moment, however, a pestilence befalls his army, decimates the ranks of his warriors, and causes such demoralization among them that Guiskard needs his entire energy to prevent their open revolt; he himself is stricken by the plague and can hardly conceal his illness from those around him. Without his dominating will, the plan is doomed to failure, for neither his son nor his nephew combines the authority and the popularity necessary to carry out his great idea. Under the pressure of these circumstances he accepts the offer of the traitors and gives orders to storm the city, but the plague fells him before even this plan can be carried out. His heroic effort to master his fate has been in vain.

Die Familie Schroffenstein left at least some hope of an escape from tragic fate, but the fragment *Robert Guiskard* seems to express only the despair of a man who realizes the futility of all human endeavor.

> In des Sinns ensetzlicher Verwirrung,
> Die ihn zuletzt befällt, sieht man ihn scheuszlich
> Die Zähne gegen Gott und Menschen fletschen,
> Dem Freund, dem Bruder, Vater, Mutter, Kindern,
> Der Braut selbst, die ihm naht, entgegenwütend.

And yet this most dreadful hopelessness of fate, as portrayed in the certainty of death just before the goal is reached, is but a transitory stage in Kleist's development. It is this utter pessimism with regard to man's power wh..ch he tries to overcome; and his struggle constitutes the deeper meaning of the heroism with which he endows his protagonist.

It is fundamentally the same problem in Kleist's comedy *Der zerbrochene Krug*. Although the comic form suggests a more optimistic approach, the content of the play reveals a close relation to Kleist's first tragedy *Die Familie Schroffenstein*. Again it is a world dominated by prejudice and material interests which menaces the happiness of the lovers, and again it is extreme and unperturbed devotion which points the way out of the chaos. The environment is as unproblematic and as near to life as one can possibly imagine, for the play concerns peasants with robust senses and an unspoiled joy in life. That is why we feel the more keenly the potential tragedy inherent in man's nature: man's reason enables and forces him to transcend the immediate experience of reality; but this human ability at the same time serves to undermine man's natural relation to others by causing misunderstanding, dissension, and antagonism. An unfortunate caprice of nature has endowed the village magistrate, Adam, with a club-foot and a bald head, but, as compensation for his disfiguration and the resulting social handicaps, Adam possesses the doubtful gift of a shrewd and unscrupulous reason. There is hardly anything which can embarrass him; he readily finds a number of explanations for the disappearance of his wig, and displays an astonishing resourcefulness in his attempt to adjourn the hearing or to find someone who might be talked into assuming the guilt of intruding into Eva's room and breaking the precious jug. In order to save himself, he even welcomes the theory that the devil himself might be involved in the case and proposes that the decision be postponed until the synod at the Hague has passed its judgment on the possibility of diabolic interference. The comic element in the play is, however, only a means of emphasizing the underlying problem: is reason as such capable of regulating the relations of man? The grotesqueness of the magistrate's character reveals the contrast between actual administration and the ideal of justice, which, however, finally prevails through the intervention of Councilor Walter; the play shows that reason without a deeper foundation in human sympathy may become the source of any calamity.

The characterization of Frau Marthe also shows the shallowness of mere reason. Reason predominates in her over maternity. Her most reasonable dependence upon conventional prejudices is comically exaggerated to the disadvantage of the deeper maternal relation. As a mother, she should be concerned above all with saving Eva's honor. But Frau Marthe's trust in the moral character of her child cannot rise above the common prejudice, which may be thus baldly put: if a man has been in her daughter's room the girl's morals must be corrupt. Frau Marthe is a petty housewife who values her material possessions incomparably higher than such ideal issues as the honor of her daughter. Conventional belief assumes grotesque dimensions in the superstition of Brigitte, who cannot think of any other cause for the indefinable odor in Adam's garden than the presence of Satan in the flesh. Ruprecht's lack of confidence in Eva's unwavering love makes her almost a tragic character. While he allows his sympathies to be influenced by gossip and superficial evidence, she is guided in her actions only by her love; she even sacrifices her good name and takes the most defamatory accusation upon herself, all to save Ruprecht from military service in the fever-infested Dutch colonies. If her confidence seems to be justified in the end, this justification is not the result of a change in the mental attitude of the other characters; it is rather due to the intervention of the representative of objective justice. Eva, in her heroic love, remains tragically isolated and essentially misunderstood in a world of conventions and prejudices, a world rationally divorced through reason from immediate contact with reality.

The comedy *Amphitryon*, which Kleist adapted from Molière's play of the same name, has been interpreted by bourgeois moralists as a glorification of matrimonial fidelity. Others, who have applied the classical pattern of Schiller, have thought that Kleist intended to present the rise of a character from worldly affection to absolute devotion to the ideal. Still others have considered the drama as a symbolic presentation of the Christian mystery of the Immaculate Conception. Others, again, have not been able to discover in it anything but a psychological study of the confused ways of human passion. These misinterpretations clearly

[33]

show that one can read almost anything into a work of art so long as one takes it in its isolation and not as an integral part of the author's whole work and expression of his fundamental problem. Kleist's desire, however, was to establish an emotional contact with this world and thereby to come to an understanding of its deepest and most vital reality. Even the god who has his throne in the isolation of Olympus suffers from the abstract and impersonal relation of man to him:

> Auch der Olymp ist öde ohne Liebe.
> Was gilt der Erdenvölker Anbetung,
> Gestürzt in Staub, der Brust, der lechzenden? (II, 5)

Man has no immediate emotional relation to God, he rather forms an abstract idea of his God and then adores this idea. This is the reason why Jupiter, disguised as Amphitryon, descends from his heavenly see in human form in order to embrace Amphitryon's wife, Alkmene. But how can she be deceived in her unerring faithfulness? Can sympathy, which supposedly alone can revitalize this world, be confused and beguiled? No. Fundamentally, Alkmene remains true to herself, and sympathy remains her absolutely reliable guide, for only a god could succeed in deceiving her, since he alone has the power to transform himself so completely into the figure of Amphitryon that he becomes for her the idealized husband. He can win her only by assuming the figure of Amphitryon; he even had to become Amphitryon in an idealized form in order to deceive her, for she would not yield to the wooing even of a god. Love for a god would mean still less for her than love for a mortal being, for love is not an abstract relation to some superior being, but a most concrete emotional experience. It is impossible for her to be a mistress because her love is complete devotion to one definite being and not merely an esthetic experience. With this idea, Kleist's relation to classical idealism is clearly determined; from the point of view of idealism, yielding to a divine being would be but a symbol of man's longing for harmony with the ideal. Romantic estheticism may consider as a value the enjoyment of the "beautiful moment" in which all consciousness recedes, so far as enjoyment symbolizes the freedom of transcending individual boundaries. For Kleist, however, there is neither a transcendent idea, nor an esthetic, passive submersion in the infinite. The essence and the foundation of his universe is the individual concrete self, which transcends its own limited sphere in active emotional experience.

Alkmene's refusal to renounce her mortal husband for her divine seducer expresses Kleist's firmly established conviction that the self is the center of all life, and that the non-self is recognized only in so far as it becomes a concrete emotional experience of the self, if we adopt Fichte's philosophical formulation of the problem. The identity of love and marriage, which is accepted in this drama as a matter of course, is closely related, however, to the main issue, the conflict between the rationalized norm and the individual will, and is therefore submitted to further poetic analysis.

This is the theme of the tragedy *Penthesilea*. Here again the subject matter, as such, is but an interesting psychological analysis of the erotic affinity between love and hatred, between fulfillment and disillusion, as carried to the extremes of voluptuousness and perversion in the anni-hilation of the beloved and in self-destruction. Such a psychological interpretation can at best reveal something of the intensity of Kleist's emotional life, but it overlooks the fact that the purely psychological problem attains its poetic dignity only towards the end of the nineteenth century, and that for Kleist it can be but the symbolical expression of his struggle for a world view. *Amphitryon*, too, is a visualization of his yearning for a new world order centered in the inner self; it is a visualization of the eternal human tragedy which is conditioned on the one hand by man's infinite potentiality and on the other by his limitation through heterogeneous norms and dead traditions.

In *Penthesilea* Kleist's reaction against his rationalistic heritage and environment finds a much clearer exposition than in his two comedies. Penthesilea is the queen of the state of the Amazons, a state founded on rationalism in a typical eighteenth century *contrat social*. Sometime in the past, the Ethiopians had invaded Amazon country, killed all the men and raped the women. They have now avenged their husbands, murdered the Ethiopians, and founded a state in which only women are allowed to live and to rule. To propogate their race, they send their daughters out on the battlefield to win fathers for their children. In this way, the most subjective concern of life becomes an abstract and objective institution. It has degenerated into a means of propagating the species and continuing the existence of the state. It is a rational deterioration of nature, which does not even serve the deeper purpose of natural selection, since only those men who are physically inferior can be won; the stronger and more desirable men are compelled to murder. This paradox is illustrated in the fight between Achilles and Penthesilea. Both seem to be predestined for one another by nature; in strength, vitality, and youthful beauty they excel all their companions, and from first sight they are convinced that nature has left no other

[35]

choice to them. But nature is not allowed to take its course. Each must defeat the other on the battle-field; Achilles is bound by his military honor, and Penthesilea stands under the unnatural law of the Amazons. In her position of leadership, the queen has the additional obligation of suppressing her most personal self in order to set an example for her followers. At first she thinks it possible to reconcile the law of the Amazons with her feelings, but the law requires that she either kill Achilles or win him by fighting, whereas love would compel her to do everything to save his life. This law which originated in hatred and rational arbitrariness excludes the possibility of a genuine love for an opponent of equal strength and worth. The mere fact that Penthesilea selects a particular warrior in this fight, for the purpose of cohabitation, is a violation of the unsentimental and impersonal procedure prescribed by the law. This dissociation of law and love and the revolt of love against the fetters of a rational order is the tragic theme of the drama. The first realization of the incongruity of strife and love is responsible for Penthesilea's break-down and her temporary captivity. Then the two confess their love, but neither of them is ready to break the traditional bonds. When Achilles finally finds a compromise solution which might save the appearance of honor and win her love, she misunderstands his challenge to a duel in which he intends to be defeated. Her feelings have achieved emancipation from the law of the Amazons, but her thinking remains under its domination. Her hatred for the fatal authority of the law has reached a stage where she cannot see in Achilles' challenge anything but the effect of law and the shameless arrogance of the stronger man, who, conscious of his invincibility, seeks to humiliate her. Her sentiment rises to the madness of sadistic hatred, which can be soothed only by the most cruel annihilation of the object of her love. Her deed is an act of inconsolable and hopeless despair; it is a manifestation of the absolute destitution of an individual who, in merciless self-denial, has emancipated herself from the usual feelings but meets with unconquerable obstacles in the attempt to live in accordance with the newly acquired ethical standards. The law of the Amazons is revealed as a complete failure, for it compels the most repulsive absurdity, the brutal murder of a lover for the sake of the very love borne him. An explicit renunciation of this law marks the end of the tragedy:

> Ich sage vom Gesetz der Fraun mich los
> Und folge diesem Jüngling hier.

Penthesilea's death is the symbol for this liberation of the inner self:

Denn jetzt steig' ich in meinen Busen nieder,
Gleich einem Schacht, und grabe, kalt wie Erz,
Mir ein vernichtendes Gefühl hervor.

.   .   .   .   .   .

Und schärf' und spitz' es mir zu einem Dolch;
Und diesem Dolch jetzt reich' ich meine Brust.

Her death is not an atonement for her guilt in murdering Achilles in the sense of Lessing's theory, for Achilles is less an independent character and real antagonist of Penthesilea than one of the indispensable pre-requisites for the unfolding of the conflict between external fate and inner spontaneity and self-assertion. Neither is her death the test of the sublimity of the moral character as we find it in Schiller's tragedies. Kleist's conception of morality differs essentially from the classical idea of the universal validity of moral principles. Her death is rather the supreme liberation from all heterogeneous determination and the absolute assertion of the spontaneous individual. The attitude of the Amazons towards men is intended to show the extent of demoralization to which the rationalization of human relations may lead. The abstract and objective order is thus represented in this tragedy as the arch-destroyer of the highest personality values. The tragic end of the play demands rather that the inner sympathetic relation should be acknowl-edged as the fundamental principle of human conduct. The ideal of humanity can be attained only on the basis of sympathy and love.

The aim, in other words, is to replace the heteronomy of a rational and inflexible order by a dynamic order which expresses the sympa-thetic relation of human personalities. In Penthesilea the problem is still illustrated in a negative way. Even if Penthesilea and Achilles had been free from the inner compulsion of a rationalized order, the realization of their aim would have been possible only in complete isolation from their people. Complete isolation, however, would be identical with loss of life itself, since life from Kleist's point of view can be life only in so far as it is in active relation to others, or again in Fichte's terminology, only so far as the non-ego is transformed into the ego. From this point of view Kleist's next question must be: What is the nature of a positive, super-individual order which would guarantee the self-realization and subsistence of the ideal personality? *Penthesilea* leaves no doubt that the order must be such that its laws can be obeyed by the individual without detriment to his inner fredeom. Such synthesis of authority and inner freedom, however, is possible only if law and order are manifestations of the moral will of the individual and derive their validity from his will only, that is if law and order become identical with the moral will of the individual.

Kleist's inner relation to Fichte's philosophy is extremely close in this drama. In Fichte's abstract terminology, its content may be summed up as follows: Penthesilea's ego is essentially activity, an active relation to the non-ego. As such, the self revolts against the limitation of its activity by the non-ego, the law of the Amazons, until the ego finally realizes its freedom from all limitations and acts only in accordance with those laws which are the creative expression of the inner self—a freedom which is symbolized by Kleist in the power of the mind to destroy the bodily existence.

The dynamic form of this tragedy corresponds to the dynamic nature of the idea. Without intermission the fighting antagonists move across the stage, which is now filled with Amazons and now with Greek warriors; out of the fighting groups single heroes emerge and disappear again in the fluctuating mass. The individuals and the groups appear without being announced in the rational way of the classical drama; there is a continuous motion against a fixed background. Long speeches are followed by excited shouting and abrupt sentences. Even time has its share in the dynamic effect: the fifth scene turns back to the beginning of the fourth scene. Thus even the formal structure is dissolved in the irrational and the organic.

In *Penthesilea* the emphasis is still on the negative side of the problem; with *Käthchen von Heilbronn* it shifts to the positive presentation of the emotional foundation underlying human relations. Käthchen is the impersonation of nature in its primal purity, naïvely free from the considerations and inhibitions of reflective reason, unerringly devoted to her love and ever willing to sacrifice her life in the service of others. Her rival is Kunigunde von Thurneck, the impersonation of rationalism, which in her is portrayed as identical with extreme wickedness. She has no genuine sympathy for anyone; all her actions are calculated, and for her any means are justified which lead to the desired end. She gives her affection to those who pay best; she jeopardizes Käthchen's life to save a property deed, and later she even makes an attempt on Käthchen's life. Her hideous body is but a symbol of the depravity of her soul, and the technical and cosmetic devices with which she tries to disguise her ugliness are symbols of a rational perversion. She typifies the absolute non-ego, which, without an inner center, becomes the slave of the material object.

Count von Strahl stands as a character between the two extremes of

[38]

the absolute ego and the absolute non-ego. Like Käthchen, he has heard the call of genuine love in a dream, the symbol of subconsciousness and sympathetic nature, but his feeling is confused by rational considerations. He rejects the daughter of a tradesman because his aristocratic prejudice forbids him to marry a commoner; yet he yields to the coquetry and to the egotistic speculation of Lady Kunigunde. Only after he has realized the brutality of her character does the vision of his dream, in other words his inner self, awaken to triumph over his prejudices; he accepts Käthchen as his bride, who is then, in a fairy-tale solution, recognized by the emperor himself as his natural child.

Kleist calls this drama "ein groszes historisches Ritterschauspiel." He uses, indeed, many of the theatrical appurtenances characteristic of the chivalresque plays which were written in imitation of Goethe's *Götz von Berlichingen*, such as the Vehmgericht, the duel, the storming of the castle, and the nocturnal tempest. On first examination of the theme it might seem that the play is but a dramatization of the Cinderella fairy-tale or of the disenchanted princess who is saved by a prince and then marries him. As in the fairy-tale, good and bad are sharply contrasted, and the solution of the conflict is a fabulous triumph of goodness, while wickedness is completely put to shame. The repeated transition from reality to the miraculous and back again to reality is of course also characteristic of the fairy-tale, a form of popular art which has been explained as the wish-dream of the people and an artistic substitute for their thwarted hopes. This particular nature of the fairy-tale thus made it especially suitable as a substratum for the presentation of Kleist's problem, for his ideal of a revitalization of the world from the inner center of the emotional self could best be presented in its imaginative setting. In a world which is not constrained by the laws of causality the poet is free to visualize his ideal and the spiritual structure of the world of his belief; here, in conformity with his ideal, emotional sympathy may prevail over all obstacles inherent in a materialistic and rationalized world.

The optimism which distinguishes *Käthchen von Heilbronn* from Kleist's earlier dramas reflects Kleist's own growing confidence in himself and his ability as a playwright. His more positive attitude toward life may be seen in this play's unmistakable insistence that sympathy be the guide in human relations. In this drama, in contrast to *Der zerbrochene Krug* and in comparison with *Penthesilea*, the ideal order prevails without the intervention of a kind of *deus ex machina*. Whereas Walter, in *Der zerbrochene Krug*, actually contributes to the solution of

[39]

the plot, the miraculous elements in *Käthchen von Heilbronn* have only symbolic significance. Wickedness and egotistic speculation are compromised by their own consequences, while natural goodness and confidence in the goodness of others are justified by their results. Käthchen's devotion not only triumphs over Kunigunde but also convinces von Strahl of the value of irrational sympathy. He emancipates himself from the domination of the non-ego, from class-prejudice, egotistic calculation, and superficial impressions. So far as his ego is dominant in his environment, it becomes a creative ego in the Fichtean sense, at least for the small circle of two loving beings. As in the earlier dramas, the problem is treated more or less as an individual issue, in spite of the fact that it is rooted in the general cultural situation of the time, in the conflict between rationalism and romanticism.

This problem gained actual significance in the year 1808, when Kleist expected an alliance between Austria and Prussia for the purpose of thwarting the imperialistic aims of Napoleon. In the *Katechismus der Deutschen* Kleist attacks Napoleon as a fiendish parricide and vandal, "als einen der Hölle entstiegenen Vatermördergeist, der herumschleicht in den Tempeln der Natur und an allen Säulen rüttelt, auf welche er gebaut ist." It is characteristic of the consistency of his world view that he attributes the fate of his nation to the hypertrophy of reason at the expense of emotional development:

> dasz der Verstand der Deutschen . . . durch einige scharfsinnigen Lehrer einen Überreiz bekommen habe; sie reflektierten, wo sie empfinden und handeln sollten, meinten alles durch ihren Witz bewerkstelligen zu können und gäben nichts mehr auf die alte, geheimnisvolle Kraft der Herzen.

Misery had befallen his countrymen that they might learn to despise material goods and strive, instead, for the supreme values of humanity: "God, fatherland, emperor, freedom, love, and faithfulness, beauty, science, and art." For these values, above all for that of freedom, the battle should be waged, even if all perish,

> auch wenn alles unterginge und kein Mensch, Weiber und Kinder mit eingerechnet, am Leben bliebe.

These words of the *Katechismus* reveal the very same contrast of reason and emotion which we found in Kleist's dramas. The same principle which he established for the relation between individuals he now applies to the relation between individual and state. In *Penthesilea* Kleist had refused the idea of the state's absolute and heteronomous authority over the individual. He had, at least implicity, maintained that this authority must have its foundation in the will of the individual. In the *Katechismus* he adds that the individual cannot exist as an isolated being, but only in interaction with others, i.e., that the individual must be rooted in the community of the nation. Both the individual and the nation are essentially interdependent. The clear recognition of this fact is a result of Kleist's imprisonment in France:

> Sie haben mich immer in der Zurüchgezogenheit meines Lebens für isoliert von der Welt gehalten, und doch ist vielleicht niemand inniger verbunden damit als ich.*

Such interdependence involves, on the part of the individual, the obligation to defend the existence of the state as the foundation of his own existence. Here Kleist's attitude is apparently much more concrete than that of the classicists, for they were mainly concerned with the preservation of the ideal values, whereas the national community was considered as a value only because it offered the most favorable condition for the realization of the ideal values. But Kleist's conception is also more idealistic and more universal than the nationalistic ideas of the later nineteenth and the twentieth centuries, since the nation for him remains the manifestation of the individual will, and since the ultimate goal is the unity of all national individualities,

> eine Gemeinschaft gilt es, die dem ganzen Menschengeschlecht angehört (*Was gilt es in diesem Kriege?*).

> Wenn sich der Barden Lied erfüllt,
> Und unter e i n e m Königsszepter,
> Jemals die ganze Menschheit sich vereint,
> So läszt, dasz es ein Deutscher führt, sich denken,
> Ein Britt', ein Gallier, oder wer ihr wollt. . .
> (*Die Hermannsschlacht*, I, 3)

In the drama *Die Hermannsschlacht* these ideas are so closely linked with allusions to the events of the time and so obscured by the passions of the day that the play is hardly more than an historical document. The king of Prussia, the emperor of Austria, the princes of the Rhenish Alliance appear in transparent disguise, and the dramatic development is often interrupted by the author's acrimonious harangues addressed to his compatriots. Yet this drama, too, has the function of further clarifying the relation between individual and state. The state is here presented as a necessary condition for the existence of the

*Letter to Marie von Kleist (?) June, 1807.

[41]

individual. As in Fichte's philosophy, the individual transcends his boundaries and becomes an exponent of the comprehensive "ego" of the state. The state exists actively by continually realizing its essential character. Any subordination to foreign conquerors, any compromise for the sake of material advantage is a denial of the state's own essence and therefore a worse evil than non-existence. Any encroachment on the individual life of another nation violates the highest ethical right of that nation and can only spring from rational and selfish motives; consequently it is radically bad. This is the conviction which determines Hermann's action. He is the highest manifestation of his nation's will-to-live, and his struggle is directed against the foe of its existence in a superindividual integration. In the same way, the individual in the ranks of the enemy is no longer an individual, but the exponent of a principle which is radically bad because the enemy attack violates the right and the obligation of another nation to realize its individuality. For this reason Hermann cannot except any particular enemy from his general moral condemnation, however good and humane its deeds may be; he must even regret any exceptional goodness, because it lessens the determination to annihilate the aggressor. Thus Hermann has nothing but a curse for the centurion who saved a German child from a burning house at the risk of his life:

> Er hat auf einen Augenblick mein Herz veruntreut, zum Verräter an Deutschlands groszer Sache mich gemacht!

He himself foments hatred against the enemy by having cruelties perpetrated by Germans under Roman disguise. To the last moment he deceives his friends and his enemies about his real intentions. On the other hand, he risks the life of his wife and his children in order to lead his people to either victory or destruction. Thusnelda, who at first has some sympathy with the enemy and yields to the flatteries of Ventidius, takes the most savage revenge when she finds that his courting was nothing but treacherous speculation. Rational and cold-blooded calculation is, indeed, the real guilt of the Romans; they want to subjugate the Germanic tribes solely for materialistic reasons; they suppress their freedom with a rationally codified law which is to be substituted for a justice based on the conscientious valuation of the individual case. Their diplomatic principle of *divide et impera* is founded upon the same rationalistic disregard for personal and national values.

An evaluation of their character would place the representatives of the tribes in a scale of values between Hermann and the Romans. Hermann stands highest as the organic personification of rising nationalism among the German tribes. The Romans with their rationalistic blindness for the inner living forces of the state represent decadent institutionalism and have consequently the least value in the organic scale of value. Between these two extremes can be placed the tribal chiefs. Some of them are imbued with Hermann's zeal for liberty, others share with the enemy the materialistic property conception of the land and its inhabitants which makes them ready for a compromise with the aggressor.

The real hero of the drama is the people, with its absolute claim to existence, with its inner activity. It is the people as an organism which constantly creates from within its individual integrity and which therefore has the absolute right to its country as the condition of its existence and it has the moral duty to defend its own integrity. The people also is the hero of the play in a deeper sense. It is the people who surpasses in its fight the limitations set by its own greed as well as by a foreign rule and thus achieves its realization in national self-assertion.

Since the play had its origin in a tense and passionate political situation, the emphasis is more upon the national issue, and the inner relation of the individual to the national community is left somewhat obscure. In Kleist's next drama, *Prinz Friedrich von Homburg*, this relation is elucidated as thoroughly as is possible in dramatic presentation. This leaves no doubt that the individual should *not* be subservient to the state and its objective laws. Any other interpretation of Kleist's meaning would be incompatible with the whole development of his thought; it would be in absolute contrast to the rejection of the rational and heterogeneous order in *Penthesilea*. We have no right to suppose of *Prinz Friedrich von Homburg* that Kleist had opportunistically yielded to the pressure of the moment and thus rob the striving and the suffering of his life of its meaning. Neither can the drama be interpreted, as is often done, as a return to classical idealism as embodied in Schiller's *Jungfrau von Orleans* or *Wilhelm Tell*. For Schiller the value of the fatherland depends on the degree to which it allows and furthers the development of moral autonomy in the individual personality:

Wir haben stets die Freiheit uns bewahrt.
Nicht unter Fürsten bogen wir das Knie,
Freiwillig wählten wir den Schirm der Kaiser.
Denn herrenlos ist auch der Freiste nicht.
Ein Oberhaupt musz sein, ein höchster Richter,
Wo man das Recht mag schöpfen in dem Streit.

(Wilhelm Tell, 1211 ff.)

[43]

Johanna's death for her country in Schiller's drama is the triumph of the free individual over all bonds of causal determination; in comparison with that, the liberation of France is only an achievement of relative value, a value dependent upon the willingness of Johanna's people to follow her example of moral freedom. Kleist's idea of the fatherland is more than the real condition of ideal freedom; it is the concrete manifestation of the will of a natural group of people aiming at the highest realization of their individual potentialities. This fatherland is never merely existent; rather it continues to realize its existence through the active will of the individual; it is an ever-creative regeneration. As the final goal was anticipated in Käthchen's and von Strahl's dreams, so the conclusion is foreshadowed in the dream of Prinz Friedrich von Homburg in the first scene of the drama: the wreath and the chain are the symbols of his striving for love and glory. The obsession of his double aim causes him to disregard the order of the prince-elector and to join the battle before his time for action has come. His striving for glory at this point is still superficial and egotistic; it is not rooted in any sympathetic union with his people. He is still motivated by a heteronomous factor, namely, the praise which might come to him for a conspicuously valiant deed; his actions still lack a foundation in the center of the ego, from which alone they can derive unity and meaning. To establish the inner center of his personality and to develop it so that it becomes an integral part of the greater ego of national life, and thus to transform a fate from outside into a will within, is the purport of this drama. The prince has to experience the consequences of an authoritative law in its extreme form of the death-sentence in order to recognize the futility and utter meaninglessness of his superficial and unfree ego.

The death-sentence threatens Homburg's whole existence because he is an extremely limited individual. In fact, there is nothing in his personality which is essentially his own but his will-to-live. The prince who risked his life in a venturesome attack, is willing to renounce his honor, his glory, and his love, merely to save his bare existence. Everything that seems to be of highest value falls away when he is consciously confronted with the sacrifice of his life. In the face of death there is only one value which stands the trial, his bodily existence; no other value has really become part of his personality. He is expected to submit to the statute because its enforcement is necessary to uphold the authority of the state. He could reconcile himself with this fate by the application of the categorical imperative to his case. His reason would tell him that the egotistic motives of his insubordination were unfit to become a universal law and that he consequently deserved the penalty. But it is no such reflection which causes him to accept the death sentence. His change of mind occurs abruptly at the moment when the prince-elector makes him the sole judge of his fate:

> Meint ihr, ein Unrecht sei euch widerfahren,
> So bitt' ich, sagt's mir mit zwei Worten —
> Und gleich den Degen schick' ich euch zurück. (IV, 4)

These words call for a rational decision concerning the justice or injustice of applying the law to his particular case. Homburg cannot help recognizing the justice of the decision under the prevailing objective and authoritative law:

> Schuld ruht, bedeutende, mir auf der Brust,
> Wie ich es wohl erkenne; kann er mir
> Vergeben nur, wenn ich mit ihm drum *streite*,
> So mag ich nichts von seiner *Gnade* wissen. (IV, 4)

Discussing the justice of the decision has value only under an objective law; but pardon under this law is impossible without abrogation, i.e., without virtual infringement of the law. Discussion and pardon are, however, natural and even essential features of a subjective law which genuinely expresses the will of the individuals who constitute the state. This is the law whose application Homburg expects. If he signs his own death sentence, he is not submitting to the same law against which he rebelled up to this scene; he is, instead, faced with the choice of becoming the destroyer or creator of the law, and by that, the destroyer or creator of the state whose foundation is in this law. By his signature he creates the subjective type of law which exists through the creative will of the individual. He signs his death sentence and stands by this decision with the absoluteness of the creative will:

> Ich will das heilige Gesetz des Kriegs,
> Das ich verletzt im Angesicht des Heers,
> Durch einen freien Tod verherrlichen! (V, 7)

By this same act, he gives the authoritative state of Brandenburg a new and deeper foundation in his own will. Finally, his love for Natalie is freed from its superficial sensuality and becomes ethically rooted in his concern for the freedom of her personality. She whose love he was willing to renounce in order to save his own life has become the last thought of his life; he is willing to die, if she can thus be saved from being married to an unloved man, as the price for a political bargain.

[45]

By these decisions he has extended the realm of his inner self to include not only the narrower circle of his friends but also the larger community of his fatherland, of which he himself has become an actively creating part. Thus he feels his self grow into the infinite unity of the universe:

Nun, o Unsterblichkeit, bist du ganz mein!
Du strahlst mir durch die Binde meiner Augen
Mit Glanz der tausendfachen Sonne zu. (V, 10)

Death has lost its sting for him, and is now the highest fulfillment of the self in the transcendental oneness. But the death sentence, too, has lost its meaning, since the will of the individual and the will to maintain the foundations of the state have reached the stage of complete harmony. The prince-elector can and must pardon him, if the death sentence is to mean more for him than brutal revenge. Homburg has earned the wreath and the chain not by his vainglorious deeds on the battlefield, but by the realization of his inner self. His victory is implicitly a victory of the state, which cannot perish as long as it is the active and everrenewed manifestation of the free will of its constituents.

The incipient rationalism in Kleist's development remains the negative pole even in this last drama; its most distinctive representative is Prince Hohenzollern, especially in the argumentation with which he tries to save his friend from execution. He attributes the real guilt for Homburg's insubordination to the prince-elector himself, who gave the wreath and the chain to Homburg in his somnabulistic dream and thereby weakened his will-power so that he disobeyed the military instructions; therefore, the prince-elector rather than Homburg should be held responsible. The prince-elector reveals the absurdity of this rationalistic argument by pointing out that a causal explanation would, in the last analysis, reduce to absurdity any concept of guilt and would undermine the entire organization of the state. This is the import of the witty answer in which the prince-elector attributes the responsibility to Hohenzollern, by going one step further in the chain of causality:

Tor, der du bist, Blödsinniger! Hättest *du*
Nicht in den Garten mich hinabgerufen,
So hätt' ich einem Trieb der Neugier folgend,
Mit diesem Träumer harmlos nicht gescherzt.
Mithin behaupt' ich mit gleichem Recht,
Der sein Versehn veranlaszt hat, warst du! (V, 5)

However, the strictly legalistic interpretation with which the prince-

[46]

elector justifies his death-sentence suffers from the same rationalism. He claims objective validity for the law, and he judges the individual case according to the rules of logical subsumption. He neither considers the motive for the action nor does he examine the formula with regard to its concrete or ideal value. In the discussion of the fourth scene of the fourth act, this objective law is deprived of its absolute validity, and the prince-elector himself begins to doubt the justice of his legal rigorism, when Kottwitz emphatically defends the relative and pragmatic value of any law. His objective rigorism yields to the subjective conception when he pardons Homburg, for the act of pardoning presupposes a more personal and emotional conception of right and justice and a freedom which stands above the law and can abrogate it, as soon as it has fulfilled its purpose of changing the inner attitude of the culprit. This drama, therefore, establishes a synthesis between the objectivity of reason and the pure subjectivity of sentiment; it makes the individual subject the creator of the law of the state and makes the law dependent upon the active will of the individual to establish a superindividual order.

Kleist's poetic creation began as a revolt against the rationalism which dominated his own life and thinking as well as that of his environment. Rationalism became the negative pole and the search for an emotional principle of life the positive pole of his work. In *Familie Schroffenstein* this rationalism is introduced as a blindly raging fate. Reason and logic prevent any immediate and sympathetic understanding and are revealed in all their absurdity, the cause of the most unreasonable chaos. As a destroyer of all sympathetic relations between men, they appear in all his later dramas. Their most important symbolic disguises are laws and the courts, which, in their objective and authoritative rigorism, cannot do justice to the organic pecularity of the individual case. Following the reasonable course brings tragedy in *Familie Schroffenstein;* the confession extorted from the servant reveals the incongruity between life and reason. Judge Adam in *Der zerbrochene Krug* adheres to legal procedure, but his distortions of the laws, although reasonable, do violence to life and real justice. The rationalistic constitution of the Amazon state makes unnatural demands on living human beings and thwarts their most natural right. The legal decision of the Vehmgericht in *Käthchen von Heilbronn* unnaturally compels the separation of the lovers. Roman law applied to a primitive people in *Die Hermannsschlacht* threatens their organic development. To save the rigid raison d'état, the Kurfürst condemns Homburg, in whom he might have lost,

[47]

by a strict application of the letter of the law, a most valuable supporter of the state. Reason in the petrified form of social convention falsifies the relation between individuals, whom nature has bound closely and strongly together. Family interests and prejudice bring about destruction in *Familie Schroffenstein*. Bourgeois morality and maternal concern over conventional exteriors make Frau Marthe blind to her own daughter's genuine moral integrity; thus Eva's true love is almost ruined by conventional mistrust. In *Käthchen von Heilbronn* Kunigunde is the conventionally desirable bride; yet her calculating greed of property and her synthetic beauty create but a deceptive external illusion of the real qualities, which the unconventional Käthchen actually possesses.

The opposite of this traditional rationalism is the search for a new order. Kleist's dramatic works show a progressive clarification of this problem, which, on the whole, is closely related to Fichte's ethical activism. The aim of this development, evident in his first drama and increasingly so in the later dramas, is the renewal of human relations through immediate and sympathetic understanding, the reexamination of everything which has lost its active contact with life and become solidified in objective and traditional forms—the transformation of the non-ego into the ego, as Fichte would call this ethical obligation. Nothing should be accepted simply because it has been of value in the past and therefore comes to us with a traditional claim. Every situation and every person should be judged and evaluated by the immediate appeal to our sympathy or antipathy, and our emotional reaction should be valid only for this one instance and should not claim any eternal and universal validity. This is the meaning of the creative and dynamic principle which distinguishes Kleist's conception of life from any rationalistic and static conception. The same meaning is presented (though somewhat obscured) in *Familie Schroffenstein*, where the catastrophe might have been avoided if a natural emotional relation between men had prevailed. In *Der zerbrochene Krug* Eva's absolute reliance upon her sentiment overcomes the danger of tragedy, but in respect of her confidence in others she remains isolated, and her victory is due as much to the objective arbiter as to her ideal character. Penthesilea emancipated herself from the heteronomous rule of an unnatural law within her and foreswears her allegiance to a state and to a rôle which have forced such a law upon her. But her attitude remains negative, she is not able to substitute a more ethical order for the one she destroys; her self transcends the individual boundaries only in the destruction of her bodily existence through the power of her mind. The

[48]

task of making the individual the creator of the laws of his existence remains unsolved. In *Käthchen von Heilbronn* this task is achieved for the relation between two individuals. All attempts ruthlessly to separate those who are united by sentimental bonds must fail in the course of time, when rationalistic speculation is unmasked. In *Die Hermanns-schlacht* and *Prinz Friedrich von Homburg* even the state itself is freed from the rational stability which characterized the *contrat social* state of the Amazons. It is transformed into a dynamic organism which has its foundation in the active will of the individual and is the manifestation of the ever-creative will of the individual to live in community with other individuals and under conditions of life under which self-created and ever renewed laws guarantee the existence of such a community.

Every one of Kleist's dramas is, therefore, evidence of a fight against the traditions of a rationalistic order of life, and of a search for a new order in which every form and every relation of life is constantly being created out of immediate contact with persons and situations. His work as a whole may be considered as a progressive solution of this problem. It is the expression of a relentless fight for an immediate experience of existence, for the dynamic penetration of the object-world with the creative will of the subject, for the transformation of the non-ego into the ego.

[49]

CHAPTER VI

FRANZ GRILLPARZER
(1791-1872)

SCHOPENHAUER'S philosophy clearly reveals the decline of the idealistic belief of the classical and the romantic periods. The philosophical
decline of idealism is paralleled by a similar development in the
political sphere, where we see the national enthusiasm of the Wars of
Liberation degenerate into the Biedermeier attitude of the Restoration
period. The Biedermeier attitude is characterized by a disheartening
doubt concerning the objective value of ideas, or at least of their applicability to public life. During this period men are content with activity in
a very small sphere and are willing to submit to the traditional powers of
the state and the church. They are no longer interested in questions of
national and international significance, but limit themselves to home
and town to avoid all the disturbing elements of life. Only the stronger
individuals preserve their natural impulse to break through the narrow
limitations of such a life, and they necessarily meet a tragic fate in the
conflict between the demands of their will and an outside pressure which
leaves practically no other choice but that of complete adjustment to
these very limitations.

  This is the prevailing mood of the Restoration period which followed
the enthusiastic rise of national sentiment during the Wars of Liberation.
The liberal ideas of a new empire and of a constitution, the romantic
idea of an organic state which would constantly recreate and regenerate
itself through the active will of every single citizen—these ideas had
been suppressed by the Congress of Vienna. The authoritarian state
persecuted these ideas; its establishment was not only a casual victory
of reactionary forces, it was a tragic necessity. Especially for the dis-
integrating Danubian monarchy would any liberalistic experiment
have been a definite menace. The old authoritarian and the new consti-
tutional principle appeared here to be almost equally justified, and
external force decided temporarily, at least, in favor of reaction; the
will to establish an order of renewed vitality succumbed to the fear of
possible destruction through such reorientation.

  His personal development as well as his environment forced Grillparzer into the same conflict. His kind-hearted, imaginative mother had

given him poetic vision; but it was also this heritage which drove him into the hypochondriac solitude which paralyzed his will, time and again. His father's severe justice, his withdrawal into himself, which isolated him from his surroundings and thus made him appear harsh and unapproachable, strengthened the passivity in Grillparzer's character. He, too, periodically mistrusts everyone and withdraws into himself, he vacillates between adjustment to his clerical profession and to social demands, on the one hand, and assertion of his inner self on the other. According to his autobiography, his character has

> etwas Rekonziliantes und Nachgiebiges, das sich nur gar zu gern selbst der Leitung anderer überläszt, aber immerwährende Störung und Eingriffe in sein Inneres nicht duldet;

he is receptive and yet extremely solitary. Like his time, he is placed in a tragic dilemma which also confronts the fundamental types of the characters in Grillparzer's dramas.

His tragedy *Blanka von Kastilien* has, as a drama, hardly more than historical value; but it is, for all that, a valuable document of the relation and the reaction of the young dramatist to Schiller's idealism and of the germination of new ideas which evolve in later dramas to a clearly visualized philosophy of life. The drama is inspired by Schiller's *Don Karlos* and distinctly reflects the themes of its model. In *Blanka von Kastilien* as in *Don Karlos* despotism and the enslavement of the individual conscience oppose civil liberty and moral freedom. In Grillparzer's play, as in Schiller's the pessimistic view that men cannot help abusing their freedom contrasts with the optimistic view that freedom is the basis of moral development. The early Grillparzer was hardly able to grasp the real significance of this idea, but, apart from his immaturity, he belonged to a generation which was too remote from the ethical and optimistic conviction of moral freedom—from the climax of the idealistic belief—to be able to accept it without modification.

The selection of the subject matter itself points towards a growing emphasis on the factor of "inclination" as contrasted with moral duty. Surrender to passion and intrigue, isolation of the criminal, growth of criminality to the point of final self-destruction—these are the stages of demoralization portrayed in *Blanka von Kastilien*. Although Grillparzer adopts Schiller's antithesis of duty and inclination, he does it without endorsing the autonomous fulfillment of moral duty, which was the principle of Schiller's classical idealism. Blanka's and Federiko's love is not simply condemned as adulterous. The relation between Blanka and her legal husband, the king, cannot be considered a marriage even from an extremely orthodox point of view, since the king has hardly ever seen his wife. Their marriage is less an inner duty than an external fate. Blanka's fatalistic resignation to her marriage appears almost immoral. Federiko's allegiance to the king is just as inexplainable from the idealistic point of view. It is decidedly heteronomous and therefore immoral according to Kant's and Schiller's ethics, the more so, since Federiko makes himself an accomplice to the crimes of the king through his loyalty to him. In fact, this immoral conception of duty is surmounted in the last act, by the union of the lovers in death—and with that Grillparzer implicitly asserts the value of life as the highest of values.

While Blanka is biased by a doubtful conception of duty, which she holds only with melancholy resignation, Jacqueline, who presents the author's view with less reserve, considers life as a higher value than moral duty:

Ihr hebet eure Träume auf den Thron
der Tugend und glaubt in dem fremden Wesen,
das seine Klauen in das Herz euch schlägt,
die Pflicht, die martervolle, zu verehren.
Nicht Gott ist's, der die Last euch auferlegt,
nein, eure Fantasie wird euer Henker!

(*Final version*, 3127 ff.)

The premarital union with Federiko is praised by the queen as a blessing and an enrichment of her existence:

und ist der Kalte wohl beglückt zu nennen,
der nie, in seinem ganzen Leben nie
so göttlich schön gefehlet, wie du's nennst!

(*l.c.*, 663 ff.)

In the final version of the play, this love idyll is even described in detail in a cave scene reminiscent of that in Gottfried von Strassburg's *Tristan*.

In *Blanka von Kastilien* life is represented as being both outward and inward attachment to others, independent of any reflection or deliberation. Blanka remains attached to her French fatherland* and meets in the foreign country nothing but misfortune, contumely, persecution, and death. Here is the nucleus of the motif which plays such an important part in Grillparzer's later dramas: a character uprooted from his home surroundings experiences moral bewilderment and then disintegration. But Federiko's search for happiness outside of his country and Blanka's

*Second version, 481-510; final version, 4957.

desolation in a foreign country are still treated as casual coincidence and not yet, as in the later dramas, as the dominating motif of the tragedy. From this point of view we can also explain the conception of duty, which is absolutely unintelligible from the idealistic standpoint of the classicists. Grillparzer's notion of duty is not a result of conscious reflection; it is no Kantian ideal which derives its validity from a potential universality and which tends towards realizing the ideal of humanity. It is rather something which exists as a fatal determination before any reflection; it is tradition—attachment to inherited values without any consideration of their fitness for the actual situation.

Life, however, appears also in its active form as will-to-live, in particular, as ruthless striving for power and prestige in the brother and the sister, the Padrillas, and as sensual passion in the king. Schiller's antithesis between moral duty and immoral inclination is preserved only with a decidedly vitalistic weakening of the principle, and sensual desire is even satisfied in the common fate of death.

Die Ahnfrau also gives evidence of Grillparzer's struggle against the idealistic tradition. The absolute determinism of fate in this tragedy is not merely a negation of the idealistic conception of the freedom of will, but also the initiation of a new conception of man. When Schiller in *Die Braut von Messina* dramatizes the blind rule of fate, his intention is to show how moral man, in spite of all causal determination, still has the ability, and therefore the obligation, to preserve his dignity as a personality. Grillparzer, however, submits his characters to the utmost cruelty of fate. They are aware of the higher ideals and want to live up to their ideal obligation, but the vital urge is stronger in them than the ability to pursue the ideal they have chosen. The Ahnfrau herself is subjected to the conflict between ideal will and vital urge; the adultery, for which she must atone, is for her as much an object of self-condemnation as of satisfaction;

> Haszt sie die vergangne Sünde,
> Liebt sie die vergangne Glut.
> (560-61)

The same conflict between free will and the determinism of an inherited past is the fateful heritage of the Borotin family. The old count is oppressed by the dreadful premonition that the end of his house is imminent, but he tries to disregard his presentiment, instead of facing it with the heroic determination characteristic of Schiller's idealism. Scornfully he meets his fate, without any resistance. Passively obeying

[53]

a traditional code of honor, he becomes a tool of this fate when he takes part in the persecution of the robber who, though unknown to him, is his own son.

Jaromir, more than any other character, betrays Grillparzer's reaction against the classical belief in the ideal. He has been uprooted from normal surroundings by his life among the robbers and thus drawn into an inner conflict with human society. His desire is to be human, and his aim, which he seeks to realize in his love for Bertha, is purity and innocence. But his ideal is coupled with a voluptuous sensuality, and it is completely lost in uncontrollable passion when he realizes that the object of his love is his own sister. Thus his ideal is, in part at least, responsible for the final catastrophe. Orestes in Goethe's *Iphigenie* overcomes the urge of his instincts and attains to the ideal of humanity through love for his sister. Grillparzer's Jaromir, however, cannot renounce his sensual love for his sister Bertha; the realization of this love—although ideal in its beginning—only drives him further into crime and destruction. This development only illustrates the poet's conviction that instincts play their part even in ideal striving and may offset its effect entirely. Day-dreaming, silence, and death seem to be the only ways out of the desolation of a fate which, cynically enough, converts all higher endeavors into their very opposite. Thus Bertha finds in everlasting sleep an escape from the entanglements of the will-to-live.

> Lieblich sind des Schlafens Träume,
> Nur das Wachen träumt so schwer.
>
> (2649-50)

In the tragedy *Sappho* idealism again proves illusory, for it would have us believe in the exceptional nature of artistic genius. Sappho, as a poetess, has remained in solitary isolation from the world. Phaon's love has re-established her immediate contact with natural life, and she begins to doubt the value and the singularity of the lofty existence of the artist, which in this drama is a symbol for any idealistic elevation above the immediate and concrete experience of life. Life itself becomes for her the highest aim of life, "des Lebens höchstes Ziel," and fulness of experience becomes more valuable than the ideal loftiness of "arme Kunst." She seeks, therefore, to return to the concreteness of life and to find new roots in the simple idyllic existence of the herdsmen. But her former detachment from the natural sphere continues its fatal hold on her; there is no retreat from a situation which has really been lived

[54]

through, since the experience of the past is an integral part of the present. Sappho, therefore, cannot return to a naïve existence; the attempt to return must become a disappointment for her, and the glory of the poet, once she has experienced it, must mean more to her than empty words, "leer bedeutungsloser Schall."

She comes to realize her failure through Phaon, who, in his first idealistic enthusiasm, confused his admiration for the poetess with love for the woman in her. He, too, is therefore disappointed in Sappho when she wants to be regarded, not as a poet, but as a loving woman. Sensuality alone, however, leads his affections to the simple naturalness of Sappho's youthful slave, Melitta. This in turn causes Sappho to experience the deepest tragedy, which again results from the non-reversibility of the process of life; she cannot even return to the sublime solitude of her poetical world. Instead of heroically resigning herself she, at least temporarily, degrades herself to the lowest level of womanhood when she persecutes Sappho and Phaon with jealousy and vengeance. She can restore her personal dignity only by fully realizing the tragic dilemma she caused when she aspired beyond the limited order of natural simplicity. She realizes that through her spiritual and creative activity she has severed herself from the natural immediateness of life and thus made a return to it impossible. She comprehends, finally, that in the attempt to return to a more naïve stage of humanity she has created a situation for herself from which the only salvation is death, since both ways of life, ideal striving as well as resignation to the pastoral idyll, left her dissatisfied. Life is resignation to one of these types of existence or else destruction in the indecision between the two. Goethe, too, had experienced this tragedy, but he was able to overcome any negative consequences of his experience by the richness of his personality. The drama *Sappho*, however, concludes with resignation and disillusionment. Grillparzer surrenders reluctantly to the conviction that man is, according to his nature, unable to rise from his natural environment to the free and unconditioned sphere of ideality. *Sappho* is the recognition of the tragedy of the mind which allows man to transcend his situation, and which creates in him the illusion of freedom and independence from the entanglements of his sensual existence. It is a symbol for the tragedy of the idealist who believes that he is able to live in lofty detachment and who can never find his way back to the foundation of life because he has severed himself from the roots of his existence.

This tragedy of the idealist implies, first, that man is essentially

[55]

rooted in the elemental stratum of his instincts and in interactive relationship with others; and, second, that man's belief in his ability to free himself from this elemental substratum of his nature is liable to induce him to actions resulting in guilt and catastrophe. Recognition of these facts is the dramatic theme of *Das Goldene Vlies*. At the beginning of the first part of the trilogy, in *Der Gastfreund*, Medea believes herself to be free: "Was ich tu, das will ich—und was ich will—manchmal tu ich's nicht" (66-67). But even then she is really free and truly herself only as an integral part of her natural environment—her family and her people; she is free in so far as her natural will to live is in harmony with her consciousness. This harmony is destroyed when her father, Aietes, violates the laws of hospitality and murders Phrixus in order to obtain the sacred fleece. The mind which raises her above the others makes her conscious of her father's rapacious guilt and the unavoidable catastrophe which such guilt must entail. Her ability to transcend the situation through conscious reflection is her tragic fate. She suffers from her inner disagreement with the others and escapes into a solitude which is neither attachment to her natural environment nor complete separation from it, neither participation in the life of her surroundings nor a decisive and final renunciation of all bonds. The complete realization of guilt destroyed her immediate contact with life, without allowing her an independent, individual existence. Thinking and willing, which idealists believed to be a distinction of man, are for Grillparzer the truly tragic gift. Man is essentially

> Ein töricht Wesen . . . . . .
> Treibt dahin auf den Wogen der Zeit,
> Endlos geschleudert auf und nieder.*

Medea may return to her people when they are menaced by the Argonauts, who have come under Jason's leadership to recapture the golden fleece; but since she lives in inner disharmony with her family and her people, she readily yields to the elemental impulse of her love for Jason, and thereby she is torn farther away from the sphere of her original, naïve existence. When she is first deceived by the illusion that the god of death, Heindar, is asking for her life, this illusion is but an expression of her yearning to return to the sphere of unbroken and unreflecting life, for Jason's love is the greatest menace to her existential rootedness. If she tenders the poisonous cup to Jason, as her father wishes, she may at least preserve the physical contact with the foundation

Argonauten, 230-32.

of her existence, but she can never be inwardly rooted again. She would suffer from the guilt of having murdered a beloved man, although he came as an enemy of her people; and she would thereby be driven into even deeper solitude and dejection than that she had experienced after the murder of Phrixus. Torn between two evils, she saves Jason, impelled by the elemental force of her love; but this choice is in no way a final decision against her father and her people.

Guiltless in the sense that her actions are determined by her natural impulse, Medea becomes thereby responsible for the death of her father and her brother and many of her countrymen, and for this guilt she has to suffer the fate of complete destitution: "Ohne Vater, ohne Heimat, ohne Götter." She follows the man who has left his own country for the sake of adventure, glory, and honor. He, too, is detached from the roots of his natural environment, and in this state he is overpowered by his love for Medea, a love which can persist only as an elemental force in a primitive, unreflecting environment, where the traditional bonds of his original surroundings are ineffective. As soon, however, as he returns to his own Greek world, this elemental tie must become fatal for both characters. Medea cannot but feel homeless in this environment of cultured consciousness, and she is thus absolutely dependent upon a love which at first she obeyed but unwillingly. She tries to forget her past and to live for the moment, but, as an essentially organic being, she is doomed to failure:

> . . . so dürfen wir nicht mehr sein, was wir wollen,
> So lasz uns, was wir können, mindstens sein.
> Laszt uns Sitte und Rede ändern, denn hier ist
> Recht, was dort unrecht . . . .
> . . . . Der Augenblick,
> Wenn er die Wiege einer Zukunft ist,
> Warum nicht auch das Grab einer Vergangenheit.*

The feeling of timelessness is a symptom of the utter dejection and desolation which has befallen Medea. In vain she endeavors to retain Jason's affection by adjusting herself to Greek culture, though that adjustment would, if successful, mean a renunciation of her most personal self. She fails in this endeavor because Jason has returned to his own natural sphere, where he is confronted with the necessity of deciding whether he should adapt himself to the elemental nature of Medea and renounce his own original world, or conform to his original Greek

*Medea, III, 1.

[57]

environment. But he cannot return; he cannot undo his immediate past; it continues to live in him as an inescapable fate, however seriously he may try to disregard the past and to live only in an abstract present. His attachment to Medea determines his fate just as her attachment to him shapes hers. He cannot become the free man again, whom King Kreon wants him to become through the expulsion of Medea. The attempt to separate his future from hers reawakens the primitive energies in her, which cannot but be destructive, since she has severed all bonds with her past and can exist as a moral personality only when supported by the love of him alone for whom she has sacrificed everything. She experiences all the dejection and misery of homelessness when she is deserted by her own children. They are born into the conflict between two worlds and cannot take root in either; their future lot is to be either slaves or criminals. It is, therefore, not only the outbreak of primitive hatred and vengeance which impels her to murder her children, but the hopelessness and the inner annihilation of uprooted man; she is the compassionate mother who desires to save her most sacred possession from physical and moral catastrophe. If she chooses for herself to continue rather than to make an end to her miserable life, her decision is more heroic than Jason's cowardly desire to escape the consequences of his fate; it requires the greatest courage to live out a life of utter disillusionment in a hollow world which has no sympathetic response for her despair.

> Was ist der Erde Glück? . . . . Ein Schatten!
> Was ist der Erde Ruhm? — Ein Traum!
> . . . Der von Schatten du geträumt!
> Der Traum ist aus, allein die Nacht noch nicht.*

The intrinsic value of a drama like this is, of course, not exhausted by the analysis of its psychological motivation. It has to be considered or rather reëxperienced as the expression of despondency in a man who, in spite of all his striving and yearning, never finds any genuine response to his personality; a man who longs to be free and realizes again and again that his will is determined by anonymous powers. *Medea* also expresses the tragic philosophical recognition that man as a consciously thinking and willing individual detaches himself from the all-embracing foundation of life—existential symbiosis—and is thereby drawn into guilt and destruction. Consciousness hinders man's immediate and natural reaction without giving him the power to shape his

*Medea, 2372-5.

individual life independently of the vital forces of his elemental nature. This inhibition of immediate reaction through consciousness is the cause of man's aberrations and moral confusion and, finally, of the tragedy of his desolation in an unresponsive world.

In *König Ottokars Glück und Ende* life is explicitly declared the absolute and fundamental value when Ottokar, shortly before his death, recognized his guilt in the sacrifice of man to his personal ambition:

> Den Menschen, den du hingesetzt zur Lust,
> Ein Zweck, ein Selbst, im Weltall eine Welt—
> Gebaut hast du ihn als ein Wunderwerk . . . .
> Ich aber hab' sie hin zu Tausenden geworfen
> Um einer Torheit, eines Einfalls willen,
> Wie man den Kehricht schüttet vor die Tür . . . (2834 ff.)

In this drama it is apparent that life is interpreted in its essential form as association with others, as activity in an organic community for the welfare of the whole. In such an organic sphere the activity of the individual is regulated and safely founded in naturally evolved institutions and norms.

The highest representative of this form of life is Emperor Rudolf, whose integration in the organism of the state has an almost religious dignity. He has subdued his egotistic will, which knew no bonds, but the regeneration of his character was due to the intercession of God. But Grillparzer had deeply experienced the truth that what is done cannot be undone. Events, once they have occurred, cannot be reversed. The past continues to influence the present. In its miraculous singularity, Rudolf's regeneration by no means contradicts this deterministic view of the fatal irreversibility of life:

> Da nahm mich Gott mit seiner starken Hand
> Und setzte mich auf jene Thronesstufen,
> Die aufgerichtet steh'n ob einer Welt! . . .
> So fiel's wie Schuppen ab von meinen Augen,
> Und all mein Ehrgeiz war mit eins geheilt.
> (1908-1912)

Rudolf appears less as a human character than as the embodiment of the author's ideal postulate, that man should find a task and a limitation of his concern for the welfare of the whole. In Rudolf is the first, abstract indication of the aim of Grillparzer's entire work: Rudolf must reëstablish on a higher level of conscious activity that inner harmony which was lost during the disintegration of man's original, organic community.

Rudolf characterizes himself as such an idealistic and abstract character:

Was sterblich war, ich hab's ausgezogen
Und bin der Kaiser nur, der niemals stirbt.

(1787-88)

In other words, defying the law of inconvertibility, he has thrown off his past; as the representative of the ideal demand he has become timeless.

König Ottokar impersonates the catastrophe of uncontrolled will. He has less restraint and less regard for others than Jason had, and what he does for his people is not motivated by any feeling of responsibility or obligation. His actions are not, like Rudolf's, the outgrowth of an objective and wise consideration of his people's needs and wants. He is the egotist who is driven only by his ambition and his indomitable desire for power, and who has no regard for human rights and no respect for the inherent value of human personality. His individual will is completely detached from any deeper roots and is therefore seduced by a rational force which drives his unfettered will from one aim to the other, without any hope of satisfaction. Such a will is doomed to that restlessness which Schopenhauer in his main treatise, *The World as Will and Idea*, considers as the fate of the consciously-willing man.

Never bound by the will of the larger group, he is supported by this group only so long as his personal aims happen to coincide with, or at least not to conflict with, those of others. It is for egotistic, dynastic reasons alone that Ottokar demands a divorce from his wife Margarete, whom he had also married for political reasons. If he invokes any legal authorities to obtain this divorce, it means no more for him than an empty formality necessary to avoid unwelcome criticism or opposition. He rejects Berta von Rosenberg because a marriage with her does not offer sufficient political advantage, and he marries Kunigunde, the daughter of the King of Hungary, not expecting more from her than an increase in territory and an heir to his throne. Without any understanding for organically developed customs, he insults the legates of the Tartars by mocking at the impracticality of their curved swords and their queues. He orders the suburb of Prague to be evacuated in order to have it settled by Germans, for he values an unrooted rational civilization more highly than indigenous culture. The arrogance of the egotist devoid of any inner attachment reaches its climax in the infatuated answer to the elective council:

[60]

Doch will ich lieber hier in Böhmen sitzen
Und eines armen deutschen Kaisers lachen,
Als selbst ein armer deutscher Kaiser sein.
Indes verschmäh' ich nicht, die höchste Macht
Vielleicht zu krönen mit der höchsten Würde . . .
Doch soll man mir die Kron' erst selber bringen . . .
Bevor ich mich entscheide was geschieht.

(1178-87)

After he has forfeited his chance of being elected Emperor, through his refusal to accept any obligation, his fatal isolation begins. He is still capable of refusing to swear fealty to the emperor, but his self-assurance soon begins to weaken and he consequently loses his fight against the emperor. Again he has neither the inner courage to carry his revolt to complete self-destruction nor the self-control to submit to the new master. Ottokar's oath of allegiance and his genuflection before the emperor, which for others symbolizes acknowledgment of the order and integrity of the empire, is an act of the lowest debasement for him who knows only himself and his egotistic aims. When his genuflection is made known to the people by Zawisch's treason, his morale breaks down completely. At this point, the enormous danger of rational detachment from the elemental foundations, the danger of unrooted life, becomes obvious. He who seemed so absolutely sure of himself is demoralized to the lowest degree of instability. He feels himself despised and destitute and thus completely dependent upon the opinion of others. Zawisch seduces his wife, for whose demoralization Ottokar is more responsible than anyone else, for he caused her to leave her natural Hungarian environment. In the misery of his debasement, he takes petty revenge on the aged knight Merenberg. Compelled more by the obsession of his humiliation than by his own conscious will, he rebels once more against the emperor. It is no longer a courageous and daring opposition, but a languishing hesitation, a reluctant submission to the final expiation. His self-assurance has subsided into passive humility; a broken man, he bows before the supreme power of death at the bier of his rejected wife:

Um was ich dich und alles gab,
Gefallen ist's von mir, wie Laub im Herbst; . . . . .
Und einsam steh' ich da. von Leid gebeugt,
Und niemand tröstet mich, und niemand hört mich.

(2662-67)

He recognizes his selfish disregard and contempt for the life of others as his greatest guilt and falls an inglorious victim to the revenge of the young Merenberg, whose father he has killed. Yet his death appears less as an atonement for his crimes than as the necessary and tragic consequence when the conscious will is isolated from its natural contacts. In such isolation his life loses its meaning, and the danger of destruction grows in the same proportion as he frees himself in his actions from the foundations of his existence.

The same problematic existence of unrooted man is represented in Duke Otto von Meran in the tragedy *Ein treuer Diener seines Herrn.* Ordinarily this character is considered only as the villain of the play and as the antagonist of Bancbanus; generally his negative traits—his irresponsibility, his disloyalty, his frivolity, and his playful superficiality—are merely enumerated; no attempt is made to analyze the motivation of these traits. Yet Grillparzer plainly states the fact that Otto was never allowed to grow into an environment which might have supported his moral character and this is the cause of his demoralization. Born in the Alps and educated in Paris, he now leads an empty and aimless life as the companion of his sister at the Hungarian court. His utter lack of self-control makes it impossible for the king to entrust him with the duties of an administrator during his absence; yet his moral character could be saved by the assumption of such a responsibility, as his sister, the queen, well realizes. Without any responsible function in the administration of the state, Otto abandons himself to fateful drifting. His will remains without direction and controlling norms; in its isolation and aimlessness even its temporary flaring up lacks the elevating effect of a strong natural instinct.

But what causes Otto's ruin is more than mere stubbornness and hysterical rage akin to that of a child denied the fulfillment of its wishes. It is something more tragic than boundless embitterment against the woman who rejected his wooing. His begging for the least bit of sympathy and human respect is the last cry of a soul drowning in the solitude of nothingness. Just as he sought a support in the duties of a public office, so he seeks his salvation from complete dejection and moral ruin in Erny, whose absolute virtue he recognizes and esteems. Again, it is his tragedy that by his attitude he has forfeited the right to be believed and trusted, so that Erny cannot but reject his most sincere plea. Thus she too, though innocently, shares responsibility for Otto's complete moral collapse, which immediately follows her escape into death. Now the extreme misery of human dejection breaks forth. The energy of his wanton youth has disappeared; like Ottokar, he loses all power of resistance to his impending fate; not even the miserable solace of complete insanity is granted him. Homeless, he is banished to the world which has always denied him the rights of a citizen.

While Otto von Meran represents the tragic disintegration of the uprooted individual, in Bancbanus rootedness is carried to such an extreme that, paradoxically, its value appears as very questionable. Bancbanus is so firmly and one-sidely adjusted to his position in the structure of the state organism that his whole existence is undermined by the temporary assumption of a higher duty. He is the unreservedly submissive and faithful servant, the official who knows only the wish of his superior and who fulfills his duty with unswerving loyalty and with literal obedience. In his subordinate position, where others do the thinking for him and assume the responsibility, he can exist without any risk or danger to himself or to others; and in that position he also serves the best interests of the state. But to entrust him with the responsibilities of a vice-regency is the most fatal overestimation of his discriminatory powers. In loyal obedience he assumes a task completely contradictory to his servile nature, a task which requires a sense of the essential structure of the state and the courage of responsible decision and action, and not a stoical passivity. This task draws him out of the narrowly confined sphere of his activity and ability and ultimately causes his destruction. It raises him above everything that is merely personal into the sphere of representative function, for which, however, he has neither the external authority nor the inner autonomy. It is one of the few reconciling, manly traits credited to him—in spite of his unmanly fatalism—that he is able to subordinate all his personal interests to the superpersonal duty; even his passivity has an element of grandeur when he saves the man who destroyed his wife in order to preserve his loyalty to the king. Schiller would at this point have exposed the sublimity of the human character; he would have shown how man conquers fatal necessity by his absolute determination to do his freely assumed duty. Grillparzer, however, does not attempt to diminish the desolating tragedy of human existence; Bancbanus suffers and humbly resigns himself to a world which punishes with inner destruction even the passive transgression of the human limits. Every individual has such limits assigned to him by the irrevocable determination of his character and by his place in the organism of the world.

Man appears in this drama in an intolerable dilemma. Uprootedness, even apart from all guilt, is fatal for him; yet a belated attempt to root himself in a more organic and responsible form of life may prove fatal. Complete rootedness, however, limits his flexibility and adaptability to such an extent that even a temporary transplantation may be his ruin, and withal he is not even allowed the consolation of Schiller's idealistic belief in inner freedom, in spite of all his determination. This double exposure of man to the dangers of both uprootedness and complete rootedness, with its consequent pessimistic and paralyzing effects, demands an adjustment which will attribute a relative significance and a living value and function to both forms of life.

The drama *Der Traum ein Leben* may be considered as an attempt to harmonize these two antagonisms. Both tendencies, that of a quiet and self-restraining contentment with one's self and that of an unrestrained striving beyond one's self, are united in Rustan. He lives in a modest rural environment, to which he is bound by his love for Mirza. Yet he has inherited the warrior spirit of his ancestors, which drives him away from his idyllic life on extensive hunting trips and engages him in serious quarrels. He gradually yields to the evil influence of Zanga, a Mephistophelean figure impersonating the restlessness of unrestrained striving. While in earlier dramas only the catastrophic results of such a striving were pointed out, striving is in this drama the transition stage to a conscious, and thus deepened, adjustment of the individual to an adequate environment.

This escape from the tragic consequences is, however, not reached by a consciously adopted change, that is, by the determination of a free will, but by the subconscious experience of dream life, a device which Grillparzer borrowed from the Spanish drama. In his dream, Rustan experiences the consequences of unrestrained striving, namely, moral degradation and destruction. With his complete devotion to external striving, he sacrifices his personal self. His actions are no longer determined from his inner centrum, in which his own desires and the needs of those in his sphere of life are integrated; they are rather determined by the accidental combination of outside conditions. They do not allow any free decision or any sympathetic regard for the wishes of others. His ambitious striving places Rustan in the paradoxical situation in which, with every success, his will becomes more dependent upon conditions beyond his control from which he intended to free himself by leaving his narrow environment. His dependence is symbolically indicated by the fact that Rustan starts on his adventures, not under his own name, but under the assumed name of the Emir's son, and by the fact that the rescue of the king, which opens the way for him to the court, is the deed of somebody else. This theft of another's deed forces him to murder the actual rescuer, and, when the crime becomes known, to poison the king himself. When he is then brought to account for the assassination, he can save his life only by destroying a whole city. Thus he is driven by his ambitious activity into an inescapable fate and to complete despair. In the realistic setting of Grillparzer's earlier dramas, Rustan would end in self-destruction; here the dream experience is sufficient to make him realize the deeper value of his self and return to idyllic reality, there to find his satisfaction:

> Eines nur ist Glück hienieden,
> Eins: des Innern stiller Frieden
> Und die schuldbefreite Brust!
> Und die Grösze ist gefährlich,
> Und der Ruhm ein leeres Spiel;
> Was er gibt, sind nicht'ge Schatten,
> Was er nimmt, ist nicht so viel!
> (2653-59)

He never, of course, was a man with a clear vision and valuable aims, but a rover and adventurer who, without any ability, pursued his vague illusions of glory and greatness. Not all striving, but only that striving which transcends the real ability of the particular individual is, therefore, condemned by his example.

The pessimistic mood which characterized the tragedy *Ein treuer Diener seines Herrn* is also mitigated in *Des Meeres und der Liebe Wellen,* in spite of its tragic ending. The end is not an expression of complete disillusionment and fatalism, but of a desire for a more natural life, in which the values which are here doomed to catastrophe would be saved. Hero's acceptance of the temple service is, unlike Rustan's dream adventures, an escape from a world of suppression and of inner desolation. Her father is a hard-hearted, ambitious, and selfish household tyrant, to whose rule mother and daughter submit only reluctantly; nor does Hero find any sympathy from her heartless brother. Thus the temple appears to her as a place where she might find justice and peace, for there, at least, there is no discrimination between the sexes and consequently no suppression of the weaker sex. Here she hopes to be free from the confusing entanglements of the world and free to live up to the demands of her self. But she fails to see the whole import of this resignation from the world and of subordination to the priestly norms. Since her womanhood has not grown to maturity, she cannot suspect the danger to which she is exposed by her unnatural renunciation of instinctive nature. In her desire for an undisturbed inner life, she violates

[65]

the laws of life, which cannot be limited and protected by human regulations. Life is not only existence for one's own self, but existence with and for others as well. With her vow of chastity she submits to a limitation comparable to that of Bancbanus in his pedantic officialdom.

At the very ceremony which is to sever her from the outside world and to confine her in the isolation of the temple, she is seized by the instinct of love, which should have been the foundation for growth into an organic environment. She shares this love with a man who, in similar solitude, is longing for a deeper relation and attachment to others. Leander grew up without a father; he lived with his mother and devoted himself entirely to her care when she succumbed to her melancholy dejection after the death of her husband. Hero and Leander are thus destined for one another by the similarity of their inner fate, and they are separated from one another by a norm which owes its origin and the rigor of its form to conscious reason. The law of the priests, which promised protection and justice, becomes a menace and an injustice; it turns out to be a distortion of the natural order, according to which reason has not the right to claim absolute mastery over the instincts, but acknowledges and respects the instinctive substratum as the primary and fundamental existence.

Placed between natural fulfillment of her womanhood and life-restricting rules, Hero cannot make a free decision any longer. The peace which she sought in the solitude of the temple is irrevocably lost, once the conflict has arisen within her; submission to the rules of the temple in this condition means the destruction of her nature. Violation of her vow and consequent liberation would involve exile from her country— the Medean fate of uprootedness and complete demoralization,—not only for herself but for her entire family. By a premature limitation of her nature she has brought herself into a situation in which will and resignation lead to the same fatal catastrophe. Her fate is the same as with so many of Grillparzer's characters: she is forced into the impasse between action and non-action, and passively she faces the inescapable end, in which life avenges any conscious effort of suppression. After she has rejected Leander's love, she is moved by compassion for a man who is in similar danger, and so she gradually yields to his passionate and hazardous wooing. Then after the love-night in the tower, only external pressure keeps her in the secluded world of the priests. She rejects the laws of the temple and embraces the higher obligation of natural life:

...... auch meine Pflichten kenn' ich;
Wenn Pflicht das alles, was ein ruhig Herz
Im Einklang mit sich selbst und mit der Welt
Dem Recht genüber stellt der andern Menschen .....
Die Götter sind zu hoch für unsere Rechte.
(1728ff.)

There is no possibility of saving Hero and Leander; for the law of the temple is a rational law and therefore absolutely rigorous. The rational principle is considered as more important than life itself; life must be sacrificed ruthlessly when a principle is at stake. That was apparent in the warning words of the priest before he discovered the violation of the law:

Doch stieszest du des Freundes Rat zurück,
Du fändest auch in mir den Mann, der willig
Das eigne Blut aus diesen Adern gösse,
Wüszt' er nur einen Tropfen in der Mischung,
Der Unrecht birgt und Unerlaubtes hegt.
(994-98)

To prevent the further violation of this law, Leander must die; and with his death Hero's life loses its meaning; for she has realized that life is more than isolated existence in and for one's self, that it is rather existence in and for others.

In *Ein treuer Diener seines Herrn* tragedy resulted from an exaggeration of the principle of the integral state order (*Standesstaat*), in which life was in danger of being degraded into a mechanical function. The same danger of a petrification of organic life is more explicitly dramatized in *Des Meeres und der Liebe Wellen*. The inner conflict of Bancbanus is here impersonated in antagonistic characters, one representing natural instinct and the other, the limitation of life by rational regulation. Furthermore, the extreme form of rootedness, the Bancbanus type, is here also considered as ruled by reason. Since Grillparzer—and this fact cannot be emphasized too strongly—conceives of life as the fundamental value and of reason only as an instrument for deepening and enriching life, the emancipation of reason and its predominance over life can only be a perversion of the natural order. This perversion, however, is in both these dramas seen to be founded in the process of life itself. In *Ein treuer Diener seines Herrn* it is interpreted as an extreme result of adjustment to organized life; in *Des Meeres und der Liebe Wellen*, as a refuge of the self from the repression and the confusion of the world. These attitudes originated as forms of life; but both the prin-

[67]

ciple of subordination and that of chaste isolation from natural life become a menace to life in the absoluteness of their claim. In this absoluteness the paradox and the immanent tragedy of life are revealed. With the help of reason life establishes limitations which violate its very essence and cause its own destruction.

In the comedy *Weh dem der lügt,* Grillparzer further elaborates the main theme of *Des Meeres und der Liebe Wellen,* but the mere fact that the author chooses now the comic form to express his ideas seems to indicate a somewhat more objective attitude toward the problem of life. This does not mean that Grillparzer begins to minimize the problematic aspect; on the contrary, his comedy, like his tragedies, revolves about the essentially unsolvable paradox of life. Both forms, the comic and the tragic, serve to reveal the disharmony between the two poles of unrestrained vital energy and rationally directed life. It is the nature of comedy to compare a claim with its realization and to point out the resultant discrepancy between the claim and its not even approximate fulfillment, however deceiving superficial appearance may be. In this drama, Bishop Gregory's demand, that nothing but the truth be told, represents the claim. All of Leon's actions are held up against it in order to determine how far an absolute principle can be harmonized with the realities of actual life.

When Bishop Gregory demands in the first act of the play that the principle of truth be upheld unconditionally in word and in deed, he does it first of all as a priest and as a representative of the absolute, divine norm. However, the postulate of truth is simultaneously characterized as a rational abstraction from the experience of life, for, because he had told a falsehood, Gregory had missed the opportunity to free his beloved nephew, Atalus, from captivity. For this reason he allows Leon to attempt the rescue but only on condition that he proceed with absolute truthfulness. Leon, however, is an unspoiled child of nature, for whom a lie, until then, had been nothing but play and an innocent instrument for reaching the ends which his amiable nature suggested to him. A desire to find rest and direction for his unsteady temperament has induced him to accept a position as cook in the bishop's household. Respect and love for his good-hearted master have led him to promise not to lie, although he is convinced that action in this world and uncompromising principles are mutually exclusive. Since he is mainly concerned with the success of his plan, he is satisfied with a merely formal fulfillment of the principle. When he says to Kattwald that he intends to escape and to take someone else along, and that he has the wrong key,

[68]

he speaks the objective truth; but just this plain statement of the truth is deception, since the professed intention is made to seem ridiculous and unbelievable by such an open confession. He also deceives by his deeds, as when he spices the meal too highly and thus makes the whole court drink too much so that during their drunkenness he may safely escape. Edrita in her natural truthfulness, plainly analyzes his insincerity:

> Es lügt der Mensch mit Worten nicht allein,
> Auch mit der Tat. Sprachst du die drohn'de Wahrheit,
> Und wir, wir haben dennoch ihr vertraut,
> War Lüge denn, was dir erwarb Vertrauen.
>
> (1137-41)

Leon can reconcile his conscience only because he gives the principle of truthfulness a relativistic interpretation. Again and again he tries to live up to the absolute demand of the principle; but when, at the end of the play, he examines his deeds in order to justify himself before his master, he must humbly admit his own depravity.

At the last moment, the success of his adventurous rescue is once more endangered. He prays for a miraculous intervention of God. His prayer is answered: his countrymen have just conquered the city in which he is seeking refuge from Kattwald's pursuit. This divine intervention must be interpreted as a recognition of his good intention to satisfy the absolute norm. It is also a symbol of how the basic problem is solved: the moral principle demands of man that he unreservedly acknowledge and conform to its imperative; but man is unable to comply with the principle; in spite of his best intentions, his actions will always fall short of realizing the ideal demand. Yet the absoluteness of the demand retains its value as a regulative principle. As Leon is led by his experience from natural unconcern to acknowledgment of the ethical norm, so Bishop Gregory learns to restrict his absolute demand to the humanly possible. He recognizes that relative fulfillment is the utmost which can be achieved by a human being actively engaged in the affairs of the world. Man cannot submit to a rigorous principle which limits any active part in life; yet the opposite situation, complete aimlessness of the human will, is also not a tolerable solution for the problem. What man must and can achieve, however, is a synthesis: the flexibility of life and the respect for a principle must both determine the direction of his decisions.

The theme of *Die Jüdin von Toledo* is similar to that of *Weh dem der lügt*. In both dramas, life as a vital impulse is contrasted with the moral norm, and the absolute validity of this norm is questioned. The solution

[69]

given in *Die Jüdin von Toledo,* however, is more closely related to that of *Der Traum ein Leben,* since in these two dramas the temporary abandonment of one's self to the aimless and boundless drift of life is considered as a transition of educational and moral value. However, the experience of a dream in *Der Traum ein Leben* is treated in *Die Jüdin von Toledo* as a reality, and therefore leaves a deeper impression on both the reader and the audience, once Grillparzer's organic law of the inconvertibility of the life-process is understood.

King Alphonse has been brought up to rule a world and yet carefully guarded from the world; without practical and independent experience, without any active coöperation on his part, he has become the responsible ruler over the destiny of his people. In Eleonore of England he finds a Puritan wife who sees in marriage only the "von Gott geadelte, greuelhafte Sünde" (1202). She is faultless and pharisaically proud of her virtue but without any sympathetic understanding for the living and unrestrained energies in man and without any deep interest in the people over which she is set as queen. She cannot, therefore, signify anything but disillusionment and repression for Alphonse's vivid Spanish temperament. He realizes that her attitude is due to lack of vitality and that life without courage is not life in the deeper and fuller sense of the word. According to Grillparzer, a character does not prove his value in a phlegmatic, passionless fulfillment of conventional norms, but in an active and immediate contact with a dangerous situation. Only by facing this dangerous situation can man perfect his inner self.

> War einer je gerecht, der niemals hart?
> Und der da mild, ist selten ohne Schwäche.
> Der Tapf're wird zum Waghals in der Schlacht,
> Besiegter Fehl' ist all des Menschen Tugend,
> Und wo kein Kampf, da ist auch keine Macht.
>
> (171-75)

By his opposition to the negativeness of the queen's virtues, the king is prepared to meet Rahel, the Jewess, who, with her demoniac vitality, is almost a symbolic impersonation of the unrestrained passion of life. Her essence is sensual self-dissipation. Her reason offers hardly any resistance to her sensuality, and even fails to exert its life-preserving function, so that she drifts helplessly into the fate of self-destruction. The king is somewhat more restrained. In spite of his conviction that the experience of danger is necessary for the development of a strong character, he only hesitatingly and with inner reluctance reaches his

[70]

decision. Anxiously he vacillates between risking and preserving his royal dignity, which, however, he jeopardizes by his very indecision. Similarly, his passion rises to a point where it endangers the interests of the state, but he never loses himself entirely and unreservedly. Hardly has he satisfied his sexual hunger when he feels the disgust of surfeit; but this reaction cannot induce him to retreat resolutely to his royal duty. As a typical Grillparzer character, he remains under the spell of his experience, and he can only be freed from Rahel by her death. Not until he stands before the dead body does he recognize the inferior value of abandoning one's self to the aimless and unrestricted impulse of life. His sensuality has made him the main culprit in Rahel's death without leaving him even the consolation that he has done everything in his power to save her from her cruel fate.

The transition from this experience to the resumption of his royal duties is only imperfectly motivated. The inner shock brought about by the realization of his guilt is so inadequately expressed that only actors of such mimic talent as Kainz succeed in giving a convincing interpretation of the change. The last scene, however, leaves no doubt about the meaning and the value of the king's transgression for his moral development. Having overcome his all too human weaknesses, he is prepared to fulfill the duties of his royal office, when, at this point, the dangers of the battle restore to him his forfeited right of existence. He will be saved less as a man than as the impersonal representative of the objective system of the state; in his subjective existence he could, according to Grillparzer's opinion, hardly be saved.

The drama in which Grillparzer's views find their final expression and their most lucid synthesis, is the tragedy *Libussa*. Here psychological insight and historical and philosophic speculation are combined with the expression of his own problems and his reaction to the situation of his time. According to the philosophy of *Libussa*, man originally lives a harmonious life in closest contact with nature. Even his reasoning is not directed toward forceful subjection of the natural energies for utilitarian ends; nature is rather the object of reverent contemplation; man admires the immutable laws of nature and of the human mind. Contemplative man hovers timeless above all human events, above earthly cares and wishes.

Libussa abandons this state of absolute harmony to enter the disquieting sphere of active life. Her first step is apparently one of utter insignificance; she goes into the forest to find medicinal herbs for her dying father. Yet this one step away from the mere contemplation of

[71]

nature determines the entire direction of her life, for it is the beginning of the exploitation of nature for human needs:

> Ein Schritt aus dem Gewohnten . . . . .
> Er zieht unhaltsam hin auf neue Bahnen,
> Nur vorwärts führt das Leben, rückwarts nie.
>
> (384-86)

This first step away from a mode of life which is complete in itself ties her to the laws of a world from which there is no return. After she has met Primislaus she can honor the memory of her father only by taking over the duties of his kingdom, for the contemplative life of her sisters appears monotonous and shallow to her after she has once come into active contact with life:

> Mit Menschen Mensch zu sein, dünkt von heut mir Lust.
>
> (404)

It is her fate that life cannot be changed by sudden decisions and that the past is a determining factor in the shaping of the present and the future. When Libussa realizes her love for Primislaus, she tries to escape by magic incantations and to leave the responsibility of decision to unknown powers. Similarly, her reign vacillates between motherly confidence in the congeniality of mankind and conscious regulation. Without rigorous norms, her patriarchal state is to be an immediate expression of human inter-dependence and cooperation, a natural organism in which the laws of nature function without the pressure of rational legislation.

> Ich bin ein Weib und, ob ich es vermöchte,
> So widert mir die starre Härte doch.
> Wollt ihr nun mein als einer Frau gedenken,
> Lenksam dem Zaum, so dasz kein Stachel not,
> Will freudig ich die Ruhmesbahn euch lenken,
> Ein überhörtes wär' mein letzt' Gebot.
>
> (429-34)
>
> In Zukunft herrscht nur Eines hier im Land:
> Das kindliche Vertraun.
>
> (444-45)

It is one of the laws of human nature, however, that the will tends to free itself from its natural bonds and to strive toward the predominance of the rational over the irrational, a development which is a menace to the existence of organic life within, as well as outside of, the individual. In Libussa's state the rational element unconsciously breaks forth in the quarrels of the peasants over the boundaries of their fields, in their refusal to accept a compromise, and in their demand for a legal decision, —a decision not based upon the sympathetic relation between men, but on the objective examination of the case and the logical application of a fixed norm:

Recht, das Recht zugleich und Unrecht und statt Vernunft Gesetz ist.
(1000-01)

With rational criticism and consistency the Wladiken demand the restoration of the rule of a male king. Thus, the appearance of Primislaus is prepared for by the needs of the state; he is to change the organic form of the patriarchal state into the rational form of a legally and constitutionally ordered monarchy. In spite of the fact that he is a man and therefore more governed by reason and will, yet he, too, must consciously free himself from a life which had been content in its close contact with nature. He, too, hesitates to abandon the harmony of his primitive life to enter the world and to accept the responsibility of ruling and of regulating life with his rational will. Therefore, he leaves the initiative entirely to Libussa. Although he loves her, he fears in this very love an impending obligation to the world; and when he finally assumes the obligation, it is only his love for Libussa which determines his decision. The character test in the fourth act epitomizes in a symbolic fairy-tale-like form the deeper significance of this transition from organic existence into a more rationally governed world. In this scene, it is not the wisdom which Primislaus shows in resisting the enticements of wealth, knowledge, strength, and beauty that wins him Libussa's hand and the kingdom; it is his shrewdness and determined will which are accepted as qualifications for his task as a ruler.

In Primislaus' rule rationally planned action characteristically dominates over instinctive and impulsive action. Under his rule people leave the country and settle in artificially created cities, in which all natural life is levelled by the limitations of space. As their needs increase, so do their claims on life; but their original peace and contentment have disappeared, and no longer is there opportunity for a contemplative life. After her last spontaneous action, the wooing of Primislaus, Libussa herself tries to return to the sphere of her primitive, organic existence, but according to Grillparzer's views, this return is denied to man. The only way out of the conflict between organic rootedness in nature and adjustment to a rational world is, therefore, extinction. This fate is imposed on Libussa by Primislaus' wish that she bless with her prophecy his rationally planned work, the founding of the city. To fulfill this

[73]

request means a further yielding to the rational world, since it implies that the religious emotion, whose source is in the elemental nature of man, must be subordinated to the aims of human reason. In a last supreme effort, therefore, which reveals the complete hopelessness of this conflict, Libussa attempts to fulfill Primislaus' wish. She returns to those depths of her inner self where she feels at one with the organic universe, and out of this forcibly restored harmony she is able to prophesy the course of the future development of the human community, a course which reflects her individual fate.

The evolution of the natural patriarchial state into a rationally ordered state is apostasy from nature; it is an inversion of the natural relation of instincts and reason; it is a dissolution of the whole into disconnected parts; it substitutes practical considerations for moral valuation; it involves a rationalization of natural polytheism into monotheistic and pantheistic abstractions and finally ends in the self-deification of man. Concrete sympathy with one's neighbors is generalized in universal love of mankind, and thus is deprived of any emotional force. Genuine sympathy is replaced by fanaticism; the ideal deteriorates into a means of propaganda to incite men to hatred and war. Equality and freedom are the slogans of the envious, who would declare themselves against any higher merit. Under the rule of reason, the world, which is severed from its natural foundation, is declining into a final state of mechanization and petrification:

> Dann schlieszen sich des Himmels goldne Pforten,
> Begeisterung und Glauben und Vertraun
> Und was herabträuft von den sel'gen Göttern
> Nimmt nicht den Weg mehr zu der flachen Welt.
> Im Leeren regt vergebens sich die Kraft
> Und wo kein Gegenstand da ist kein Wirken.
>
> (2390-95)

Only one hope remains: it may mean a simultaneous beginning of a new integration, a regeneration of the old state of harmony with nature:

> Doch an die Grenzen seiner Macht gelangt . . . . .
> Wird er die Leere fühlen seines Innern . . .
> Beschwichtigt das Getöse lauter Arbeit,
> Vernimmt er neu die Stimmen seiner Brust . . .
> Dann kommt die Zeit die jetzt vorübergeht,
> Die Zeit der Seher wieder und Begabten.
> Das Wissen und der Nutzen scheiden sich
> Und nehmen das Gefühl zu sich als Drittes;

Und haben sich die Himmel dann verschlossen,
Die Erde steigt empor an ihren Platz.
(2470 ff.)

Libussa shows more distinctly than any of Grillparzer's earlier dramas
how closely his dramatic problem is connected with those of the nineteenth century transition period. He could not see in this period anything
but a disintegration of the organic form of human society and an
increasingly materialistic spirit. This view of Grillparzer's also explains
his rejection of the Young German emancipation, which for him could
only be identical with the disintegration of organic life. *Libussa* is a
step further in the solution of his main problem, for in it he sees the
decline of organic life and its replacement by rational regulation—the
change from rootedness to uprootedness, to use the terminology applied
to Grillparzer's earlier dramas—as inherent in the evolutionary process
of life. In addition to that, he at least hesitantly admits the possibility of
rhythm in this evolution, according to which the decline would be followed by a renewed integration.

In the tragedy *Ein Bruderzwist im Hause Habsburg* the disintegration which Grillparzer considered as a contemporary problem is projected into the time of the Reformation just preceding the Thirty Years'
War. It contains the author's political creed, and it reflects his position
regarding the revolution of 1848. On the one hand, he recognizes the
political mistakes caused by the indecision of the responsible statesmen,
but he also believes that it is impossible to halt the course of events,
and that the application of severe measures will only hasten the outbreak of the catastrophe. Our analysis of *Libussa* has shown that Grillparzer considered the victory of democratic ideas as a catastrophe
for the state as well as for human culture in general. This attitude
toward the events of his time together with some of his personal traits,
is embodied in the character of Rudolf II. Rudolf is afraid of any active
contact with the reality of the world and is predisposed to a contemplative life. It is, therefore, his tragedy that he is placed in a position in
which he is least allowed to be himself and in which he must represent
the world, in the most impersonal office of a king. His longing soul,
however, lives in a timeless stage of inner harmony with nature, which
man, in his development, has left behind him; thus he finds in the lowest
animal more truth than in man:

Drum ist in Sternen Wahrheit, im Gestein,
In Pflanze, Tier und Baum, im Menschen nicht.
Und wer's verstünde, still zu sein wie sie,

[75]

Gelehrig fromm, den eignen Willen meisternd,
Ein aufgespanntes, demutvolles Ohr,
Ihm würde leicht ein Wort der Wahrheit kund,
Die durch die Welten geht aus Gottes Munde.
(411-17)
Dort oben wohnt die Ordnung, dort ihr Haus,
Hier unten eitle Willkür und Verwirrung.
(428-29)

His conservative attitude towards the religious strife of the time accords wholly with his belief that originally all men lived in naïve and idyllic unity but later fell from this state of grace into strife. It is not personal intolerance which makes him an opponent of the Protestant demands, for the exterior form of religion is of no significance to him; belief is a matter of the heart and "reint sich selbst in reinen Herzen" (335). He can respect the nobility of character in the Protestant duke Julius von Braunschweig, but he sees in the Protestant movement a menace to the organic unity of his people and with that a menace to the achievements of science and art, which can thrive only so long as this unity is preserved. Freedom of belief is for him the slogan behind which an undisciplined urge for power is hidden:

Mag sein, dasz diese Spaltung im Beginn
Nur miszverstandene Satzungen des Glaubens,
Jetzt hat sie gierig in sich eingesogen
Was Unerlaubtes sonst die Welt bewegt.
(1233-35)

The result of striving for freedom and equality will thus be a complete debasement of all that is great.

But the decline cannot be prevented. Rudolf's consciousness of the approaching end does not give him any power over the course of events; it only increases the tragedy of his position in a chaotic world. The only reason for his existence is to keep alive the memory of the times when men still lived as an organic community:

Mein Haus wird bleiben, immerdar,
. . . . . weil es einig mit dem Geist des All,
Durch Klug und scheinbar Unklug, rasch und zögernd,
Den Gang nachahmt der ewigen Natur
Und in dem Mittelpunkt der eignen Schwerkraft
Der Rückkehr harrt der Geister, welche schweifen.
(1277-83)

He lives in the utter solitude and dejection of the wise man who realizes the fatality of apostasy from natural existence, but who is doomed by

[76]

his position to participate in the universal guilt. His knowledge forces him again and again to actions which are intended to retard the advent of the final chaos, as, for example, the war against the Turks or the signing of the charter; but his efforts only help to hasten the process of disintegration. So he departs from this world, deprived of his imperial dignity, a broken man who can find no consolation in the value of his deeds, and whose only hope is the salvation he expects in accordance with his religious belief. The empire he leaves is helplessly drifting into the suicide of the Thirty Years' War.

Kleist's struggle was directed against the rationalized forms of life which, according to his belief, undermined all human relations. His aim was a regeneration on the basis of a sympathetic understanding among men. His point of departure and attack was the rationalistic tradition. Grillparzer's work rests on the same antagonism between rationalized forms and sympathetic understanding, but for him the ideal of organic and sympathetic relation between men is a value of the past, and the growing rationalism is a menace of the future. This explains the different mood of the two dramatists. Kleist remains, in spite of his personal fate, the idealist who believes in the values of the idealistic system and in the necessity, as well as in the possibility, of their realization. Grillparzer's work, however, leaves the impression of a man who defends a hopeless position and who is too pessimistic to offer any effective resistance to the impending catastrophe. He has lost Kleist's faith in regeneration through the moral will, and he tries to reconcile himself in a long and tiring struggle against unavoidable decadence.

In his first dramas, though they were written under classical influence, Grillparzer abandons the idealistic view that man might by his moral will master his destiny. In *Blanka von Kastilien* the brutal, irresponsible, and shrewdly calculating characters prevail. Even the sympathetic characters are far from possessing the moral automony of their classical model, Don Karlos; their attitude, moreover, is mainly determined by tradition and desire. In the *Ahnfrau* Grillparzer consciously rejects the sublime freedom of the moral character, as portrayed in Don Cesar in *Die Braut von Messina;* he deprives his hero of all moral stability and allows him to reach the lowest stage of demoralization in his uncontrolled love for his sister Bertha. Grillparzer stands with his emotionalism nearer to Goethe than to the enthusiastic rationalist Schiller, and the theme of his drama *Sappho*—the suffering caused by the onesidedness of man—is closely related to that of Goethe's *Torquato Tasso.* But Grillparzer's ideal is no longer that of the harmonious development

[77]

of all potentialities in man, the ideal of a man who is equally well equipped to achieve greatness in art as well as in life; his representation of the fate of Sappho is more a complaint against the fact that she had to pay for her idealistic striving the price of detachment from the vital foundation of existence.

From *Blanka von Kastilien* on, we notice a steady growth and clarification of the conviction that the abstract moral values must be subordinated to the one fundamental value of life. The significance of life, however, lies not so much in the individual existence as in active and reactive coexistence with others, in participation in an organic community; and action in this community is determined more by impulse than by the conscious will. In this community man finds a moral support; apart from it he loses himself and drifts toward moral and physical destruction. Moreover, severance from the natural community with others constitutes the metaphysical guilt of individuation, and it is here that we may seek the cause of man's tragic fate. The possibility of such a detachment from the existential roots is psychologically founded in the fact that man is able to transcend by his thinking the living context of life and thus disregard it in his action, too.

This tragedy of uprooted existence we were able to trace in the fate of Blanka von Kastilien, who finds on the foreign soil of Spain nothing but contempt, distress, and ruin. The abduction of Jaromir in *Die Ahnfrau* gives this idea a deeper psychological interpretation, but in the development of Medea, Jason, Kunigunde (*König Ottokars Glück und Ende*), and Otto von Meran (*Ein treuer Diener seines Herrn*) we have the most convincing impersonations of the theme of uprootedness and the degradation of man in a foreign environment. *Ottokar* clarifies psychologically this same theme even better than *Die Ahnfrau*, for it is Ottokar's conscious will which carries him beyond the limits of possibility within an organically integrated world. Organic rootedness, which up to then had been considered as the foundation of moral and physical life, is dramatically exposed in its own problematic nature in the tragedy *Ein treuer Diener seines Herrn*. Bancbanus fails because he is too completely adjusted to a very definite position in the organism of the state and has thus lost all his flexibility. *Der Traum ein Leben* continues the same view in a more positive direction: here the transgression of the narrow boundaries of adjusted life is considered as a valuable experience of one's personal limitations, and, at least, it is in the subconscious sphere of dream-life, not fatal.

The catastrophe of the two lovers in *Des Meeres und der Liebe*

Wellen is the expression of the postulate that life be considered the paramount value, whereas the extreme control of life by rational norms is rejected as contradictory to the principle of life. This theme is continued in *Weh dem der lügt*, with the result that the norms are acknowledged as regulative principles, but not as being capable of rigorous application. Even more emphatically than in *Weh dem der lügt* King Alphonse in *Die Jüdin von Toledo* must first prove his qualifications for royal responsibility; temporarily unrestricted activity in the world is demanded of him, before he becomes, in the truest sense, king. This, however, does not essentially change Grillparzer's earlier view that such a detachment from the normal environment constitutes an inexorable danger. It is rather the basis of his fundamentally tragic conception of life: full experience of the world is necessary for the greatest possible vitalization of character, but it is necessarily connected with danger menacing the very existence of character. Stability and complete adjustment to given circumstances, on the other hand, entail a lack of vitality which is just as incompatible with the essential principle of life. Bancbanus is as guilty as King Alphonse.

In *Libussa* this tragedy of human existence is applied to the whole of cultural development. It can almost be established as a natural law that culture transcends the boundaries of organic harmony, that human affairs are more and more subjected to the conscious guidance of a rational will, and that cultural and moral degeneration stands in direct proportion to its remoteness from the state of primitive harmony. Grillparzer leaves only one hope for a possible regeneration; the return to the original state of harmony, in which the rational will subordinates itself to the natural conditions of life. *Ein Bruderzwist im Hause Habsburg* gives in historical projection a similar view of Grillparzer's own time as a period of general disintegration, in which all action becomes tragic guilt.

Considered as a whole, Grillparzer's dramatic work presents a steadily progressing elaboration and clarification of his world view. This view is founded on the supposition of an original harmonious existence, in which man does almost instinctively what is right because he is guided in his actions by an immediate sympathetic understanding of others. In his first group of plays Grillparzer develops the consequences of detachment from this foundation. His characters feel the tragic conflict between rootedness in a natural environment and the inevitable entrance into the world of conscious action, in which they are exposed to uprooting and destruction. In the second group of plays,

[79]

he accepts existence in a world of rational activity as man's destiny and as an evolutionary tendency founded in human nature and therefore at least partly justified; a tendency which leads to final catastrophe, but which permits, at least for the general evolution of culture, the hope of ultimate reintegration.

Although he takes, for the most part, a derisive attitude towards German idealism, Grillparzer's views show a distinct relationship to Schelling's philosophy; for he, too, assumes that individuation is an apostasy from the natural unity of existence, and that the final aim of the evolutionary process is a new harmony. With Schopenhauer, Grillparzer shares the view that man is part of a universal will and thus an integral part of an instinctive and non-reflective principle; that man separates himself from instinct by his intentional reason; that in consequence of the separation he must submit to the fateful antagonism of blind instinct and conscious will; that this will can never be satisfied; that man, when he clearly recognizes the dilemma of existence, will avoid acting and will seek the harmony of contemplation; and, finally, that there is no redemption for those still in this stage of the dilemma except liberation from all will in the nothingness of Nirvana.

Grillparzer's metaphysical views also have some points in common with Hebbel, which is not surprising, since both dramatists have the same idealistic background. Like Hebbel, Grillparzer sees a metaphysical and tragic guilt in the individuation of man, and in their later dramas both authors try to interpret this guilt less as human "hybris" or arrogance than as an unavoidable stage in the development of the individual, as well as of mankind. Grillparzer, however, lacks the conviction of progress which would somewhat mitigate this necessity of guilt. Where Hebbel sees in a particular stage the development toward higher forms of morality, Grillparzer deplores the disintegration of an original organic unity. Hebbel's response to tendencies of the middle of the nineteenth century is North-German, logical, and rationalistic, whereas Grillparzer's response is Austrian, musical, and irrational.

CHAPTER VII

CHRISTIAN DIETRICH GRABBE
(1801-36)*

GRABBE betrays even more than Grillparzer the inner disharmony and
disillusionment of the Restoration period. His birth placed him between
the bourgeois and the proletarian classes: he shares with the bourgeois of
the late-romantic and Biedermeier period the political disinterestment
and contemplative characteristics while the proletarian in him tends
towards an anti-idealistic, concrete positivism. Tension in his character
is also presaged in the contrasting temperament of his parents: his
mother is passionate; his father, rational and unimpassioned. In Grabbe
himself are combined qualities which, at least in part, seem incompatible: industry, intelligence, contentment as against an unrestrained
imagination, and boundless intemperance. Grabbe is a man who longed
for inner harmony and the sympathy of his environment, but again and
again he was agitated by his uncontrolled vitality and demoniacally
driven to the wildest extremes, only to be thrown back into a stage of
exhaustion and apathy. Correspondingly, his work is characterized by
the antagonism between romantic subjectivism and an intense desire
for exaggeration, on the one hand, and a realistic objectivity, a critical
valuation, and a recognition of the limitations of concrete existence, on
the other. In particular, the emotional side,—the organ of romantic
self-transcendence—is counteracted by analytical reason, the organ of
self-limitation and self-control. The opposing tendencies within his
character reflect the general situation of a time which begins to turn
from patriarchal self-sufficiency and the modest pleasures of the smallest
sphere to a materialistic and utilitarian mode and aspect of life. This
disharmony and consequent reorientation, which stirs Grabbe and his
period, is also characteristic of his dramatic work, in which these opposite tendencies seek a tolerable balance. For this reason alone earlier
interpretations must be rejected which find in Grabbe's work chiefly the
problem of the leader-personality who fails through the stupidity of
the masses. Such an interpretation presupposes a belief in the absolute
value of the great individual which Grabbe, despite the fact that he

*This chapter appeared in German in a somewhat more detailed essay, "Die realistische
Tendenz in Grabbes Dramen," in *Smith College Studies in Modern Languages*, July, 1931.

possessed qualities of genius, was just as incapable of endorsing as his contemporaries Grillparzer and Schopenhauer.

There is no direct evidence for Grabbe's earlier belief in the values of the idealistic world view. Its significance, however, for his formative years can be inferred from the desperate disillusionment of his first dramatic works. His tragedy *Herzog Theodor von Gothland* can be compared, with respect to the part which it played in his development, with Grillparzer's *Blanka von Kastilien* and even more with *Die Ahnfrau*. Grabbe's struggle with traditional views and values in the first drama is even more desperate and pathetic than Grillparze-'s, and its dynamic exuberance is almost pathological. At the beginning of the drama, Herzog Theodor is a man of outstanding value, the champion of the freedom of his people, the happy husband of a noble woman, the father of a worthy descendant, the pride of the king and of his countrymen. He is inspired by a passionate love for his brother, a love which rivals the most idealistic figures of mythology. This emotional exuberance, however, becomes fatal for him, since it obscures his sense of reality. A relatively insignificant incident is sufficient to shatter his belief in the ideals which dominated his life. The sudden death of his brother raises in him the suspicion that his less beloved brother, the chancellor of the king, might have murdered his idol. The mere thought of this possibility makes him incapable of examining soberly the factual situation, and so, in auto-suggestive delusion, he kills the alleged murderer. Blindness of passion spells ruin for all his ideals. He drives his once beloved wife, with his father, out into a murderously cold winter night. He drags his only son and heir with him into physical and moral destruction. He who once had been the only hope of his people in the fight against an undefeated enemy, now fights on the side of the same enemy against his own people and even forces the people, who elect him their king, into a most barbarous war. All human sympathy has died in him; people and mankind mean nothing to him but a mass not worthy of any better fate than to be slaughtered by the thousands. Completely isolated, and surfeited with life, he meets his death.

> Noch niemand ging mit den Idealen für der Menschheit Wohl ins Leben, der es nicht als Bösewicht, als ausgemachter Menschenfeind verlassen hätte (IV. 1).

Such words most plainly reveal the duke's, and even the author's own tragedy. The duke began with an unshaken belief in an ideal world, in the freedom to do what is good, in God and in immortality, in the

[82]

eternal laws of the universe "on which the world is founded . . . and which no fleeting century can destroy." But he ends in absolute Satanism born of utter despair:

wir sind erschaffen, weil wir in der Hölle verderben sollen; . . . die ganze Naturordnung ist auf Mord aufgebaut (III. 1).

It is complete disillusionment with all existence and all values;

die Hölle? O, die ist zum wenigsten etwas Neues—und ich wette: Auch an die Hölle kann man sich gewöhnen.

Kleist, in his fate-drama *Familie Schroffenstein*, lets a world of illusions break down, because reason has emancipated itself from the rule of sympathetic emotion; Grabbe, conversely, makes blind emotionalism responsible for the catastrophe of human relations: Gothland's tragedy is that of disregarded reality. He becomes demoralized when in his romantically exaggerated emotionalism he loses the ability objectively to consider the factual situation. Confounded by misfortune, he withdraws into himself and experiences in his inner solitude his deepest tragedy, the complete destruction of his faith in humanitarian values and, finally, the destruction of the fundamental belief of the idealistic system, the belief in the value of the self. Subjective Romantic idealism thus ends in a complete nihilism of values. This negative result, however, is the first stage of Grabbe's search for a world view, in which the individual is not considered as a detached self, but as existentially integrated in a human environment.

Grabbe's despair of ideal values is also illustrated in Gothland's son Gustav, who, on account of his Romantic idealism, succumbs to an inexorable debasement of his character (II. 1). In the same way, we must interpret the fate of Theodor Gothland's father, who is forced by his loyalty to the king and his duty as a judge, to extirpate his own family; a principle which has been set up as a norm is here directed against life itself and thereby proves its own worthlessness and absurdity. Berdoa,—from the historical as well as from the psychological point of view the most preposterous figure of the drama,—in his infernal hatred most consistently expresses the young poet's despair that values cannot possibly be realized. *Herzog Theodor von Gothland* is a document characteristic of the decline of Romanticism and Idealism with its passionate violation and exaggeration of all realistic probabilities. Exaggeration even appears in the structure as a whole. In its single scenes and in the dialogue, it is almost entirely built upon such con-

[83]

trasts as Christianity and Satanism, immortality and nihilism, love and basest harlotry, humanity and bestial sadism. Most characteristic in this respect is Gustav's seduction in the first scene of the second act. In a review of his own work (1827), Grabbe himself finds the significance of his work in the fact that it grew out of the crisis of his idealistic beliefs:

> Dennoch spürt man in seinen Stücken überall nur die Trümmer einer zerstörten Subjektivität. Der Verfasser hat Ruinen gemacht, um daraus neu zu bauen.

The comedy *Scherz, Satire, Ironie und tiefere Bedeutung* emphasizes less Grabbe's despairing doubt of the fundamental values of idealism. Rather it criticizes a world which has accepted the ideas of previous periods in their most distorted form. In this play, Grabbe derides almost everything which the conventional mind has taken over as a secure possession or with the claim of infallibility. The pretenses of the nobility are caricatured in the superficiality and avarice of von Wern- thal and in the brutality of the Freiherr von Mordax. The rage for titles in an empty-headed society is ridiculed by the friendly reception of the devil, who introduces himself with papal titles. The world of the lower bourgeoisie is presented as so hopelessly stupid that it entrusts the education of its children to a drunkard and considers the possession of intestinal worms as a sign of aptitude for the study of theology. And it is hypocritical enough to condemn the works of Casanova in public while devouring them in private. The intellectual products of this society are, or course, on a corresponding level. The ladies enjoy the sentimentalities of late-Romanticism, but reject everything which is of a more concrete vitality as coarse imagination. This society worships the theologians whose beliefs are criticized by Grabbe as primitive and fetishistic. It has the highest esteem for the conceited, but actually stupid, scientists, who repudiate any factual evidence which might shake the validity of their preconceived theories. It has the same deep respect for those idealistic philosophers who content them- selves with reducing the concrete world to an empty formula such as "the essence of all existence," the "Inbegriff alles Existierenden, von dem kleinsten Würmchen bis zu dem unendlichen Sonnensystem" (II. 2.). This satire reaches its climax when, at the end of the drama, a strong punch is served and the "vermaledeite Grabbe" appears in per- son to join the drinking party; for this indulgence is the only thing which the author believes himself to have in common with such com- pany. Society is treated in this comedy as a group deprived of any intelligence, and held together by a few traditional valuations, unreasonable formalities and primitive needs. The author here shows he has lost his belief in any inner community of man which would derive its force from living values. Only one choice seems to remain, the choice between the nihilistic despair of Herzog Theodor or else some kind of an adjustment to reality, which, however, he finds extremely disappointing, since he has approached it with the expectations of an idealist. This explains why the prevailing mood of this so-called comedy is not a self-sufficient humor which can consider the weakness of man as an imperfect manifestation of a perfect idea, but is, to use Grabbe's own words, "das Lachen der Verzweiflung"; he is deeply stirred by the imperfection of reality and tries to face the intolerable by refusing to take it too seriously. The grotesque and apparently chaotic structure of the play is, therefore, not mere license or lack of artistic capability, but an adequate expression of the inner rift in Grabbe's relation to the outside world. Disharmony pervades even the details of the scenes; time and again the author creates a mood of sublimity and suddenly interrupts it by a remark or a situation of coarse and caustic realism; thus, when the school-teacher declares to the father of his pupil:

> Ihr Sohn gehört zu den eminentesten Köpfen: Ich werde ihn nicht nur in die tiefsten Geheimnisse der Dogmatik, der Homiletik und der übrigen Nebenwissenschaften der Theologie einweihen, sondern auch in den plastischen, idyllischen und metaphysischen Hauptwissenschaften unserer Landprediger, als im Schweineschneiden, Kuhschlachten und Mistaufladen unterrichten (I. 1),

or when he lets Mollfels tell his sweetheart of his tragedy:

> Unvermutet schallt aus dem Tempel der Ausspruch, dasz die Göttin den Untergang der erhabenen Prinzessin Salvavenia beschliesze. Das Volk heult, die Glocken läuten, die Prinzessin jammert, als ob sie dem Satan schon in den Krallen säsze, und alles stürzt in wilder Verzweiflung von der Bühne. Hierauf tritt Ossian ein und iszt ein Butterbrot (II. 4).

As a grotesque comedy it differs, in spite of many similarities, from the Romantic comedy, as in Tieck's *Der gestiefelte Kater*. The Romanticist regards life with complete esthetic freedom. In spite of all criticism of philistinism, contemporary writing, social and political conditions, the Romantic comedy remains an expression of the freedom of the creative mind. It blends poetry and life in such a way that both appear as the illusive products of an infinite mind; and then it places itself, in a last ironical climax, above this infinite mind, in order to deride its inability to manifest itself in perfect forms. With all his suffering from the finiteness of reality, the Romanticist retains his consoling belief in the freedom and the infiniteness of the mind. Grabbe is still under the influence of these ideas, but he has lost his faith in them, and so the comparison between idea and experience poisons his attitude towards reality, which, after all, he cannot fail to recognize.

The fragment of the tragedy *Marius und Sulla,* marks a certain progress towards solving Grabbe's dilemma. Earlier Grabbe had doubted the validity of idealism and disdained reality; in *Marius und Sulla* we see him gradually attaining a more positive attitude toward reality. In the first part of the fragment, which was conceived in 1823, Marius is still a character like those of Grabbe's first dramas, whereas Sulla, the hero of the second part (written in the year 1827), is a much more positive and realistic figure. Marius is the gentler and more sentimental one of the two generals; old and broken in vitality, his eyes are turned backwards to a glorious past. In mournful melancholy, he sits on the ruins of Carthage fatalistically expecting "wie arg es das Schicksal mit mir zu treiben denkt" (I. 1.). His proletarian descent has fostered in him a feeling of inferiority which makes him dependent upon the opinion of others. Therefore, he is inspired, like Gothland, by only the one thought of annihilative revenge on his own native city. He is in continual danger of forgetting the actuality around him; and so he dreams of "the happiest and greatest hour of his life," the moment at which

> Bürger zitternd nahen und ihm als einer Gottheit, die gesühnt werden musz, Opferstücke vor die Fusze legen (II. 6).

Only the fearful cry "Sulla" awakens him from his dreams. The conclusion of his reflections on his life sound like a parody on idealism:

> Wenn ich so an die Hergänge
> Des Römerreiches und meines Lebens denke . . .
> . . . . so erscheint
>
> Die Himmelswölbung mir beinahe als
> Das Inn're eines ungeheuren Schädels
> Und wir als seine Grillen! — Ich bin eine,
> Die er, wie sehr ich auch mich sträube, im
> Begriff ist zu vergessen!

In spite of his seventy-two years and against all the dictates of common sense, he clings to his dignity and defends it, together with the memory of his former grandeur, until "unter sehr poetischen Floskeln" he is overcome by death.

[86]

Sulla's character, however, belongs to a period which the author himself characterizes with the following words:

> Dennoch spürt man in seinen Stücken überall nur die Trümmer einer zerstörten Subjektivität. Der Verfasser hat Ruinen gemacht, um daraus neu zu bauen.*

Sulla is intended to be an ideal of Grabbe's own personality,

> nicht *das* Ideal, denn sonst wäre er sehr wenig,

that is to say, he shall not be an idealization, since Grabbe has passed this stage of belief and disillusion. Sulla represents the type of a self-assured realist, who, in spite of his passion, is guided by his reason, a man who does not indulge in lamentations over the past, but recognizes only the tasks of the future. He is a *Realpolitiker:*

> Sein Entschulsz ist klar und vollendet: schonungslos will er die Zeit von ihren Auswüchsen zu reinigen versuchen. Mit Schrecken will er sie niederwerfen, um dann desto sicherer das Bessere wiederaufrichten zu können. Geschehe auf diesem Wege, was da wolle, ernstliche Gewissensbisse braucht er nicht zu fürchten—dazu ist er in sich selbst zu abgerundet (III. 1).

In the ruthless pursuit of his own ends he is capable of considering man as mere

> Spinnen und Fliegen . . ., welche der Knabe gleichgültig und mitleidlos zerrupft, weil er ihr Jammern nicht versteht (I. 3).

In cold blood and with cruel irony he orders the execution of a mother and her children, because she cannot give any reason why her life should be spared. He allows the proscriptive murders to continue for weeks; he decimates his people with the cold-bloodedness of a physician at the operating table. The plan for the Sulla scenes was to present the dictator's brutalities in such a way that they would appear as inexorable necessities in the attempt to cure a hopelessly infected people which had degenerated from its former greatness and become a stupid, cowardly mob, the easy prey of demagogic abuse. For Sulla was planned to be a tragic hero, "zu einer riesenhaften, wahrhaft tragischen Höhe weiterzuschreiten" (III. 1). Sulla was not, like Marius, to murder for the sake of revenge but to restore the ideals of the Roman past. He hopes to regenerate the blood of his people by granting the rights of citizenship to ten thousand soldiers, and when he finally gives his people a new constitution he considers his task as completed; for

*Letter, Dec. 28, 1827.

he recognizes that the regeneration itself is beyond his power, that it is rather the task of the people themselves. Therefore, he resigns in the moment of complete control, when "der Erdball wie ein gekrümmter Sklave unter ihm liegt" (V. 2). He cannot wish his people to be slaves, for he has not fought for selfish aims. For the sake of his ideal aim, the regeneration of the Roman spirit, he has to abdicate his power at the climax, not because the Romans are slaves, but in order that they may not become slaves. This is what he symbolically expresses by taking off his laurel-wreath and handing it to Metella, his wife, with the jocular request that she season the food with the leaves. He does not speak with cynical pessimism, as is often thought. His words are rather meant as a last and urgent warning to the Romans to live up to their ideals; they soberly and realistically express the realization that a people cannot exist by the will of a dictator, but only by its own will. The fragment does not state whether Sulla's confidence is justified. For our purpose, it is sufficient to note that the sentimental and retrospective Marius is defeated by the positivistic and rational Sulla. The romantic victim of incontinence is contrasted with a character of realistic self-determination and self-limitation. This corresponds to Grabbe's own inner development from the disharmony of "Gefühls-zerrüttung" to a more objective attitude towards life—in part as a result of his work on this dramatic fragment. The same polarity, the same antagonism between two views of the relation of man to reality, the same tendency of development from idealistic detachment to realistic acceptance of the world is dramatically symbolized in the tragedy *Don Juan und Faust*. Grabbe's testimony supports this interpretation when he says that the author's own spirit seems to be engaged in a death struggle with itself. In *Don Juan und Faust* he attempts to show the "destruction of the too sensual and the too spiritual nature in man." With these words he ascribes to his drama the function of establishing a balance between these two opposite tendencies which oppressed the poet and his contemporaries; thus he wishes to counteract the menace of a materialistic reaction to the idealism of past generations.

Don Juan is here conceived, in harmony with the older tradition, only as a lover of life's sensual pleasures; there is no attempt to exhaust the tragic possibilities of his character, which lie in the inability of man to satisfy even his most natural desires. For Grabbe's Don Juan any true affection, any sympathetic attachment is nothing but hypocrisy. Women are ranked in the same category with good eating and drinking; they are but a kind of Epicurean pleasure. We

CHRISTIAN DIETRICH GRABBE

are, however, somewhat reconciled to Don Juan's sensual attitude towards life by his vivid imagination and his wit, and especially by the fact that his attitude is in part, at least, a reaction against the mediocrity around him, and, finally, by his consistency of character and determination to his very end; he prefers to continue as Don Juan in hell rather than to renounce his individual nature:

> Was
> Ich bin, das bleib' ich. Bin ich Don Juan,
> So bin ich nichts, werd' ich ein andrer!
> Weit eher Don Juan im Abgrundsschwefel
> Als Heiliger im Paradieseslichte! (IV. 4)

Don Juan represents in this drama the same stage of development which Grabbe had reached in *Herzog Theodor von Gothland*, the stage of cynical disrespect of all personality values. Only in the earlier drama Grabbe had presented the catastrophe of a growing disillusionment in idealism. In this play the result of his disillusionment is embodied in Don Juan, a static character, one of two extreme types, neither of which represents the final solution reached or desired by the author. In this drama he also continues the social criticism of *Scherz, Satire, Ironie und tiefere Bedeutung*. Don Juan is what this society would be, if it only dared to be itself; he is sensual, selfish and materialistic; but society is less than he, and deserves Don Juan's criticism, for it does not even dare to live according to its true nature.

At the beginning of the drama, Faust has reached a similar stage of disillusionment, with the difference, however, that he is not driven to the extreme cynical dissipation in a senseless surrender to the transitory moment. Faust faithfully continues to strive for the absolute, even after he has despaired of finding in religion and science an approach to the indestructible essence of existence. He is unable to abandon himself to the superficial experience of reality like Don Juan; reality oppresses him with its finiteness and instability. Therefore he concludes a pact with the devil, from whom he expects, first, the completion of his theoretical knowledge and, second, guidance in the way in which he "might have found peace and happiness." These stipulations preclude from the very outset any satisfactory solution of his life problem, since they are consciously limited to theoretical experience and eliminate practical, i.e., immediate contact with life. With this restriction, however, a tragic outcome is unavoidable at this point of Grabbe's development towards a more realistic conception of life.

The execution of the pact proceeds in three stages, the first of which

[89]

is the way of knowledge. Faust's journey through the universe increases only the quantity of his knowledge, but fails to provide any insight into the essence and the meaning of cosmic energy. The second stage takes Faust into the sphere of the will, of striving for power. His diabolical companion is now his slave; he rules from his solitary seat in the clouds over the powers of the earth. With the use of magic he murders his wife in order to possess Donna Anna, and when she refuses to yield to his desire he destroys her, too. Through her death, however, he realizes that there is something higher and more essential than knowledge and will, namely, humanity, in which a sympathetic feeling defeats all egotism, transcends the limitations of the individual, and attains to a superindividual interrelation of men.

> In diesen Tränen, die ich weine, spür'
> Ich es: es gab einst einen Gott, der ward
> Zerschlagen—wir sind seine Stücke—Sprache
> Und Wehmut—Lieb und Religion und Schmerz
> Sind Träume nur von ihm.
>
> (IV. 3)

When it is too late, he recognizes his sin against life, which cannot be embraced with only a part of ourselves, with the reason or the will, but only with our entire living personality.

These three stages reflect Grabbe's development up to this point, as we have followed it in his dramas, especially in such characters as Gothland, Marius, and Sulla: (1) disillusionment and doubt of religion and idealism, (2) egotistic and materialistic desecration of reality, (3) the recognition of reality with its superindividual life experience. When we compare this last stage with Sulla's attitude, however, we notice a further decided progress in the humanization of the author's relation to man; the tyrant is replaced by a humane character, who within the course of the drama attains full appreciation of human sympathy.

Grabbe comes herewith rather close to the views of Grillparzer, with whom he shares the development away from idealism. Like Grillparzer, he arrives at a conception of life which places the individual in a definite environment and forces him into tragedy through detachment from his environment. Such tragedy could already be traced in Grabbe's first drama *Herzog Theodor von Gothland.* In *Don Juan und Faust,* it is the final truth which Faust at last realizes. In *Kaiser Friedrich Barbarossa,* the dependence of man upon his time and environment is treated in a way which reminds one of Grillparzer's *Sappho* and *König Ottokars Glück und Ende.* Barbarossa rises with his

[90]

ideas far above the average understanding of his contemporaries, and his most objective and competent judge, Pope Alexander, recognizes in this fact the cause of his ultimate failure:

> *Papst Alexander.*
> Weit sieht man von den Höh'n des Vatikans:
> Was du erstrebtest, kann zur Wahrheit werden.
> Doch du gingst her *vor* deiner Zeit. Wer aus
> Der Zeit tritt, wird ihr fremd!

> *Kaiser Friedrich.*
> Ich glaube,
> Auch Zeitverhältnisse sind zu bewältigen,
> Denn Menschen waren's, die sie schufen!

> *Papst Alexander.*
> Unter
> Der Leitung Gottes!

Translated from the religious symbolism of the Roman Catholic Church into the profane language of this world, this means: Man may transcend the conditions of his time in his thinking, but in his actions he remains dependent upon the concrete situation. Barbarossa has all the qualities required for complete domination of the political world: he excels his contemporaries in his extraordinary will power, in the clear vision of his aims and in a personal selfcontrol which allows him to exploit even the most dangerous circumstances to his advantage. But he meets the fate which, according to Schopenhauer, is the result of the reasoning power of man; in his thinking he transcends the limits set to his will, and then feels the urge to put these thoughts into practice. But in this attempt he necessarily isolates himself and exposes himself to the dangers of complete failure and destruction. In spite of all his power over a world of concrete facts, Barbarossa is led away from the basis of reality by a keen imagination which anticipates the possibilities of a distant future; he is a Romanticist in important as well as in trivial issues. He, the emperor, enjoys participating in the contests of the troubadours and the tournaments of the knights; in Provençal *reverie* (*Schwärmerei*) he worships his Beatrice; princes and kings belong to his indispensable retinue. Similarly, his ultimate aims, conquest of the Orient, liberation of the people from the rule of the priests, and unification of the world under his own scepter, lie far beyond the limits of realization in the realm of Romantic imagination. They are only thinkable aims, and the attempt to convert his ambitions into reality is a fateful overestimation of the creative power of the pure mind. Accordingly, the last scene of the drama, in which the emperor takes leave of his beloved wife and his occidental empire, must be interpreted as tragic. It is the tragic self-deception of idealistic detachment from reality when, in apparent triumph, he departs with the words: "Und Sterben selbst! Im Kreuzzug ist's Gewinnen!" The exultation over the defeat of the Guelfs and the triumphal march at the close of the drama stand in sharp contrast with Mathilde's vision of the future glory of the Guelfs and the passing splendor of the Hohenstaufen dynasty. The words of Heinrich VI at the bier of his father confirm the tragic detachment of the imaginative mind from the concrete, historical conditions of the king's enterprise:

> Grosz warst du, doch dabei zu groszmutsvoll,
> Ein Held warst du, wie nie ein besserer,
> Doch statt als Deutschlands Herrscher zu regieren.
> Hast du auch nur als Held gehandelt!—Wozu
> Der Kreuzzug und sein eitler Ruhm? Was nützt
> Der Ruhm, wenn man die Macht ihm opfert? Sie
> Nur kann ihn aufrechthalten!
> (*Kaiser Heinrich der Sechste*, I. 2)

Barbarossa's failure in his phantastic attempts is the starting point for the second Hohenstaufen tragedy *Kaiser Heinrich der Sechste*. Heinrich wants to avoid the mistakes of his father by pursuing a realistic policy. Without any scruples he abandons even his most loyal adherents to suit his political advantage, and shrewdly exploits even religious motives for his imperialistic aims. Only in one respect does he remain a true Hohenstaufen, and that is the cause of his downfall; in spite of his better judgment, he too cannot help striving far beyond the limitations of reality:

> Hätt' ich auch die ganze Welt — Schaut nicht der Himmel dort, so tief
> und sehnsuchtsvoll, . . . dasz die Busen hoch klopfen müssen, auch zu ihm
> zu stürmen . . . ? . . . Doch besser wär's, wir hätten ihn schon im Leben
> (V. 1).

After reconquering southern Italy, he yields to the lure of his father's phantastic aims, the hereditary imperial crown, the conquest of Palestine and Africa, the subjugation of the papacy and the Lombardian cities. Death, however, overtakes him at the very moment when he adopts these projects of his father. Heinrich's death has been explained as an expression of Grabbe's extreme pessimism, as the effect of a blind fate which destroys the most valuable personalities shortly before the realization of their highest aims. But this death is not as utterly absurd and unmotivated as it first appears to be; it is a historical symbol for the fatal consequences of disregarding the limits of reality. Whether Heinrich VI dies or not is not essential; in any case, his striving has carried him away from the foundations of his power; it has isolated him from any human contact so that he is doomed, dead or alive. His sudden death does not interrupt a successful enterprise, it only contracts into a single moment the inescapable course of events and thereby emphasizes the principal thesis of the play, the confinement of all human striving within the limits of reality. Only if one disregards the fact that the catastrophe began when Heinrich shifted his political center from Germany to Italy, can one interpret his death as the work of a brutal destiny which cruelly destroys men at the very moment when they are about to achieve their greatest deeds. Grabbe, however, has long since passed beyond such a cynical conception of the world order; when he wrote this drama, he had come to the conclusion that man is limited in his activity by concrete conditions, about which his imagination tends to deceive him with most tragic results. Over against these rulers with their superhuman aims, the antagonists in these two Hohenstaufen-dramas, especially Heinrich der Löwe, Pope Alexander, the consul of Milan, and Tancred, ruler of the Normans, represent the cold concreteness of reality. Their resistance brings the phantastic and capricious politics of the emperors to a tragic end. Instead of respecting their adversaries as legitimate living powers or letting them die from their own inner weakness, these emperors dissipate their energies in the attempt to suppress them. This attempt, however, is doomed to failure, because instead of weakening the enemies of their imperialism it unites and strengthens them in their defense. In the political sphere they make the same tragic mistake which Faust made when he suppressed his active human nature in favor of a theoretical aim beyond the reach of human understanding. An almost grotesque illustration of the tragic condition into which the emperors have fallen through their lack of realistic judgment is the war with Heinrich der Löwe, which Heinrich summarizes in these most pregnant words:

Wie hab' ich nicht gekämpft,
Gesiegt, gelitten, um den groszen Zwist
Der Welfen und der Waiblinger zu beenden—?
Es war umsonst—Jetzt endet ihn 'ne Hochzeit!—
Wie auch der Mensch drauf losstürmt—Nie erreicht er
Das Ziel, führt Gott es ihm nicht zu—
(*Kaiser Friedrich Barbarossa*, III. 2)

[93]

In these words Heinrich der Löwe implicitly admits that he, too, has failed to adapt his means to the demands of the concrete situation and that he must therefore share the responsibility for the unnecessary sacrifice of human lives in the civil war. He fails, although he was much more strongly attached to his home-land than the emperor and although he sought an expansion of his territory only in neighboring districts. In Grabbe's earlier dramas the people were treated as a mob without any human qualities and values; they were sacrificed for personal and egotistic aims or despised as an uneducated mass. In the Hohenstaufen-dramas, however, they are obviously recognized as the concrete condition of effective political action. The isolation of the Hohenstaufen from the mass of the people causes the downfall of their dynasty; Tancred's Norman kingdom is doomed in spite of its leader's determination, because his effeminate people have lost the will to self-defense; the kingdom of Heinrich der Löwe, however, will subsist, because it has grown organically with the support of the people.

The people's significance is fully recognized in *Napoleon oder die hundert Tage*. Napoleon himself rose out of the revolution, grew through the revolution and remained, to a certain degree, dependent upon it, since the European courts did not recognize him as the legal ruler of his country. But he, too, transcends the realistic conditions of his power; he opposes the tendency of his time, the trend towards liberalism; in his personal vanity and his attempt to emulate the European princes, he adopts their extravagant ideology, their pretention to rule by the grace of God and their ridiculous pride of ancestry; he talks himself into the unrealistic conviction that "the earth would be happiest if the greatest nation (i.e., Napoleon's own people under his leadership) would rule and be strong enough to enforce its laws everywhere," and that it is his own mission to "scourge Europe, the infantile old man" (I. 4). As far as the realistic evaluation of the conditions and the exploitation of given possibilities are concerned, he is infinitely superior to all his adversaries, particularly to the Bourbons; but his imagination drives his thirst for power far beyond the limits of possible realization. He might have remained the first consul of France; but his absolutism could not hold out against the liberal tendencies of his time; and the conquest of Europe was bound to fail, because it neglected the most important factor of a realistic policy, the will of the conquered people. It is only self-delusion which causes Napoleon to ascribe his military defeat to the "stupidity, the negligence or the wickedness of one single miserable individual" (V. 5), i.e., to Grouchy; it is rather his own blindness regarding the situation which allows him to entrust to Grouchy a task for which he is entirely unfit, and it is the same blindness which causes him to underestimate the energy of Blücher, his Prussian opponent. His downfall is to be attributed at least as much to his character as to outside factors.

It is, therefore, a complete misinterpretation of Napoleon's character and fate, if one sees in him only the misunderstood genius whose ideal purposes are defeated by the inertia of a mass of weaklings and of wicked traitors; in fact, he does not fall as a victim of treachery, unfavorable circumstances, and misfortune. Grabbe describes him as entrusted with the fulfillment of an important historical mission: he destroys old-fashioned institutions and unifies the political structure of Europe by dethroning a number of incapable rulers; but in the egotistic pursuit of his phantastic aims, he fails to consider the other equally important tendencies of his time. It is not the aimless mass which causes his ruin, but living, positive forces such as the French liberalism of Carnot and Fouché, the absolute regard for honor and duty of the English commander Wellington, and above all the Prussions' love for their country, their confidence in their king, their admiration for their poets of liberty, Schiller and Körner, and their loyalty to Blücher, their capable general and honest comrade. By his selfish conceit and his fundamentally autocratic ambition Napoleon himself assumes part of the responsibility which he derides in his closing words:

> Statt eines groszen Tyrannen, wie sie mich zu nennen belieben, werden sie bald lauter kleine besitzen—statt ihnen ewigen Frieden zu geben, wird man sie in einen ewigen Geistesschlaf einzulullen versuchen—statt der goldenen Zeit wird eine sehr irdene, zerbröckliche kommen, voll Halbheit, albernen Lugs und Tandes . . . (V. 7).

Grabbe believes in the potentialities of the people and their significance as a substratum for any development and expresses this belief in his *Napoleon* drama.

A theoretical formulation of his conviction we find in a letter of the year 1831:

> Alle Staatsrevolutionen helfen aber doch nichts, wenn nicht auch jede Person sich selbst revolutionert, i.e., wahr gegen sich und andere wird. Darin steckt alle Tugend, alles Genie.

Accordingly, a people can be happy and successful, only if it has the inner determination to be so. As far as the relation between a people and its leader is concerned, the very best leader is of no avail, if his people is unwilling or incapable of following him, and, further, a people which really has inner power and purpose may be successful even with a less efficient leader. The negative of this thesis could be induced from the final scene of the fragment *Marius und Sulla;* it was even more evident in the decline of the Norman rule in southern Italy, in spite of Tancred's efforts to preserve the old glory (*Kaiser Friedrich Barbarossa*). The positive form of the thesis was emphasized in the Prussian victory over Napoleon under Blücher. In the *Hannibal* tragedy both forms are clarified and dramatically contrasted. At the same time, the emphasis is further shifted from individual superiority to the coöperation of the people. In this play for the first time, Grabbe makes the people the subject of tragic fate.

The Carthaginians are petty shopkeepers and cowards, who try to save their country from impending destruction by cruel human sacrifices; they are short-sighted egotists who are more interested in the luxurious caravan of a sheik than they are disturbed by their fateful victory at Cannæ. They allow their menaced country to be ruled by mad intriguers like Melkir, Hanno and Gisgon, whose main concern is to ruin the influence of the Barkas family, and who cannot realize the danger even at the moment when Hannibal's army is defeated by the Romans before the gates of the city. Yet they are capable of great deeds; when they realize the deception of the Romans, they prove their inner value in a most courageous, desperate fight and finally in their self-destruction under the burning ruins of Carthage. Their death shows, although too late, that there still existed in this people living values and energies worthy of a better destiny; thus their destruction assumes tragic proportions for it symbolizes the inexorable demand of reality.

Their leader, Hannibal, is drawn into this tragedy in the same way as the other heroes of Grabbe's dramas. He is not, however, like Napoleon, Barbarossa and Heinrich VI, a conqueror whose phantastic ambition drives him beyond the natural limits set by the defense of his people. He is entirely satisfied to fight for the existence of his people, and the means by which he chooses to do so are ingenious and within the sphere of possible realization. The destruction of Rome is just as possible as that of Carthage, which is carried out by the Romans; and the success he is able to achieve in spite of all difficulties entirely justifies his strategic plan. If he fails nevertheless, it is because even the best leader depends in his action upon the cooperation of his followers, and that he can be successful only if his will is the exponent of the less conscious will of the people. Hannibal's real tragedy, then, lies in the fact that his aim is far too comprehensive to be understood and adopted by his countrymen with their short-sighted egotism and materialism. It is based on the delusion that he might be able to arouse their enthusiasm for an extraordinary action, and so convince them that he is fighting for the victory of one party and the extermination of the other. By reason of such expectations, he, too, transcends the realistic basis of his action; and he must, according to the logic of Grabbe's drama, meet his defeat, because his aim lies beyond the range of the power at his disposal. If any one of Grabbe's heroes fails on account of the stupidity and inertia of the masses, it is Hannibal. Yet this pessimism is not the last word of the author; it is complemented and mitigated by the contrasting success of the Romans.

Their power rests on their community of purpose: they, as a people, are kept together by the common aim of preserving and promoting their state. Their leaders lack any great vision, and the best of them has neither the genius nor even the extraordinary human qualities of Hannibal. Among them there is even such a superstitious simpleton as Fabius Maximus Cunctator who retreats with his forces before a herd of oxen. In spite of such lack of leadership, the Romans win on account of their unyielding and determined realism, which always visualizes only the nearest aim, but subordinates to this the whole strength of the people.

Grabbe gives in the Romans a perfect illustration of the realistic view of life, in which leader and people are integrated by one strong will to exist and dominate the Mediterranean. In the Carthaginians he pictures a people which has almost lost its inner unity and its determination to defend its unity against attacks from the outside; they realize too late the necessity of defense and so they meet their tragic fate. The other, "idealistic" extreme is represented by King Prusias, who lives in the most ridiculous aloofness, completely unaware of the realities which threaten his fairy-tale existence. In Byzantian segregation from his people, he leads a life of pure ceremonious form, absolutely devoid of any content. He is, therefore, helpless when the Romans demand the extradition of Hannibal; his royal honor does not allow him to betray his guest and ward; his fear of all contact with reality prevents him from protecting Hannibal against the energetic demands of the Romans. In this dilemma, he saves the appearance of his royal honor by absenting himself during the attack on his protegé. This casuistry is a persiflage of all formal ethics, which in Prusias' action is deprived of its real core, the good intention. Characteristic

[97]

of Grabbe's development toward a more realistic view of life is also his derision of theoretical thinking in the dialogue between Prusias and Hannibal about the strategy pursued in the Punic Wars:

> Prusias: . . . Bisweilen hast du deine Reiter rechts, bisweilen links, bald in der Mitte, und mit deinem Fuszvolk geht's ebenso.
> Hannibal: Meine Entschuldigung sei, dasz ich mich nach Zeit und Orts-gelegenheit richten muszte—
> Prusias: Die gilt nicht, weder in der Kunst noch im Krieg: das System nur ist ewig und nach dieser Richtschnur müssen sich Heere richten, Gedichte ordnen, und das System stirbt nicht, geschäh' ihm auch ein Unfall.

In *Die Hermannsschlacht,* the theme of the *Hannibal* drama is further developed in its positive aspect. The Germanic tribes are animated, although on a more primitive level, by the same spirit of self-respect and self-determination as the Romans in *Hannibal.* They are still somewhat awkward in their cooperation; they are held together in a more or less negative way by hatred of their oppressor and fall back into their primitive habits as soon as the immediate goal is reached. Their love of freedom, however, their bravery and physical strength, and their natural sense of justice are qualities which promise a greater future. In spite of the fact that Hermann does not attain his real aim, he is the least tragic of all of Grabbe's heroes. His respect for the actual situation precludes from the very beginning the extreme tension between leader and followers which we observed in the earlier dramas. By clever calculation he succeeds in widening the rift between the Teutons and the Romans, in deceiving the Romans about his intentions, and in gathering together his countrymen for unified action. But his influence ends, and tragedy begins, when his aims overstep the boundaries of immediate necessity, when he confronts his people with a final purpose beyond their political maturity and understanding, the conquest of Rome. This tragedy, however, loses significance in view of the greatness of his actual achievement and the consternation with which the Roman emperor regards the future of his empire. The drama does not close with the sarcastic invitation to the banquet, to which his countrymen respond as fervently as they reject his plans against Rome; rather it closes with the vision of the dying Augustus, who sees his empire crumbling under the attacks of the Nordic tribes and the advance of Eastern Christianity. In spite of the resignation with which he abandons greater projects, Hermann's achievement preserves an historical meaning and is thereby relieved of absolute tragedy: his deed saves the liberty of the Teutons, and paves the way for the defeat

[98]

and the conquest of the Roman world; the conquest of the Germanic tribes is not regarded with the scepticism with which the Italian campaigns of the Hohenstaufen emperors were condemned. The negative and pessimistic side of this thesis, the failure of an ingenious leader through the inertia of his followers, loses prominence in *Die Hermannsschlacht*, for the counter-action is not represented by any character who can claim the sympathy which Hannibal or even his Carthaginians excited. The Romans are no longer the great people they were in the *Hannibal* drama, a people able to overcome all exterior difficulties by their inner vitality, determination, and subordination to one purpose. They are no longer guided by men who embody the will of the people, but are dominated by rulers for whom they serve but as an instrument for egotistic ambitions. The legions no longer fight in the vital interests of the people; they are a mechanized military body without individual will and enthusiasm, under a commander who is himself but an instrument. Their administration of justice has lost all immediate contact with life and has become a sterile system of laws. The scribe, who, in view of imminent death, thinks of nothing but obtaining the signature of a contract which becomes absolutely meaningless in event of defeat, is a caricature of the disintegration of national life; his human substance has, like that of Prusias, vanished into an "idea" devoid of all contact with actual reality. In his abstractness he is the extreme opposite of the Teutons, who immediately after their victory fall back into the most concrete enjoyment of life. He impersonates the fatal end of a development, whereas the Teutons are still at the very beginning of their development toward an ideal humanity in harmonious balance between animalistic self-satisfaction on the one hand, and meaningless standardization of human reactions and complete abstraction from the exigencies of the moment on the other.

As in the case of Grillparzer, Grabbe's development leads away from idealism to a mere realistic view of life. Grillparzer began by challenging the moral presupposition of the idealistic system: the postulate of indeterminism. He found in man's organic relation to his environment the foundation of his morality and even of his entire worth as a human being. The cause of man's decline, on the other hand, appeared to him to be his individuation and the consequent rule of reason. Grabbe differs from Grillparzer especially in the decidedly positive value he attributes to reason. His first reaction against idealism is not directed so much against its indeterministic belief as against the

[99]

role which the Romantic development of idealism ascribes to the irrational and the emotional. Unlike Kleist, he cannot see in the latter a unifying force, but only the danger of obscuring the conditions and limitations of reality and of instigating the will of man to impossible aims. Thus, he comes to a conclusion similar to Grillparzer's: man's action is determined by the concrete conditions of character and environment; but man is led to tragic disregard of these conditions by his ability to transcend these foundations in his thought and will. Grillparzer, however, attributes a special value to the irrational feeling of rootedness in an organic environment and sees in such an organic attachment the only possible mode of existence. Grabbe, on the contrary, believes that a rational understanding of the necessity to adjust oneself to actual conditions is a prerequisite for effective action and he has not the slightest doubt of the value of a rational regulation of life, so long as the object of our aspiration remains within the sphere of the existentially possible.

In Grabbe's development from idealism to realism, *Herzog Theodor von Gothland* is the dramatic expression of the first revolt against a traditional world view; emotional perturbation obscures the recognition of the real issue, and scepticism regarding the reliability of the emotions causes doubt of all social and moral values, of all human relations and beliefs. A cynical contempt for man and a fatalistic resignation to the meaninglessness of existence itself characterize Grabbe's first examination of his philosophical heritage, a heritage which his feeling and imagination is disposed to accept. In *Scherz, Satire, Ironie und tiefere Bedeutung*, Grabbe turns with equal despair against a society which thrives on traditional judgments and habits, and has lost all spontaneity and inner responsibility, together with all understanding for the immediate moral demands of reality. In *Marius und Sulla*, Grabbe proceeds to a more positive attitude toward life. In Marius' fate he shows the demoralization and inner isolation of the sentimental man, who in the last analysis is not concerned about anything but his own self. He must yield to Sulla who respects the limitations of individual activity and is therefore spared the miserable end of the aging Marius. Sulla's attitude, however, is too much determined by regard for the success of his action; it is altruistically directed by the welfare of the community, but is devoid of human sympathy. In this respect, *Don Juan und Faust* marks a decided progress in the conception of the problem; for here Grabbe tries to find the human mean between animalistic sensualism and cynical materialism on the one hand, and the "ideal-istic" detachment from all living contact on the other.

A similar balance is sought in the later historical dramas for the relation between leader and people. The outstanding leader personality is here conceived in the same problematic relation to his people as the mind in its relation to the body in *Don Juan und Faust*. The leader's ability to envisage the more remote potentialities of the future makes him neglect the realistic conditions necessary for executing his projects and, thus, he exposes himself to that tragic isolation which is equivalent to catastrophe. In this way, Barbarossa and Heinrich VI are by their phantastic projects of conquest drawn away from the concrete basis of their power, the German soil, and both meet their fate as soon as they approach the realization of their goal; this very approach parallels their growing isolation. Similarly, Napoleon's efforts to attain his phantastic ends are vain, for he fails to consider the concrete political conditions and the spiritual tendencies of his time. In *Hannibal* the emphasis is shifted to the side of the people; the success of the leader depends absolutely upon the cooperation of his followers, and the harmony of the "intellectual" and the "material" principles is made the basic prerequisite of survival. Harmonious cooperation is emphasized even more in *Die Hermannsschlacht*, since Hermann partly achieves his aims, although the unachieved part of his projects can only be realized in the future when his people will have overcome their primitive stage of materialistic narrowness. Here we find at least a first pregnant, functional explanation of the tragic surplus of energy in the leader personality: the distant, unrealized aim seems to provide the necessary impulse which alone can awaken the inert masses to action; the prospect of eventual realization of this remote aim stimulates them.

The development in Grabbe's dramas indicates a progressive adaptation to the demands of reality. The extraordinary individual is gradually deprived of his superhuman halo, and the mass of the people is increasingly recognized as the spatial and temporal condition for the realization of heroic action. Simultaneously, leader and people are brought into closer organic relation; the leader becomes a life-function of the people, its thinking and directive organ. With that, the tragic meaninglessness of the masses as well as that of the surplus of energy in the individual is considerably mitigated. In the later dramas, too, there still are leaders who remain without a following because their people have lost their vitality, as, for example, Tancred, the Norman, and

[101]

Hannibal, the Carthaginian. They are, however, not considered the rule but are merely illustrations to support Grabbe's positive view; they admonish his contemporaries to become worthy of greater tasks by furthering their inner development. To quote Grabbe's own formulation of this idea in the little dramatic sketch *Barbarossa im Kyffhäuser*:

> Neue Götter,
> Unnennbare Welten
> Dringen herein—
> Doch nie sind Gott und Mensch und Welt des Glückes wert,
> So lang keiner sich selbst bekehrt!

Grabbe's view of life develops in and through his dramas from a desperate, nihilistic conception to a moderately tragic one; the denial of all tragedy would, of course, be an unworthy superficiality, since tragedy is an inescapable consequence of the natural limitation of all human will. In a quite rational development he arrives at a relative harmonization of the two antagonistic poles which we found in extreme tension at the beginning of his dramatic career. The solution which he finds for this antagonism compares with that of Hebbel, for neither of the two dramatists ever succeeds in relieving the extraordinary individual entirely of tragedy; but both find a meaning for his surplus of will and intelligence in the fact that these provide an aim for further development and the impulse for its realization. Hebbel, however, who excels Grabbe considerably as an artist and a thinker, also projects this explanation into the metaphysical background of life, while Grabbe remains entirely within the sphere of reality and in this respect stands in closer contact with the realistic tendencies of the nineteenth century than Hebbel.

CHAPTER VIII

GEORG BÜCHNER

(1813-1837)

THE collapse of the idealistic faith and the process of reconciliation with the realities of their time is the characteristic crisis through which most of our nineteenth century dramatists had to pass. Almost the only variation in the crisis is the degree of intensity with which it is experienced by the several authors. For Grillparzer it was more a continuous act of resignation, whereas Grabbe had to pass through a period of revolt and despair. Büchner's reaction might best be termed a rebellious resignation. His early death did not allow him to reach the stage of complete reconciliation with the world, and the three dramas he left behind are more the expression of his disillusionment. For he too came to doubt the idealistic claims which he ardently embraced with one side of his nature while rejecting them with equal determination with the other.

From his father he inherited a factual soberness and a stern objectivity, while his mother endowed him with romantic sensibility and an emotional devotion to things and people. His romantic turn of mind was responsible for his protest against the boring and pedantic treatment of the classics at the Gymnasium and his predilection for the private study of the works of Shakespeare, Goethe, Herder, and the romanticists. But his anti-illusionistic search for truth caused him to study with equal devotion the medical and natural sciences and critically to examine the systems of idealistic philosophy, so that we find him in his first drama in decided opposition to any idealistic interpretation of history and life.

Büchner regarded the reactionary Metternich régime with the eyes of a Late Romanticist. Late-Romantic political theory conceived a community of the people (*Volksgemeinschaft*), in which the state would express the inner life and integrate the will of its citizens. Büchner's personal experiences at Gieszen, however, where he finished his medical studies, made him despair of all bourgeois attempts at a national regeneration on the basis of the vague ideology of a liberal constitution, a united empire, and a German-Christian faith. The petty chicaneries of intimidated officials, the philistine resig-

[103]

nation to the contemptible autocracy of the German princelings and their henchmen, the denunciation of one of his revolutionary accomplices, evoked in him a disgust for the "enervated modern society whose life consists only of attempts to dissipate the most horrible tedium, a society which, as far as I am concerned might as well die out, because that would be the only change which it is still possible for it to experience."* His revolutionary attitude is not liberal, but socialistic, and is based on the reflection that it is never "the ideas of the educated classes, but only the needs of the masses which can bring about a change."

> Das Verhältnis zwischen Reichen und Armen ist das einzige revolutionäre Element in der Welt; der Hunger allein kann die Freiheitsgöttin, und nur ein Moses, der uns die ägyptischen Plagen auf den Hals schickte, könnte ein Messias werden.

But even the masses become immovable, he thinks, as soon as they have a chicken in the pot.†

Büchner sees in the masses the degrading and retarding factor in history, but he sees in them also the only lever by which society can be raised to a higher plane. In this view he again concurs with Grabbe, except that in his short dramatic career he does not come to a positive presentation of the idea. He hardly develops beyond a pessimistic attitude toward historical progress. Such a mood is despairingly expressed in a letter written during the spring of 1834, after he had studied the history of the French Revolution:

> Ich fühlte mich wie zernichtet unter dem gräszlichen Fatalismus der Geschichte. Ich finde in der Menschennatur eine entsetzliche Gleichheit, in den menschlichen Verhältnissen eine unabwendbare Gewalt, allen und keinem verliehen. Der einzelne nur Schaum auf der Welle, die Grösze ein bloszer Zufall, die Herrschaft des Genies ein Puppenspiel, ein lächerliches Ringen gegen ein ehernes Gesetz, es zu erkennen das Höchste, es zu beherrschen unmöglich. . . . Das Musz ist eins von den Verdammungsworten, womit der Mensch getauft worden.

Büchner, the revolutionary who had hoped to lead man to a higher level and who had seen his endeavors fail because of the pettiness and stupidity of his revolutionary comrades and his opponents, despairs of historical progress and of any possible upward evolution of mankind. His opposition to the idealistic belief is complemented by his con-

*Letter to Gutzkow, 1836.
†Letter to Gutzkow, 1835.

ception of man as a being essentially determined by instinct causality. Reason is for him, as it was for Schopenhauer, a power of secondary importance only, an instrument to stimulate the instincts and deceive them about their low and hideous nature. The surface of consciousness deludes man with the ideas of freedom, moral aims, and progress toward a better human order. Below this surface of pretense, in the stratum of the subconscious, the shining illusion fades away; the individual, like mankind in general, is apparently subject to blind fate and the causality of base instincts, a revelation which, at least for a time, causes Büchner to deny the value of all action and striving.

That is the inner despair from which Büchner suffered when he wrote his tragedy *Dantons Tod*. At the opening of the play, the first phase of the French Revolution is past, the phase which, in spite of all its brutality, demands our admiration as a revolt against an intolerable social and economic system. Now the revolution has entered the stage of personal revenge and ambition without any higher human aims, the stage of development which, historically, marks the transition to a military dictatorship and the degradation of liberty and equality to battle-cries of international carnage. Danton, the courageous leader of the Revolution, has withdrawn from public activity; disillusioned and in despair of finding any sense in the historical process; he has yielded to the hypocritical, fanatic Robespierre, who cannot see in Danton's retirement anything but treason against the ideals of the Revolution and who has, therefore, selected him as the next sacrifice for the bloodthirsty mob. Danton could still be saved, if he would devote his entire energy to this purpose. But the consideration of the impossibility of leading the masses to a higher aim, and the consciousness that he himself has inaugurated this murderous fury by ordering the September massacre have driven him to fatalism and cynical resignation. After only a short rebellion, he prefers death on the guillotine to the continuation of an aimless and meaningless existence.

In the form of an historical drama, Büchner examines the postulates of idealism and the ideals proclaimed by the Revolution. Over against the classical ideas of God and a reasonable world order, he sets a metaphysical scepticism.Whereas the theologians and the philosophers writing under the influence of the Christian dogma deduced from the harmony and the order of the world the existence of a divine organizer, Payne (III, 1) rejects the belief in a creator because of the intolerable imperfection of the world. If God existed, would he not have done better to leave the world uncreated than in such a state of imperfection?

[105]

Müssen wir, wenn sich unser Geist in das Wesen einer harmonisch in sich ruhenden, ewigen Seligkeit versenkt, gleich annehmen, sie müsse die Finger ausstrecken und über Tisch Brotmännchen kneten? aus überschwenglichem Liebesbedürfnis, wie wir uns ganz geheimnisvoll in die Ohren sagen. Müssen wir das alles, um uns zu Göttersöhnen zu machen? Ich nehme mit einem geringeren Vater vorlieb; wenigstens werde ich ihm nicht nachsagen können, dasz er mich unter seinem Stande in Schweineställen oder Galeeren habe erziehen lassen. Schafft das Unvollkommene weg, dann allein könnt ihr Gott demonstrieren.

While the theologians and philosophers demonstrate the existence of God from the existence of a human conscience, Payne refers to the *petitio principii* in this argument:

Erst beweist ihr Gott aus der Moral und dann die Moral aus Gott! (III, 1).

According to Danton's view, matter cannot be reduced to nothing, but he wishes that such an absolute liberation from the intolerable burden of existence might be the aim of evolution:

Das Nichts ist der zu gebärende Weltgott (V, 5)

is his version of Schopenhauer's pessimistic longing for the Nirvana. Man may convince himself of the harmony of the universe by rational arguments:

Man braucht nur einen etwas höheren Standpunkt zu wählen, und alles wird zu Harmonien (V, 5).

The assumption of harmony, however, is for Büchner's disillusioned feeling a blasphemy and a derision of the misery of human fate:

Aber wir sind die armen Musikanten und unsere Körper die Instrumente. Sind denn die häszlichen Töne, welche auf ihnen herausgepustet werden, nur da, um höher und höher dringend und endlich leise verhallend wie ein wollüstiger Schrei in himmlischen Ohren zu sterben? (V, 5).

Only the brutal and cold-blooded judge, Saint Just, recognizes the existence of a world order, but this order is a horrible naturalistic system, in which he and his murderous gang hold high positions as executors of the universal will:

Soll überhaupt ein Ereignis, was die ganze Gestaltung der moralischen Natur, das heiszt der Menschheit, umändert nicht durch Blut gehen dürfen? Der Weltgeist bedient sich in der geistigen Sphäre unserer Arme ebenso, wie er in der physischen Vulkane und Wasserfluten gebraucht. . . . Das Gelangen zu den einfachsten Erfindungen und Grundsätzen hat Millionen das Leben gekostet, die auf dem Wege starben. Ist es denn nicht einfach, dasz zu einer

[106]

Zeit, wo der Gang der Geschichte rascher ist, auch mehr Menschen auszer Atem kommen? (*End of Act II*).

In a similar manner, Danton rejects the idea of moral freedom. At the beginning of the Revolution, he believed that the destruction of the aristocratic order would help to further the moral progress of mankind. The degeneration of the revolutionary idea in its practical application, however, demonstrated the idealist's dependence upon powers beyond his control, and thus drove him as political leader to involuntary brutalities. Now the will of man seems to Danton to be determined by instinct. All human striving is hedonistic, and, in the last analysis, the highest human desire is identical in motive with the basest sensuality, since the satisfaction of the instinct is the driving energy behind all human action. Again it is the murderers of the Robespierre party who consider themselves the representatives of virtue and who silence their conscience with moral platitudes. Robespierre's virtue partly consists in the petit bourgeois' resentment against the suppression of his own desires; he makes the fight against vice his revolutionary watchword because it is the safest way to further his selfish political aims; but he fights against vice only to the extent to which it serves his purpose, while he allows the masses to satisfy their immoral desires in the wildest orgies. Such a view of life, of course, deprives the idea of immortality of all meaning; Danton has only one fear, namely, that death might fail to obliterate *all* of his memories of life.

The revolutionary ideals seem to him just as futile as the classical postulates of God, moral freedom, and immortality, at least when the attempt is made to realize them in human society. Fraternity is replaced by murder from the basest motives of revenge, craving for sensation, greed, and ambition; only the word is retained as a propaganda slogan and as an ideological disguise for the real facts. Equality is maintained on the lowest level of society; anyone who has no holes in his sleeves and who does not wipe his nose with his fingers is an aristocrat and faces execution on the guillotine. The democratic ideal of freedom, too, is only for harlots and scoundrels; on the whole, the people are but the instrument of an imbecile leader whose tenure, in turn, depends upon compliance with the instincts and demands of the mob. Justice, finally, is degraded to a bloody farce; those who are to die are removed from the trial for contempt of court, when they try to defend themselves (II, 6), and he who shows any sign of fear thereby confesses his guilt (II, 7).

[107]

The idealist of the classical and the romantic periods is willing to sacrifice his life for the ideal, like Schiller's Jungfrau von Orleans and Kleist's Prinz von Homburg, after he has recognized the higher meaning of his sacrifice. Grillparzer's König Ottokar, on the other hand, recognizes that human striving means nothing in comparison with the fundamental value of life. Büchner, like Grabbe in his first drama, *Herzog Theodor von Gothland,* despairs completely of the value and of the meaning of life. His Danton, to be sure, makes a last desperate effort to save his life; but it is the unconscious vital instinct which impels him to wage his battle of self-defense, while his conscious mind rejects life as not worth living. Man is essentially solitary and isolated from his most beloved friend by the fact that only the base sense organs are capable of leading him from his inner prison into the open (I, 1). Life is an eternal repetition of the same experience; a million times, millions of people do the same thing; and even such an exciting spectacle as the Revolution becomes a boring habit, one gets "tired of always playing the same string on an instrument which gives only one tone" (II, 1). So it is, according to Danton's opinion, hardly worth while to save one's life;

> ob sie nun an der Guillotine oder am Fieber oder am Alter sterben! . . . Es ist recht gut, wenn die Lebenszeit reduziert wird . . . das Leben ist nicht die Arbeit wert, die man sich macht, es zu erhalten.

Danton's Tod presents the tragedy of a leader who begins his revolutionary work believing in the idea and the possibility of its realization, later, however, recognizes that he has set in motion a chain of events which follow their own causality. Danton sees that the murders which he intended as a means of bringing about a better order become for the sensation-hunting mob a spectacle, and for the scoundrels among its leaders an instrument for entrenching their own power. He realizes the tragic dilemma of depending upon the masses for accomplishing change, and yet being forced to fight against them because they cannot understand higher aims and therefore degrade the noblest intentions to their own level. It is the tragedy of the idealist who sees his highest striving wrecked by the pettiness of his fellow men and who therefore begins to doubt the validity of the ideals themselves and to ask whether these ideals are not, after all, but a disguise for the sensual instincts. It is, finally, the tragedy which results from the problematic situation of life itself, of life which comes to consciousness in man; for by his consciousness he is im-

[108]

pelled to ask whether his existence has a value and a meaning, but he is not capable of giving a definite and reassuring answer to the question, so that the same consciousness which raises him above other creatures also drives him to despair and death. It is the tragic paradox that the highest evolution of life in the human mind also becomes its greatest danger. Yet even this extremely pessimistic drama leaves one dim ray of hope; beneath the extreme resignation we can discover a postulate which might have led the author to a more conciliatory attitude towards life if only longer life had been granted to him. This postulate is indicated in the remark with which Danton justifies his withdrawal from the revolutionary movement:

> Ich habe es satt, wozu sollen wir Menschen miteinander kämpfen.

These words indicate the only remaining possibility for continuing to bear the burden of life: if life is hardly worth living, and yet is the only recognizable value, then man ought, on the basis of this universal and inescapable tragedy, to renounce all hatred and strife and live in mutual sympathy and tolerance. This postulate follows as inexorably from the events of this play as the supreme virtue of compassion follows from Schopenhauer's pessimistic metaphysical speculation.

The comedy *Leonore und Lena* does not translate the author's *Weltschmerz* so vividly into dramatic symbol and lacks therefore the full artistic value of *Dantons Tod*. Büchner's intention was to criticize the higher social stratum of society just as Grabbe had done in *Scherz, Satire, Ironie und tiefere Bedeutung;* but he failed to imbue it with the same compulsion of despair. He ridicules the German system of small states, the fatuity of the princelings and their courtiers, the romantic vagaries and the blasé pessimism of his younger contemporaries. As far as this is a genuine expression of the author's own state of mind, it had all been said with incomparably more dramatic force in *Dantons Tod*. The main complaint in the comedy, too, is that life is deprived of any worthwhile content, and that the attempt to escape tedium is the real impulse of man's activity:

> Sie studieren aus Langeweile, sie beten aus Langeweile, sie verlieben, verheiraten und vermehren sich aus Langeweile und sterben endlich aus Langeweile, und — und das ist der Humor davon — alles mit den wichtigsten Gesichtern, ohne zu merken, warum. . . . Alle diese Helden, diese Genies, diese Dummköpfe, diese Heiligen, diese Sünder, diese Familienväter sind im Grunde nichts als raffinierte Müsziggänger (I, 1).

With this reduction of all motives to one of escape from tedium,

Büchner also destroys the basis for any differentiation of values. All types of man in this comedy suffer from the same ailment, from which there is but one relief, withdrawal from the world into eternal nothingness.

Human fate, imperfect and conditioned as it is by causality, is also the theme of the fragmentary tragedy *Woyzeck*. *Woyzeck*, too, expresses the same deep compassion with the tormented creature man, which inspired the author to dramatize the all-too-human decline of the French Revolution. Woyzeck is a sort of "everyman," the representative of his many companions in distress, who, poor and exploited, live their dull and meaningless existence. As a soldier he loves his brave companion Marie; he is the father of her child; but he is too poor to pay for the blessing of the church and to lead the regulated life of a middle class family. He would like to be as virtuous as his well-nourished captain, who is moved at the thought of his own goodness, would have him be But there is no virtue without money, and so these poor creatures are condemned to misery in this world as well as in the next:

> Ich glaub', wenn wir in Himmel kämen, müszten wir noch donnern helfen.

The regimental surgeon uses him as a subject of his experiments. For a quarter of a year he has kept him on a diet of peas, and the students observe its effects on his pulse and his eyes. Marie, a strong and sensual woman, as good and as uncontrolled as an animal, drives him to despair by her relations with other men, and what she does not achieve by her faithlessness, her seducers achieve by their mockery. The thought of murdering her comes to Woyzeck first in ghostlike apparitions; like an animal sniffing the air, he has vague premonitions of some indefinite disaster; it torments him in his feverish dream in the guard-room. Thus, the actual murder does not strike us as a wicked deed, but as a catastrophe of nature which had to overtake any man so oppressed and inhibited within the fatal sphere of his most primitive desires. The somberness of the atmosphere is emphasized by naturalistic dialogue and the pregnancy of the scenes, in which a few words suffice to create an impressive vision of the whole environment,—as for example, the scene in the Jewish pedlar's store where Woyzeck buys the knife for the murder. When the words flow more abundantly, they serve to characterize the more pretentious and the better educated people who, because of their very education, are inferior to the more genuine and valuable naturalness of Woyzeck and even Marie. We feel a deep sympathy toward them, but there are doubts about the real human value of the virtuous captain, and we abhor the surgeon for whom human beings are mere objects of experiments and for whom other people's illnesses are a boon from heaven.

The fragment *Woyzeck* complements the heroic tragedy *Dantons Tod*. *Dantons Tod* presents the tragedy of the leader whose higher intentions have been frustrated by the degrading forces of the masses. *Woyzeck* examines the tragedy of the proletarian man himself, the causality of his animal behavior, the determinism of his environment, which prevents him from rising to the higher stage in humanity to which he is entitled by his natural goodness. Büchner expresses in *Woyzeck* his social belief, which we quoted from his letters, that human society cannot be reformed by the decrepit members of the educated class; that a reform must begin with the material distress of the proletariat. With these ideas, the author anticipates socialism. Such ideas are closely related to Büchner's conception of man as basically instinctive in nature, rooted in his environment, and barely capable of rising above his animal origin, however much his intellect may tempt him to consider himself the free master of his destiny. With this conception, Büchner comes rather close to the deterministic naturalism of the late nineteenth century. What distinguishes Büchner from naturalism is the idealistic point of departure. Inverted idealism remains with him in the negative form of disillusionment and fatalistic resignation, for which he found further support in medical and scientific studies.

Chapter IX

FRIEDRICH HEBBEL

(1813-63)

GRILLPARZER's dramatic work shows the Austrian character with its joy and yet also weariness of life; Hebbel's work reflects the austere North-German character. In Hebbel a sober sense for the demands of reality, reason, and will are combined with a vivid imagination and emotional depth. The imaginative and emotional qualities, however, are concealed and suppressed by the rational element and therefore find only a scant and restrained expression in the poetic work.

Hebbel's childhood experience increases the tension between inner life and pressure from the outside. The natural amiability of his father was almost entirely shattered by his abject poverty. It was the mother who saved the boy from being forced into a trade, and who made it possible for him to attend a school and cultivate his imagination by reading. After his father's death, Friedrich accepted a position as errand-boy and scribe in the house of magistrate Mohr. But this position brought only new suppression and humiliation for his proud and ambitious character. At the same time, however, the library of his master provided him with the opportunity of meeting pressure from the outside with counter-pressure from within through increased knowledge and the first attempts to form his world view. Finally, he was led out of the disconsolate narrowness of the Schleswig-Holstein parish by the intercession of Amalie Schoppe, an author and editor in Hamburg.

In this city, he found assistance and motherly care in the modest home of Elise Lensing; this moderately educated seamstress also had a sympathetic understanding for the inner distress of his awakening talent. She sacrificed her hard-earned savings, her honor and her life. Hebbel could do nothing for her but, by accepting her help, provide her with an object for her absolute and self-sacrificing devotion; otherwise, her reward was social disgrace. However one may detest Hebbel's ingratitude, the poet in him needed this consciousness of guilt. It became one of the principal themes of his dramatic work; for in his plays he waged the fight for the rights of women, which he had so shamelessly violated in his actions. This relationship to Elise Lensing is the beginning of that metaphysical speculation about life which led him close to the

Hegelian system. While Elise was desperate in destitution and sorrow over the death of their child, he sought to justify his attitude in the inherent guilt of the life process itself, which designates a few select individuals the protagonists of the divine evolution, and as such compels them to break away from tradition and go their tragic way of guilt. To save his art, he had to violate the standards of bourgeois morality and the most sacred human rights. He abandoned Elise and married the Viennese actress, Christine Enghaus; freed by this marriage from economic worries, he found the philosophical and poetic solution for his life problem.

Hebbel's intellectual heritage, like Grillparzer's, was the idealism of the classical period. In his early poems, he follows Schiller in his praise of immortality as an elevating "Lichtgedanke." He believes in moral freedom and the essential goodness of man, but never to the extent of an unconditioned, enthusiastic conviction; the thought of the transitoriness of life and the unending disappointment of human striving disquiets him. He would like to have conclusive evidence of God's existence and the immortality of the soul, but he misses the absolute feeling which should support these ideas.

> Wenn sich sonst der einzelne Mensch in seiner Beschränktheit und Bedürftigkeit ins Allgemeine, ins Ganze und Grosze, hinüberflüchten konnte, so hat dieses selbst jetzt kaum einen letzten kümmerlichen Opferbrand, an dem sich das erloschene Feuer dereinst wieder entzünden läszt, hineingerettet in eine edlere Menschenbrust. Die Menschheit ist wahrhaft scheintot, und nur die Schmerzen in ihren edelsten Gliedern bürgen für die Möglichkeit eines Erwachens (*Tagebücher* Nr. 628).

Happiness in a future life appears to him as a fancy of despair and a prophecy of insanity (*Tagebücher* Nr. 689). Although he does not absolutely doubt the destiny of mankind, he believes that his own period is undergoing a serious crisis, for it is deprived of any great idea which might hold mankind together and lead it on to a higher stage.

> Unsere Zeit ist eine schlimme Zeit . . . Die Weltgeschichte steht jetzt vor einer ungeheuren Aufgabe; die Hölle ist längst ausgeblasen und ihre letzten Flammen haben den Himmel ergriffen und verzehrt, die Idee der Gottheit reicht nicht mehr aus . . .; das Leben ist ein Krampf, eine Ohnmacht oder ein Opiumsrausch . . . (*Tagebücher* No. 689).

The sombreness of Hebbel's first novelistic essays is ordinarily explained as an imitation of the technique of *Schauerromantik.* Such an explanation, however, must be supplemented by mention of the author's inner affinity to this literary form. These first novelettes

[113]

express scepticism, doubts, and despair over the world and its meaning. In *Holion*, for instance, man is a puppet of the world-spirit,

> aus nichts entstehend, kämpfend und zu nichts kehrend;

in *Brudermord*, valuable beings are led to their downfall by a fateful concatenation of circumstances; in *Die Räuberbraut*, noble and innocent love ends in crime, in *Anna*, docile submission to an unjust punishment entails an appalling sequence of disasters. The very ideal values, friendship, love, beauty, have this pernicious effect. The young Hebbel considers himself part of a meaningless world. This lack of meaning, however, shows Hebbel beginning to search for a new relationship between individual and universe which simultaneously might serve as the basis for reorganizing human society. The foregoing quotation from his diaries continues:

> Woher soll die Weltgeschichte eine Idee nehmen, die die Idee der Gottheit aufwiegt oder überragt?

This passage obviously establishes the connection between his personal despair and the problem of his time. In his time he sees the disintegration of an order based on religious and idealistic beliefs, and the need therefore of theoretical and practical reorientation.

Since his belief in the existence of a personal God and an eternal, unchangeable sphere of ideas had been shaken, the only idea which offered itself as a foundation for his new world view was the romantic, idealistic conception of evolution. Not without an inner struggle and a certain horror, he adopted the idea of an absolute process of life:

> Dies ist der Fluch alles Werdens, der die Menschheit, wie den Menschen, durch jedweden einzelnen Zustand verfolgt; es ist ein stetes Wiedergebären durch den Tod, und wem, der das im Tiefsten an sich selbst erfuhr, steigt nicht ein Ekel, selbst gegen das Herrliche und Werte auf, da er voraus weisz, dasz es früher oder später einem Herrlicheren, und so ins Unendliche fort, weichen musz (*Tagebücher* Nr. 575).

At first he finds at least some comfort in the not too inspiring thought that every stage of the evolutionary process is to be filled with appropriate action and that this action helps the world spirit over the despondency of an emptiness without action. The individual, therefore, has no meaning and value for himself, only as an instrument of the world spirit does his existence receive a relative significance. How far he has moved away from the idealistic belief in eternal values is apparent in Hebbel's interpretation of the deeds of Joan of Arc. Schiller's drama

[114]

FRIEDRICH HEBBEL

is for him nothing but a play which celebrates on the stage the French victory over the English. Correspondingly, his Johanna is a "theatrical virgin, a peacock," and not the impersonation of man's struggle for moral freedom. Hebbel himself does not conceive Johanna under the aspect of a static, universal and eternal order of values, but under that of the evolution of the universe, in which the self-developing divinity manifests itself. Her appearance is a historical miracle which paves the way for the French Revolution:

> Die Gottheit wählte ein gebrechliches Mädchen, um schon durch ihr Werkzeug anzuzeigen, dasz sie keiner irdischen Mittel bedarf, um ihre Zwecke zu erreichen, die sie als notwendig den Bewegungen der Geschichte gesetzt hat.*

Johanna is not a sublime end in herself; she is but an instrument of history, who is chosen for the tragic task of acting against her womanly nature, a task which dooms her to destruction as soon as she has fulfilled her mission in the service of the divine evolution.

> Die Gottheit selbst, wenn sie zur Erreichung groszer Zwecke auf ein Individuum unmittelbar einwirkt und sich dadurch einen willkürlichen Eingriff...ins Weltgetriebe erlaubt, kann ihr Werkzeug vor der Zermalmung durch dasselbe Rad, das es einen Augenblick aufhielt oder anders lenkte, nicht schützen. Dies ist wohl das vornehmste tragische Motiv, das in der Geschichte der Jungfrau von Orleans liegt. Eine Tragödie, welche diese Idee abspiegelte, würde einen groszen Eindruck hervorbringen durch den Blick in die ewige Ordnung der Natur, die die Gottheit selbst nicht stören darf, ohne es büszen zu müssen. (*Tagebücher* Nr. 1011).

Although the divinity is not yet wholly identified with the universe and still has personal traits, it is no longer endowed with the omnipotence of the Christian God, but bound by the laws of the evolutionary process.

This fatalism of the evolutionary process takes dramatic form in *Judith*. There it is connected with the contemporary problem of women's emancipation and the increasing importance of the masses. Schiller's Johanna began with an irrational impulse and an unaccountable feeling that she was sent by the Holy Virgin, and developed through her love to the stage of absolute freedom, that is, from moral heteronomy to autonomy. In Hebbel's *Judith*, however, the ideal motives are but an instrument of the instincts to deceive the moral consciousness. As in Grillparzer's *Ahnfrau*, ideal striving is unmasked and reduced to the longing of the sexually disappointed woman for an energetic and

Geschichte der Jungfrau von Orleans.

[115]

fearless man; this motive enters at least as one of the most important causes. That is why Hebbel places Judith "in the middle between woman and virgin." Since Manasse was frightened away from her during the wedding-night, she despises weak men and is unconsciously attracted by the brutal energy of Holofernes. But her subconscious motive is concealed from consciousness by an ideal disguise; her secret desires become God-willed duty; God's people can be saved only by the sacrifice of her womanhood. The religious and patriotic motive is finally strengthened by that of human sympathy for her starving and lost people and by the self-respect of the woman who wants to avenge the disgrace done to her sex by Holofernes. Her people's complete despair of their power to withstand the attack of the Assyrians, and of Jehovah's readiness to save them from catastrophe, gives her the final impulse to go to the enemy's camp. In Holofernes' presence she yields again to her erotic inclination for the indomitable energy of man; without Holofernes' haughty disdain for her femininity she would not find the courage to fulfill her religious and patriotic mission. Thus, offended womanhood becomes the last and decisive motive of her deed. It is the cruelest tragedy which could befall her when she realizes the importance of her sexual desires in the motivation of her deed. It is enhanced only by the realization that she has sacrificed the most courageous man, "the first and last man on earth" to save her cowardly countrymen, and by the fear that she might bear a child to Holofernes, who, according to the custom of blood-revenge, would have to murder his own mother. Whether her deed receives a meaning at least in the sphere of the superindividual, whether the preservation of Judaism means progress in the evolution of the world and thereby a propagation of the aims of the world spirit, this question is not clearly and definitely answered in this drama. Above all, the sacrificed individual does not recognize this world significance; the author dismisses his protagonist— as well as the reader—with a cruel indecision, without an answer to the most vital question as to the sense and value of this supreme sacrifice or of any idealistic decision.

The tragedy *Genoveva* gives at least a preliminary answer to this question, as also to the personal and the contemporary problems which the drama necessarily presents. In the character of Genoveva, Hebbel glorifies his deceased mother, who, after her death in 1838, seemed to him a martyr to her motherly vocation. Above all, he glorifies his sacrificing friend Elise Lensing, whose generosity and inexhaustible love impelled him to this dramatic confession of his guilt, and for whose suffering he is seeking a metaphysical reason. Perhaps he also tries to liberate himself from the moral demands of his conscience by a theoretical solution of the problem. In the preface to his drama, the author states that every play is alive only insofar as it helps to express the highest and truest interests of the author's own period. The main problem of his time is, in his opinion, the removal of the antagonism between the two sexes, the emancipation of women as it was proclaimed by the Young German Movement. In *Judith* he had presented what he considered the negative side of the problem, the catastrophe of a woman who transcended the boundaries of her nature by taking an active part in historical development. In contrast to the emancipated woman, Genoveva is Hebbel's ideal of the motherly woman who, in harmonious self-reliance, resists the temptations of the world and in unshaken love submits to persecution and martyrdom. Unlike Judith, she does not break down in her effort to solve the problem of the meaning of life and human suffering; she finds a meaning in her existence and in the world as a whole.

> Die Zeit ist um, wo der befleckte Ball
> Der Erde neu entsündigt werden musz,
> Wenn nicht der Donner aus der Hand des Herrn,
> Die schon sich hob, zermalmend fallen soll.
> Er tat im Anbeginn den Gnadenschwur,
> Dasz er das arme menschliche Geschlecht
> Nie tilgen will, wenn alle tausend Jahr'
> Auch nur ein einziger vor ihm besteht.

The meaning of life found here is comparable to Emperor Rudolf's solution in Grillparzer's *Ein Bruderzwist im Hause Habsburg*; it lies in the representative significance of ideal goodness. The embodiment of goodness in at least one human being is God's hope for the regeneration of the world. This meaning is still of a rather static quality and still reminds one of the classical presentation of goodness in Goethe's *Iphigenie* and even more of Max Piccolomini's fate in Schiller's *Wallenstein*. Genoveva's tragedy, however, is not simply, like that of Max, a tragedy of the ideal in a realistic world dominated by instincts, but the tragedy of a human being which by his greater perfection at once furthers and disturbs the world order. Genoveva's perfection is not only necessary for the preservation of mankind, as the above quotation indicates, it is also responsible for Golo's criminal development and Genoveva's own suffering. At this point, however, the Judith problem as to the sense of human suffering rises again. What meaning has Genoveva's tragic life? Hebbel gives us no satisfactory answer in this play. Rather our interest is drawn from the passive and static character of the too perfect heroine to the villainous Golo. Through Golo Hebbel confesses his own passion and guilt toward Elise Lensing; as the impersonation of his most personal experience, Golo becomes the real protagonist of the drama. In him the whole paradox of human ways as well as the dialectics of evil are revealed. To make this passionate and rash character act fiendishly, but from human motives, is, according to Hebbel (*Tagebücher* Nr. 1475), the intention of this drama. His love for Genoveva's moral perfection and beauty is the innocent, and yet guilty, beginning of Golo's moral decline. Genoveva wins such power over him because he is essentially a noble character; and because he is noble, he sees guilt in his reverence for her, and thus loses his moral self-esteem; his love for the ideal in her merges with hatred for the woman who confused his conscience and deprived him of his self-respect. Since God did not punish his suicidal climbing of the tower, he holds even God responsible for his continued demoralization. He expects Genoveva, whom he adored for her blameless character, to hand him the sword with which he promises to commit suicide in order to save her. Since he cannot possess her, he destroys the object of his love:

> Genovevas Schicksal musz erfüllt werden, damit Golos Hölle ganz werde; er kann nicht ganz selig sein, so will er doch ganz verdammt sein. Er läszt sie ermorden und ist nun als Verbrecher, was er ehemals als Mensch und Mann war, denn dahin drängt ein ewiges Gesetz der Natur, nur fallende Engel wurden Teufel, nicht fallende Menschen (*Tagebücher* Nr. 1475).

While in *Judith* the ideal motives derive from the lower instincts and ideal motivation itself is questioned, in *Genoveva* ideality and sensuality are contrasted. There remains, however, some relation between the opposite poles; goodness appears as the cause of evil and evil deeds spring from a good character; both, good and evil, disturb the harmony of the world. These dialectics of ethical conduct are but a psychological occurrence in the individual sphere, without any attempt, however, to explain this phenomenon as a metaphysical necessity. The treatment of the problem offered in *Genoveva* thus points forward to a philosophical interpretation of good and evil Can both be derived from the same root? That is the question which Hebbel asks himself in his diaries and which in Golo's development is answered only from the point of view of psychological analysis. Both

[118]

the psychological and the metaphysical interpretation must, however, be derived from the world process itself; for only a metaphysical integration of all the phenomena of life is capable of satisfying a truly searching mind.

Hebbel's dissatisfaction with his endeavors to find a meaning in human life is apparent in the comedy *Der Diamant*, written about the same time as *Judith* and *Genoveva*. The fate of royal majesty is to depend on the speed of digestion in a wretched Jewish usurer. He has swallowed a diamond, and is persecuted and threatened with murder by the pharisaic Christians, until nature relieves him of the precious stone and the persecution. This harassed creature speaks the words which mock Hebbel's own metaphysical longing and thus reveal his deepest concern:

> Eine Tat hast du ausgeführt, die in den Sternen beschlossen war, die ausgeführt werden muszte, wenn die Prinzessin nicht eines jämmerlichen Todes sterben, wenn dem Königshause der bitterste Verlust erspart werden sollte! Hättest du die Hütte des Bauern nicht betreten, hättest du den Stein nicht, wie auf den Wink des Schicksals, instinktmäsig zu dir gesteckt und dem einfältigen Besitzer dadurch die Augen über den Wert seines Schatzes geöffnet, würde man ihm auf die Spur gekommen sein? Nimmermehr. Also . . . (V, 4).

In Genoveva's fate, Hebbel demonstrated how the preëminence of the individual in the average conduct of life leads to tragic catastrophe. With this view, he arrived at the real basis of all human tragedy: the antagonism between infinite striving and the finiteness of human nature. It is a variation of Grillparzer's theme of man's dependence upon his existential situation, but Hebbel had not yet succeeded in establishing an intelligible relation between man's tragedy and the evolutionary process of the world, although we have seen preliminary formulations in his essay *Die Geschichte der Jungfrau von Orleans* and in the *Judith* tragedy.

In *Maria Magdalene* both ideas are clarified and given a somewhat more satisfactory solution: man is born into a narrow sphere of existence, from which he can emancipate himself only at the risk of destruction, and yet this sphere must be transcended if life is to be continued in its essential form of the evolutionary process. A twofold tragedy is inherent in this process; a living reaction, although it grows out of the immediate and sympathetic experience of a situation, degenerates into the dead formula of tradition and convention and menaces all life not yet standardized. This petrifaction of life into formal standards

[119]

is the fate which leads the characters of this drama to catastrophe; it is a fate which operates with irrevocable causality and which may be conjured up by any incident. An insane woman has hidden a piece of jewelry. All efforts to recover it fail. Karl, who worked in the house, must have stolen it, especially since he is known to be somewhat frivolous in his revolt against his narrow bourgeois environment. The constable, whom Karl's father, in line with a traditional evaluation, had despised as belonging to a dishonorable profession, takes his revenge by premature arrest of the son. Karl's sick mother dies from chagrin over the accusation of her favorite child. The severe father, however, has no doubt of Karl's guilt; for him anyone who does not completely subordinate himself to the standards of the petite bourgeoisie is capable of any crime. Since his self-respect depends wholly on what others think of him, he urges his daughter Klara to swear that she will never expose him to public disgrace with the words:

> Ich kann's in einer Welt nicht aushalten, wo die Leute mitleidig sein müssen, wenn sie nicht vor mir ausspucken sollen (II, 1).

Klara, however, is threatened with disgrace, for she has given herself to Leonhard and has tried to forget her real lover, the secretary. Since she could no longer endure the mischievous intimations of her friends that she had been abandoned by him, she follows the general custom of seeking a marriage of convenience. But Leonhard abandons her when her father, out of compassion for the misfortune of his old master and friend, gives away her dowry. The secretary cannot save her, in spite of his forgiving love, until he has saved his honor and killed Leonhard in a duel, for Leonhard, as the illegal lover, might mock him with Klara's betrayal. So strong is the traditional conception of honor in him, the freest of all characters in this drama, that he "makes himself dependent upon one who is worse than himself" (III, 11):

> Darüber kann kein Mann weg! Vor dem Kerl, dem man ins Gesicht spucken möchte, die Augen niederschlagen müssen? oder man müszte den Hund, der's weisz, aus der Welt wegschieszen.

Thus, the submission to a system of rules and prejudices and to the bonds of tradition drive the most valuable individuals to destruction, and we are left with the impression that a system in which the highest values are destroyed must be utterly senseless. In the discussion between the secretary and Meister Anton (III, 11), the guilt for Klara's death is clearly attributed to the dependence of everyone on possible gossip.

[120]

Human fate depends on an attitude lacking in any immediate sympathy and based on the standards prevalent among the masses. Recognition of this fact is almost identical with the demand to overcome such a nonsensical and destructive order, "to replace an externally founded morality by an inwardly founded one," or in the terminology of classical idealism, a heteronomous by an autonomous conscience; this change is, according to the Preface to *Maria Magdalene*, the "world-historical task" of Hebbel's time. Insofar as Klara's death leads to such insight, it arouses deep sympathy and intensifies the will to bring about the change; her tragic fate has gained a meaning in the metaphysical process.

The meaning is not to be found, as in Schiller's dramas, in the assertion of the moral personality; Klara's death is not, like Maria Stuart's death, a victory over her sensuality and an atonement for moral guilt; for Klara's yielding to Leonhard is considered as morally indifferent, not as immoral. Nor can the meaning of her death be found in the strength of Klara's character (as in *Judith* and in *Genoveva*). Her death gains meaning only through its significance for the advancement of the process of life. Without Klara's deviation from the rule and without her tragic death no progress in morality could have been achieved. Hebbel demands that the drama take part in conflicts and further their adjustment. We may discover in this play several levels of adjustment. The play is subjective and individual, for in it Hebbel seeks a new moral order, in which his companion Elise Lensing may live without disgrace as the mother of his child. It relates to his time because it moderately advocates women's emancipation. In this Hebbel goes no further than is compatible with the essentially passive nature of woman, the existing order of the sexes and the predominance of man. The play is universal because it raises to tragic importance the eternal conflict of the generations and the lack of understanding of the older for the younger generation. Finally, it is symbolic of the metaphysical striving of the author, who considers it the function of drama to "make clear the existing state of man and the world in relation to the idea." The state of the world in the bourgeois environment of this drama has reached a point of stagnation. It can only be overcome by the world spirit through the sacrifice of a valuable individual. Only in a new and higher order can such an individual lead that existence to which he is entitled on the basis of his moral value. This tragic world view is presented with much more lucidity than in the preceding dramas, but the effect is even more oppressive and

[121]

pessimistic. The reason is, first, that the sacrificed individual is still an entirely unconscious and passive instrument, and, second, that the emphasis in this drama is placed on the passing epoch and those views which are diseredited by their catastrophic effect; the coming epoch with its higher morality is merely indicated.

The Preface to *Maria Magdalene* shows that Hebbel now consciously adopts Hegel's metaphysical conception of a world-spirit manifesting itself in the dialectical evolution of history. Hebbel, however, does not adopt Hegel's esthetic theory without important modification. Hegel derives tragedy from the conflict of equivalent values, between which the tragic hero must choose; by his choice he necessarily violates the other value and disturbs the harmony of the moral world order. Harmony is reëstablished by the destruction of the transgressing individual. Hebbel follows the example of K. W. F. Solger in combining Hegel's idea of dialectic evolution with the tragic conception of equivalent values. Hegel's tragic conflict occurred between values existing simultaneously, with equal claim for consideration. Hebbel, however, places the conflict between values representing different stages of the evolutionary process, one representing a declining order, the other a newly arising order; thus the dialectic process itself becomes the foundation of his tragedy. To the general will, which was realized through traditional and conventional rules of conduct, he opposes the will of the individual, in which the more active and advanced values of a new epoch begin to take form. The individual representative of a coming order of higher values is destroyed in this struggle; but his very destruction furthers the decisive change to the new order. Hebbel's new principle, however, still awaits adequate dramatic presentation.

Before Hebbel attempts further to solve these metaphysical questions and apply his tragic theory, he gives in two minor plays clearer expression to the ideas he has developed so far. For the moral demand raised by the catastrophe in *Marie Magdalene* he finds a positive form in his tragedy *Julia*. This drama does not progress in the treatment of the problem; it merely shows Hebbel's personal interest in clearly presenting his stand on the social problem of illegal motherhood. The father who is attached to the old ideals, in his dependence upon the judgment of others, kills all human sympathy in himself, while Count Bertram wins a new meaning for his meaningless life by saving the threatened honor of his friend's daughter with his name. The situation, however, does not, as in *Maria Magdalene*, arise from environment and a problematic transition period with its conflicting tendencies; it is

[122]

rather badly motivated and lacks the convincing power of the earlier dramas.

In *Maria Magdalene* Hebbel showed the failure of human sympathy in the narrow environment of the petite bourgeoisie. Similarly, in *Ein Trauerspiel in Sizilien*, the ideal of justice as a living issue degenerates when an attempt is made to realize it in an imperfect world. Here it faces the danger of being suppressed by egotistic interests and made a tool in the hands of its official administrators. This disproportion is here dramatized in a series of paradoxical situations: a murder which is the result of cowardice and the boasting of a robust conscience; a lover who is accused of murdering his beloved; an innocent person who "confesses" the guilt of murder; a thief who assists in the administration of justice. Such confusion appeals more to a rational wit than to our esthetic sensibility. Horror and laughter alternate disharmoniously. The pessimistic view of a senseless and miserable humanity finds preliminary psychological relief in laughing at human weaknesses, before a more comprehensive interpretation of the world is attempted. These small paradoxes reflect the one great fundamental paradox of life, which has its origin in the dialectic progress of the evolutionary process of life, in the antagonistic rhythm of norm-fixation and norm-creation.

In *Judith*, paganism and Judaism, sensual possessive love and the right of personality were treated as antipodal principles; but a final judgment as to the value of the sacrifice made was not expressed. In *Genoveva* we missed the final and satisfactory explanation for the necessity of Genoveva's suffering. In *Maria Magdalene*, the theme was unmistakably treated as a problem of the transition to a new form of morality; by the continuation of the same theme in *Julia* this final aspect is even more strongly emphasized. But in all these dramas only the views of the passing epoch were fully represented; the expression of the new and higher moral order was obscured by the fact that the pioneers of the coming order were still rooted in the old order and became victims of the older and lower order predominating in environment and characters alike. Especially the chief victim of *Maria Magdalene*, Klara herself, lacked any insight into the significance of the tragedy which befell her.

In *Herodes und Mariamne*, these questions are brought to an extremely lucid and impressive dramatic solution. Furthermore, the theory of the tragedy inherent in periods of transition is here most consistently applied. The characters are contrasted in a forceful antithesis

[123]

as representatives of successive and antagonistic stages of historical evolution. The principles of antagonist epochs, moreover, are brought to the consciousness of the principal victim in their irreconcilability and in their proper evaluation. Through his consciousness the conflict becomes a fight of conviction and a comprehending sacrifice for an aim recognized to be of higher value; thus the tragedy of the sacrifice is essentially alleviated. The tragic pessimism of the earlier dramas gradually yields to a feeling for the sublimity of human will.

This change from a pessimistic to a heroic point of view is a reflection of the happier circumstances of Hebbel's life which began with his marriage to the Viennese actress, Christine Enghaus. The dramatic problem itself is based on the ambivalence of the feeling of love, conceived to be both affection and respect for the other personality on the one hand, and possessiveness, doubt, jealousy, and vexation on the other. This psychological aspect has its model in Hebbel's own experience; and it is part of the vital function of *Herodes und Mariamne* to overcome the inner discord. There is also a connection with the contemporary problem of emancipation and with Hebbel's philosophical ideas, and all this is integrated by projecting the whole into a historical situation of the past which provides both artistic remoteness and esthetic objectivation.

King Herod represents the final stage of a despotic order which sees in the individual only an instrument for the satisfaction of personal whims. Artaxerxes, whose life task is to feel his pulse in order to measure the time for his master, perfectly illustrates this system. Josef is the model of a cowardly subject, who, to please the tyrant, helps with an assassination and meekly accepts the order to murder his sister-in-law, Mariamne. Herod himself is proof of the idealistic principle that arbitrariness is only apparent freedom. He possesses energy, reason, resolution, and an extraordinary courage, which allows him to extricate himself victoriously from the most dangerous situations. He has, however, the fault of his virtues, the unavoidable accessory of an autocratic relation to one's fellow-men, namely, mistrust and doubt in the sincerity and devotion even of those who have the greatest affection for him. Since he sees every man but as a personal possession and demands mechanical obedience from him, he must fail whenever he meets individuals with an active consciousness of their own personal value, and at this point he encounters that causality which leads to the destruction of himself and his world. He passionately loves Mariamne, the Maccabean, but his despotism has impelled him to kill her brother

Aristobulos, when the boy allowed himself to be used by his ambitious mother Alexandra as an instrument of intrigue. As a consequence of his brutality, Herod can no longer believe in the unconditional devotion of Mariamne; more than ever she is only a precious piece of property for him, which he cannot cede to anyone else. When he is summoned to Antony to account for Aristobulos' death, he fears that she might marry Antony, who persecutes him only for the sake of Mariamne; therefore he demands from her the promise that she follow him to death. The more willing she is to die for Herod, the less able is she to give such a promise, presupposing, as it does, a lack of trust in her love. Herod, however, must, according to his nature, misinterpret her refusal as lack of love, and he therefore "places Mariamne under the sword," thereby violating her personality rights as well as those of his brother-in-law, Josef, whom he entrusts with the order of execution. Even this infamous despotic infringement upon Mariamnes' inner rights, does not shake her love for Herod; but she does long for an occasion when Herod can, through an absolutely trusting love, make restitution for humiliating her,

> ein Frevel, den man höchstens wiederholen, doch nun und nimmer überbieten kann (1646).

She must, therefore welcome the moment when he is called to fight against the Arabs; for this order "places his fate in his hands, and he can turn it as he wants to." He has to decide, however, upon more than his fate; upon him rests a world-historic responsibility, that of helping the idea of God in mankind to reach a higher moral level. Therefore God did "what he never did before, he turned the wheel of time backwards; it stands again where it stood before." Herod, however, does not recognize his mission, he represents a passing epoch and is incapable of taking part in the initiation of a new order. Mariamne's joy is for him only a sign that she hates him since his first order to kill her. He believes that "he has to fear now from her revenge what he may have unjustly feared from her inconstancy" (1952-54). He remains subject to the causality of his first distrust, since he lacks all understanding for the inner value of man. His first order could be excused because it was motivated by his love, whatever its imperfections may have been; but the second order is a conscious disrespect for the human personality in Mariamne as well as in the friend whom he appoints as her executioner. It is an extreme manifestation of the despotic principle, which no autonomous and self-respecting personality can accept. Mariamne

[125]

cannot exist in such a world; her life would pass in horror of complete destitution, because she would suspect in everyone who approached her a third executioner. If she forces Herod to murder her and if she takes care that he does not recognize his crime until after her death, this is to be explained not merely as vengeance for the brutal disillusionment of her passion, for it also reveals the meaning of her sacrifice. It shows the absurdity in the relation between arbitrariness and freedom, since arbitrariness is here seen as the cause of an extreme dependence. It further shows the absolute impossibility of tyrannically humiliating man; for that which is essentially human in man cannot be possessed as a thing; it must be gained by constant wooing for trust and confidence. To pave the way for this new idea, Mariamne sacrifices her life. The three magi symbolize the coming victory of the idea which Mariamne impersonates, and thus emphasize the meaningfulness of her sacrifice. Mariamne's tragedy is of the same type as that found in Hebbel's dramas from *Judith* on; but it has been completely clarified, especially with regard to the meaning of the sacrifice. It is her personal tragedy, that she represents a stage of morality for which her environment is not yet prepared. Metaphysically speaking, she disturbs the established order of the world-spirit, and is, therefore, guilty, and must perish from this guilt; simultaneously, however, her guilt is a necessity, since it alone makes a further development of the world-spirit possible. In *Herodes und Mariamne*, Hegel's dialectic process has found adequate dramatic visualization. Herod develops within the course of the drama to an extreme position which demands a turn to the extreme antithesis. This antithetic attitude is developed in Mariamne; it has its origin in the unbending will to power of the Maccabeans, which is impersonated in Alexandra; in Mariamne this will appears in the morally refined form of personal self-respect and respect for the personality of others; and finally, her ideal is established as a general principle of morality in Christianity.

In this drama even more than in *Maria Magdalene*, the poet sympathizes with the character representing the advanced stage in the evolution of the moral principle, while the representative of the passing world order is treated as an entirely negative character. For the development of the philosophical problem, this means that Hebbel does full justice only to the last stage of the evolutionary process and that he has not yet reached the point of view of Hegel, who sees truth and reason not only as one separate stage, but as part of the evolutionary process as a whole. This view is anticipated in minor dramatic sketches, before it

FRIEDRICH HEBBEL

reaches its final form in greater works. In the fairy play, *Der Rubin,*
inertia and striving are still antithetically opposed as evil and good,
as greed for power and altruism. The two-act fragment *Moloch,* however, reveals the integral view and the value of the past for the evolutionary process. If, after the destruction of his native city, the Carthaginian Hieram introduces his cruel god to the barbarian and godless
inhabitants of Thule, he does it only to stir up the savage people of the
north against the enemies of Carthage, the Romans. He tries to use
their longing for a higher culture, which is inherent in even the most
primitive tribes, as an instrument for his revenge. But the religion of
fear and brutality which he imposes upon them grows into a deeper
religion of supernatural faith and is accompanied by a considerable
advance in the cultural level. The world-spirit develops in these scenes
beyond the primitive stage; it manifests itself in the evolution of
morality. Every stage has its own morality and each stage, even the
barbarian, is necessary for transition; to that extent its existence is
valuable and meaningful. But at the same time, it is doomed to lose
its value and meaning because it has to be superseded by a higher stage
of development. In the more personal sketch, *Michel Angelo,* those
who envy the great artist are not only treated with indulgence, but are
given even a decisive contributory function in the creation of the work
of art. This valuation of the past stage and of the negative in its positive
function in the evolutionary process of life and the world as a whole,
paves the way for the solution of the metaphysical problem and thus for
dramatic presentation in the grand manner.

In *Genoveva* Hebbel had demonstrated the tragedy of perfection above
the average; it was Genoveva's virtue which became the cause of Golo's
crime. In *Agnes Bernauer* the simple fact that the heroine is of extraordinary beauty disturbs the normal flow of life and leads to destruction. Agnes' beauty disturbs the social order by exciting the jealousy
of her companions, who lose their admirers to Agnes; she endangers the
religious order, since these companions cannot repent and apologize
for their jealousy, as they ought for forgiveness of their sins. She finally
upsets the political order when she, a woman of the lower middle class,
wins the love of the hereditary prince Albrecht at a time when class
distinctions were supposed to dominate all human relations, when even
the commoners were divided into the patrician class and the guilds, and
the members of other guilds looked down upon the barbers' guild to
which Agnes' father belongs. She is placed in a period of transition
in which the worst injustices of class distinction have been but newly

[127]

overcome; complete individual freedom, which would allow beauty and goodness a right to the throne without any social discrimination, is the moral postulate which results from the tragic catastrophe of this drama. As a human being Duke Albrecht, too, has an absolute right to love and marry Agnes in spite of her humble origin; he must have the freedom of choosing his mate, if marriage is supposed to be based on love and faithfulness (II, 10). As an individual it is his right and as the representative of a higher moral idea it is his duty to help this idea to triumph over the norms which suppress the development of any deeper human relation in favor of class prejudice. Duke Ernst tries to grant him his right by excluding him from the succession to the throne and by substituting his sickly nephew in his place. But Albrecht is not only a private individual, but also a representative of the state. As a ruler he impersonates traditional morality as it has been consolidated in the state. His individual right and duty conflict with his responsibility toward his subjects. Duty to the state is represented most consistently by Ernst, who completely subordinates all his personal interests and feelings to the throne and who fulfills his obligations toward the state with utmost rigor. Toward Agnes and Albrecht he is as humane as the interest of the state allows and as legalistic as this interest demands. He delays the execution of Agnes as long as possible without risking a civil war or disintegration of the state, and he tries to give the condemnation a strictly legal foundation, so that it cannot be interpreted as an act of personal revenge. Since he is willing to protect the human rights of the individual in the beginning, so he recognizes at the end that the interest of the state could not be served without injustice to the principle of humanity; that is his intention when he acknowledges Albrecht as Agnes' widower and submits to his son's judgment. Albrecht, on the other hand, realizes that it is impossible simply to ignore the right of the state in favor of the right of the individual; he cannot neglect the right of tradition in favor of the obligation towards moral development. In this play, too, a superior value is sacrificed to the traditional order; this value is even destroyed, and the author makes no particular effort to attribute to such sacrifice a meaning in the historical evolution, so great is Hebbel's interest in doing justice to the conservatism of Ernst. Yet Ernst represents that very stage of evolution which Hebbel had considered as of negative value in all his dramas through *Herodes und Mariamne*. However, our sympathy in all five acts remains with the innocent victim, Agnes, and only with difficulty can we be won to see any justice in Ernst's application of the raison d'état. For the development of Hebbel's views *Agnes Bernauer* means that Hebbel himself sees the rational necessity of recognizing the passing order of values, but that his emotional sympathy remains on the side of moral progress.

The trend toward a more conservative interpretation of life can be attributed to the fact that Hebbel's marriage with Christine Enghaus had relieved him of his concern for Elise Lensing and the problem of emancipation, for which his relation to her had been responsible. It further reflects Hebbel's scepticism with regard to the revolution of 1848. In the historical projection of the contemporary problem, the development is therefore not brought about by any catastrophic event; on the contrary it is delayed and the advent of a new order is indicated only with reserve.

In *Gyges und sein Ring* Hebbel finally arrives at a complete understanding of the past, conservative stage of development and he succeeds in presenting it in a sympathetic form without subduing the evolutionary idea as much as he did in *Agnes Bernauer*. Even the selection of characters indicates the conservative view. Kandaules, the radical representative of progress, reveals, in spite of his more sympathetic traits, certain similarity with Holofernes and Herodes, who represented the passing epoch. Like them, he violates essential personality rights by his external relation to his fellow-men. By the insult to her womanly honor, Rhodope may be classed with Judith, Klara, and Mariamne, and by her self-contained harmonious nature also with Genoveva and Agnes, all of whom, consciously or unconsciously, were exponents of the moral development of mankind and of the evolution of the metaphysical Idea. But Rhodope is as sympathetic in her conservatism as the representatives of progress were in the earlier dramas. In spite of that, however, the idea of progress is not repudiated; for the hero continues in the line of characters like Golo to represent youthful sympathy and enthusiasm, the secretary in *Maria Magdalene,* and Soemus in *Herodes und Mariamne.*

As to the esthetic form, *Gyges und sein Ring* is Hebbel's most harmonious and classic drama. The action is limited to the essentials, and with its emphasis on the inner action, it easily conforms to the classical rules of unity of time and space. The symbolism of the ring and the veil allows the poet to discuss the most difficult situations in a delicate and chaste manner. The lucidity of form reflects here the clear and objective solution which Hebbel has finally found for his philosophical problem.

[129]

Rhodope's beauty is a symbol of the restful harmony and inner security provided by an old culture; but she pays for this harmony with her seclusion from all active contact with the world and with her submission to an extremely rigid moral system. She, too, desires to be like the others, to be allowed to enjoy the world as her servant Lesbia does. But the customs of her country forbid as an unpardonable sin that which is only natural to others.

> Dir sang's die Amme nimmer vor,
> Dasz Mannes Angesicht der Tod für dich! . . .
> Auch der Besten ist Opfer, was mir einz'ge Freude ist (454-57)

Within her own moral world, she acts with the freedom which is the criterion of a living order. The dictates she accepted in her childhood as heteronomous law, become, in her moral striving, autonomous norms:

> Sie suchte jeden [Wunsch], der sich regen wollte,
> Mit Scham und Angst bis unter das Bewusztsein
> Hinabzudrücken, denn sie warb allein
> Um eure [der Götter] Gunst und nicht um eure Gaben,
> Sie wollte danken, aber nichts erflehn! (916-20)

Despite the temptations of a dissenting environment and without any intolerance, she adheres to her traditional ideal of womanhood. That means she may not be seen by anyone but her husband. She demonstrates her inner freedom with regard to this form of morality, especially after Gyges has violated her womanly modesty to please his friend Kandaules:

> Hört' ich's doch
> In frühster Jugend schon, dasz die Befleckte
> Nicht leben darf, und wenn mich das als Kind
> Durchschauert hat, jetzt habe ich den Grund
> Für dies Gesetz in meiner Brust gefunden:
> Sie kann nicht leben, und sie will's auch nicht! (1269-73)

Her obedience to the traditional code of morals is the more rigorous, the more it is directed against herself. In order to fulfill the law, she even resorts to deceit and sophistry. She places Gyges before the alternative either of killing Kandaules in the duel and of marrying her, or of succumbing to Kandaules' sword and taking the responsibility for her suicide, but her real intention does not become clear until after the marriage ceremony, when she commits suicide, the very thing which Gyges sought to prevent by his tragic victory over Kandaules. One is reminded of a similar act of Mariamne, when she withholds the evidence of her innocence from Herodes until after the execution. This

[130]

sophistry points to a pathological trait in Hebbel's own character. The obvious dramatic intention of such strange conduct, however, is to emphasize the merely relative value of Rhodope's morality. If a moral system demands or even allows such legalistic sophistry, then it has lost its contact with life and has become empty formalism; it must be rejected and replaced by a moral system which does greater justice to the actual conditions of life.

The radically negative character of Rhodope's morality with its emphasis on renunciation of the world and suppression of nature, however, is not in itself a moral progress, although it may be necessary as a transitional stage in the establishment of a new moral order. This is the dramatic function of King Kandaules. With respect to culture, he is the merest novice; he is the champion of progress trying to take over the achievements of a higher culture without being inwardly prepared for its adoption. He suffers from the fact that a king is reverenced for his crown, and the crown for the rust it has gathered (50-52). He wants to be honored for his personal value and not for reasons of tradition, but does not consider that his rational conception of the royal dignity justifies his enemies' plan to replace him by a stronger and abler man. Rhodope, with all her dependence upon traditional customs, submits to a moral system which has become an inner principle for her; with all his will to be free, Kandaules remains dependent upon the situation and the opinion of his environment: therefore, he uses the concealing power of Gyges' ring to watch his enemies, an act which the tactful Rhodope abhors because it is a sign of cowardice and depravity. Kandaules' dependence upon situation and environment becomes fatal for him as well as for Rhodope and for his friend Gyges; because of it, he is unable to appreciate and enjoy his happiness alone:

Ich brauche einen Zeugen, dasz ich nicht
Ein eitler Tor bin, der sich selbst belügt,
Wenn er sich rühmt, das schönste Weib zu küssen. (531-33)

His apparent freedom is accompanied by a lack of tact and an intolerance which, in the last analysis, are but symptoms of an uncertainty regarding the new cultural values, a sign that these values have not yet become a natural part of his self. Because his esthetic judgment is still that of a barbarian, he needs Gyges' judgment of Rhodope's beauty; and he is capable of violating her modesty because, in spite of all his external progress, he has remained on the moral level which considers a woman as personal property and not as a self-determined personality.

[131]

It is part of Kandaules' tragedy that the violation of Rhodope's feminine rights is necessary to make him realize he was wrong in trying to free the world from tradition without being able to substitute a higher system of values for the rejected values.

> Drum prüf' er sich vorher,
> Ob er auch stark genug ist, sie zu binden,
> Wenn sie, halb wachgerüttelt, um sich schlägt,
> Und reich genug ist, ihr Höheres zu bieten,
> Wenn sie den Tand unwillig fahren läszt. (1816-20)

Gyges, however, is capable of solving this problem, and that is the deeper meaning in his surviving Rhodope and Kandaules. He must survive, according to the dramatic idea, since he most nearly deserves to be the champion of the evolutionary process. He represents, in the terminology of Hegel's historical dialectics, the synthesis of those factors of which Rhodope represents the thesis and Kandaules, the antithesis. In appearance also, he combines Rhodope's beauty with Kandaules' physical strength. Rhodope is, within the limits of her traditions, complete master of her inner self, whereas Kandaules, with all his antagonism toward the traditional values, is dependent upon his environment. Gyges, however, in this drama develops to a point where his inner freedom is capable of inspiring and lifting his environment to a higher cultural and moral level. His inner stability allows him to be as tactful and tolerant towards the old order as Rhodope is toward the new order, and thus he can be of greater service to the idea of progress than Kandaules with his precipitous, reformative will. This synthesis in Gyges' character is reached only through experience, and it is symbolized by the fact that his imperturbable friendship for Kandaules is complemented, and not superseded, by his love for Rhodope and that he, the friend and lover, has to assume the tragic guilt for the death of those whom he has cherished most. It signifies that development to a higher level of existence tragically entails the sacrifice of preceding levels; the realization of the higher value is possible only when the lower value is rejected. It is the tragedy of human development that the older stage of the evolutionary process is, after all, in spite of its own specific values, only a period of transition; that the champions of new ideas still are under the influence of the old order and participate only superficially in the new order, and, because of this conflict, are doomed to catastrophe; that the real representatives of the new order willingly or unwillingly are instruments for the destruction of old values. Even more than in *Agnes Bernauer*, Hebbel refuses in *Gyges und sein Ring* the radical and revolutionary attitude of Young Germany in the fields of politics and morals and attributes the higher moral value to conservative evolution.

According to a note in Hebbel's diaries (*Nr.* 5477), the principal object of the trilogy *Die Nibelungen* was to revive the interest in the medieval epic by a new dramatic interpretation, and when it was staged the author permitted the omission of the story of Siegfried's mythical birth for the sake of theatrical effect. This means that Hebbel had completed his world view in all its essential points with his previous drama, *Gyges und sein Ring*, and that he was no longer vitally interested in an absolutely clear presentation of his idea. But it also goes without saying that he interprets the Nibelungenlied, too, from his metaphysical point of view, and that only the evolutionary idea which he read into the story made it possible for him to complete his project. The theme of the trilogy is the antagonism between Teutonic paganism and Christianity, and the final victory of the latter. Behind this historical setting, one may still discern, although obscured by a vague generalization, Hebbel's main problem, the struggle for an autonomous moral order; but the personal concern with which the author presented his problem in the Preface to *Maria Magdalene* has given way to a merely formal treatment.

According to a passage in *Kriemhilds Rache* (II, 2) which was eliminated in the final redaction, the primitive energies of man,

> die ihn unmittelbar, als ganz allgemeine und interesselose mit dem Weltganzen zusammenknüpfen (*Tagebücher* Nr. 5933),

seek to unite and produce a superhuman type through the symbolical marriage of Brünhilde and Siegfried. This transcending of human measure is forestalled not only by the hatred of mediocrity for greatness, but also by the laws of nature which prohibit exceeding the merely human limit. Hagen's assassination of Siegfried is committed in the unconscious service of nature and the idea seeking its realization in mankind. The murder of Siegfried and the violation of Kriemhild's most personal rights not only prevent the exaggerated growth of primitive forces, they also unfetter the last energies of paganism, which, deprived of any meaning and direction, cause the ruin of the pagan world order and thereby necessitate a new order of higher human and moral values. Etzel, the last pagan, cedes his empire to the Christian king, Dietrich, because he sees that mankind is inevitably doomed to

[133]

self-destruction under the pagan obligations of faithfulness, allegiance, and blood-revenge:

> *Etzel:* Nun sollt' ich richten — rächen — neue Bäche
> Ins Blutmeer leiten — doch es widert mich,
> Ich kann's nicht mehr — mir wird die Last zu schwer —
> Herr Dietrich, nehmt mir meine Kronen ab
> Und schleppt die Welt auf Eurem Rücken weiter —
> *Dietrich:* Im Namen dessen, der am Kreuz erblich! (5451-56)

Gyges und sein Ring gives as complete and systematic a presentation of Hebbel's world view as possible within the form of the drama. He had found a meaning for man's existence in his contribution to the evolution of the world-spirit, and he had succeeded in finding a relative value not only for the champions of new ideas and values, but also for the representatives of the passing stage. But in spite of that, the final impression at the close of *Gyges* remained rather depressing. The fate of destruction lowered man, especially in the early dramas, too much to the level of an "instrument of God." Even characters such as Mariamne, Agnes Bernauer, Rhodope, Kandaules, and Hagen were still on the boundary line between superindividual fate and individual will; they were at least as much a sacrifice of inexorable necessity as they were free men capable of choosing the way of tragedy when confronted with a moral decision. *Demetrius* brings this transition from the tragic to the sublime. The hero of the drama chooses with freedom and consciousness the road to catastrophe in order to save the higher value of moral personality. Demetrius was born into a materialistic environment as a noble character. This materialistic world is fatal for him because he cannot degrade himself to such an extent as to become the tool of selfishness. As an illegitimate child of Tsar Ivan the Terrible he is compelled by the representatives of the Roman Catholic Church to accept the roll of legitimate pretender to the throne. The Jesuits try to use him in their attempt to be readmitted into Russia; the cardinal-legate intends to abolish the schism of the Russian Orthodox Church with his assistance and thus win the papal see for himself; the Polish voivode Mniczek follows him, because he wishes his daughter Marina to be the Tsaritsa; and the Russian Grand-dukes expect all kinds of favors and privileges for their allegiance. Demetrius, however, can only fight for his presumed royal rights, without yielding to any unjust concessions, and this only as long as he believes in the validity of his claim. When his claim is challenged, he feels obliged to surrender everything he has gained through the fraud of others. Only one thing could save him in this case, the voluntary recognition of his Tsaristic dignity on the basis of his royal qualities; his courage, the nobility of his character, and his incorruptible sense of justice. But just these qualities have no appeal for the champions of his rule; they want nothing but a tool for their egotistic aims, and since he cannot debase himself, he is lost. In an absolutely free decision he chooses a death in which his moral personality triumphs over fate.

One may interpret his fate pessimistically and see in it the resignation and despair of an idealist in view of the materialistic and egotistic tendencies of his period. But the drama allows also a more optimistic interpretation: Demetrius, to be sure, is doomed because his higher morality cannot be understood in a world ruled by barbarous selfishness, but he impersonates the regulative idea for a future development. This latter interpretation is more probable, since it is supported by the general trend of Hebbel's thought. Both views, however, are compatible, since even a pessimism concerning the tendencies of the time leaves room for the wish and the demand for a change to the higher aims. In that case, the *Demetrius* drama would be no advance over the stage reached in *Gyges und sein Ring*, except that Demetrius acts with extreme moral integrity and determination and yet with such a natural feeling for the ideal values that the tragic impression is superseded by admiration for the sublime. The fragmentary condition of the drama, however, allows no clear decision between these two interpretations.

Hebbel, too, grew up in the idealistic tradition; in his youth, he was an admirer of Schiller's poetry, and his first poetic attempts drew their inspiration from this classical model. Yet, as the son of a proletarian, he had to struggle too hard with reality, so that he soon began to conceive the world as ruled by destiny rather than shaped by the free will of man. In addition, he was disillusic 'd by his observation of the ungodly and materialistic trend of his ti..ie, so that he could no longer share the classical belief in the existence of a sphere of ideal values. This fatalism is especially expressed in the prose essays of his adolescent years and it still prevails in his first dramas, especially in *Judith*. The idealistic tradition, however, is so strong in him that, at the same time, he tries to reïnterpret the world on the basis of idealism Since he can no longer seek the meaning of life in a moral power above the imperfections of the world, he places the ideal and its realization in a distant future and conceives the world as the Idea in the process of realization. The evolutionary concept allows him to combine the im-

[135]

perfection of reality with the perfection of the ideal. This explains why his work impresses us as realistic: in its careful, and sometimes very complex, motivation (*Judith, Maria Magdalene*); in the modernity of its theme, the relation between sexes, even though Hebbel treats a modern problem in historical symbols; in the conception of man as strongly determined by tradition and environment. Man is always "a fragmentary existence which depends upon those present, but also upon the deceased."* But man depends also upon the "unborn" generations, since in them alone the meaning of the present is fulfilled and revealed. Man is for him a transitory moment in an evolutionary process, the meaning of which he seeks to discover through his dramatic work. From *Judith* on, the question is repeated over and over again, whether life and the sacrifice of life in the imperfect form in which we experience it, has a higher, transcendent meaning. In *Judith* Hebbel scarcely dares to give an affirmative answer to this question. In *Genoveva* he finds a representative and symbolical meaning for the existence of the valuable individual, but the question how goodness can become the cause of evil in a divine world order, remains unanswered. In *Maria Magdalene* Hebbel attributes to the destruction of the valuable individual a relative significance for the evolution of the world, for such an individual by his death under imperfect existing conditions reveals the need for a higher moral and social order under which he would not be doomed; his sacrifice thus becomes the impulse for a reorientation and a progressive evolution. Even more obvious is the function of the valuable individual in *Herodes und Mariamne;* Mariamne's moral self-respect helps to overthrow the old world order, in which individuals were treated as instruments without any respect for their personality. Mariamne unequivocally and clearly symbolizes the progressive tendency in the world-spirit, but a positive value is still one-sidedly attributed to the evolving higher order impersonated by her, whereas the passing order is considered as of negative value. With *Moloch* Hebbel turns to a more totalitarian interpretation, comparable to that expressed in Hegel's philosophy of history (cp. p. 18). To every stage of the evolutionary process, even on its most primitive and brutal level, is attributed a positive function in the process of life, and it becomes of negative value only when the evolution has reached a higher stage; thus evil is explained as the residue of a lower level of moral evolution. In its individualistic aspect, this problem is treated in *Agnes Bernauer.* Here Hebbel makes a special attempt to have the antagonist, i.e.,

*Tagebücher, Nr. 6335.

the representative of the declining order appear in a favorable and sympathetic light, and to explain his attitude as necessitated by the situation of the world at its actual stage of development and not as arbitrariness or passion or as the mechanized reaction of a declining period in the moral evolution of mankind. *Gyges und sein Ring* offers an absolutely clear and systematic presentation of the development in its various stages. The relative value and the inherent tragedy of each stage are demonstrated as far as possible in the symbolic language of drama. In *Demetrius*, finally, the self-sacrifice of the morally superior individual appears in its highest freedom and consciousness, and simultaneously the tragic impression seems to be mitigated by the sublimity with which the moral will of the idealistic individual faces death. It is the highest task of man in the universal order to maintain and defend the Idea which has come to consciousness in him against the degrading forces of his environment, even if he so risks destruction.

One fails to do justice to Hebbel's work if one overemphasizes his dependence upon Hegel's philosophical system. The similarity between the ideas of the philosopher and the dramatist can and must be partly explained as a similar reaction to the same situation, as an attempt to reconcile the idealistic heritage with the realistic tendencies of the time; only at a later stage of his personal development does Hebbel become acquainted with Hegel's ideas and adopt them on account of the affinity betwen the philosopher's way of reasoning and his own. The philosopher only helps to clarify the poet's personal problems and the world view which grew out of his own experience. The slow and consistent development of thought in Hebbel's work is in itself a proof that the poet does not merely translate the logical language of the philosopher into his own symbolical language, but that he rather fights a relatively independent battle to find a meaning for his life.

[137]

Chapter X

OTTO LUDWIG

(1813-65)

Otto Ludwig was born in Thuringia in 1813, the same year in which Hebbel and Wagner were born. He shares with Hebbel the desire for dramatic expression and theoretical reflection, and with Wagner the inclination to express his inner tension in musical form, but he lacks the dramatic instinct of the former and the musical ingenuity of the latter. Thus he remains an artist of promise, but few of his works ever reached the stage of artistic perfection.

There is no particularly strong contrast in the character of his parents which might have produced conflict within Ludwig's early character or habits. His father combined a lyrical tenderness with the appearance of roughness, firmness, and stubbornness. His external harshness, however, was in part acquired in his official position as a magistrate; this position also contributed to his early death when he was unjustly accused of stealing from a trust fund. Otto Ludwig's mother was a good-natured woman with an inclination for poetry and music. On account of his sickly disposition, the boy was spared any excessive disciplinary pressure and was left quite undisturbed in his artistic pursuits. Economic considerations forced him to work for several years in the store of his good-hearted, but very prosaic, uncle. Real tension, however, entered into Ludwig's life only when he left the petit bourgeois environment of Eisleben for the social and more cultured atmosphere of Leipzig and Dresden to which, in fact, he never could completely adjust himself.

The nature of his home environment—the organic and traditionally rooted life of the small Middle German town—remained the world of his desire even after he had settled in the city. City life was at first repulsive to him; it seemed to him to be superficial and estranged from the common roots of life and impressed him as unnatural and spoiled by French romanticist and liberalistic Young German ideas. This experience of the contrast between nature and civilization occupied his conscious and subconscious being to such an extent that it may be said to be responsible for his finally turning, at the age of thirty, from musical to dramatic expression.

From the literary point of view, this tension expresses itself in the conflict between the romantic heritage, on the one side, and Young German liberalism and realism, on the other. Nature, love, sympathy, laws organically evolved out of the experience of the past, genuine interest in one's work, harmony with the will of the community—these are the positive values and principles which Ludwig defends in his works. Contrasted with these as evils are superficiality, insensibility, utilitarianism, and opportunism in all human decisions; the rigorous legalism and lack of human consideration in the modern labor contract; and the lack of principles in politics. Where Kleist in his enthusiastic idealism demanded a radical regeneration on the basis of sympathetic reaction, Otto Ludwig, in accordance with his less problematic nature, develops a more moderate point of view. Not only in rationalism but also in exaggerated emotionalism does he see a negation of value and a source of guilt and suffering. He attributes to poetry the task of reëstablishing the original unity of man and nature and of preventing violation of the organic symbiosis, either in the direction of unnatural rationalism or of emotional exaggeration.

His ideal aim is similar to that of Grillparzer. In spite of all his opposition to the materialistic and rational tendencies of his time, he does not, however, regard contemporary development with the pessimistic melancholy of the Austrian dramatist. He is too remote, in his thinking, from idealistic philosophy to be either an optimist or a pessimist.

> Der Idealist ist ein Mensch, der im Jünglinge stecken geblieben ist. Die vollständige Unbekanntschaft mit der Wahrheit des Lebens läszt den Jüngling, was er je von den Dingen gehört, und wie er selbst sich dies ausgebildet hat, in jeden einzelnen Fall übertragen . . . Er hat noch kein Auge für die Gestalt der Dinge, er hat ein Bild vor Augen und sieht doch nur sein Phantasiebild. Er gesteht sich nicht ein, was er wirklich sieht und hört . . . Der Idealist liebt und achtet niemand, als sich selbst, d.h. als das Phantasiebild, das er sein Ich nennt. Denn die Dinge und Menschen, wie sie sind, sind ihm schlecht und gemein; sie sind nicht wert, geliebt zu werden von einem Wesen, so vollkommen, wie es sein eignes Ich sich eingeredet hat, das er aufbaut aus dem Konstraste seiner Einbildung mit der Wirklichkeit.

Ludwig wants to embrace the world in its entire reality, with its good and bad sides, with its virtues and its defects. In his work, therefore, he tends away from idealism and proceeds from the diversity of observed reality to the unity of the artistic form. His aim is not the visualization of the idea, but the integration of the observed heterogeneity in the idea. In laborious studies and sketches he tries to find the harmonious mean between idealism and naturalism.

[139]

Dem Naturalisten ist es mehr um die Mannigfaltigkeit zu tun, dem Idealisten mehr um die Einheit. Diese beiden Richtungen sind einseitig, der künstlerische Realismus vereinigt sie in einer künstlerischen Mitte . . .*

In his dramas he seeks to visualize a world which stands midway between objective truth inherent in *das Ding an sich* and the laws which our mind is compelled to apply to them,

> eine Welt, in der *die Mannigfaltigkeit nicht verschwindet,* aber durch Harmonie und Kontrast für unsern Geist in Einheit gebracht ist; nur von dem, was dem Falle gleichgültig ist, gereinigt . . . Der Hauptunterschied des künstlerischen Realismus vom künstlerischen Idealismus ist, dasz der Realist seiner wiedergeschaffenen Welt so viel von ihrer Breite und Mannigfaltigkeit läszt, als sich mit der geistigen Einheit vertragen will, wobei diese Einheit zwar vielleicht schwerer, aber dafür groszartiger ins Auge fällt.†

It is characteristic of Ludwig's dramatic work that it gains in literary significance the closer it approaches this "ideal-realistic" aim. His development is a gradual breaking away from the romantic tradition and the establishment of his own, moderate point of view. At the beginning he betrayed distinct traits of romantic emotionalism. In the farce-like comedy *Hanns Frei* the children oppose the marriage proposed by their elders; they refuse to be made the objects of calculation. But when their guardians accept the shrewd advice of captain Hanns Frei and forbid the children to see and meet each other, they are then seized by an irresistible love. It is in Hanns Frei's character that we notice the first sign of the function of reason as a mediator between calculation and passion.

A similar mediation is attempted by the Maltese knight in the tragedy *Die Rechte des Herzens.* He prevents the cold-hearted and calculating ruler from giving his daughter to a prince in order to restore his depleted finances. Actually the king would like to see her marry the Polish nobleman exiled from his country for participating in the revolution whom she therefore has adored in romantic admiration since she first saw him. But only when it is too late does the father find a formula which would allow him to consent to the wishes of the lovers and at the same time save his dignity; before he is ready to yield, they are united in death. This tragic irony of "too late" is a theme characteristic of the fate-drama; it is, however, not sufficiently motivated in this drama. Since our sympathy is with the romantic passion and the adventuring

---

*Otto Ludwig. *Nachlaszschriften* ed. Moritz Heydrich. Halle. Vol. 2, p. 197.
†*Ibid.*

spirit of the lovers, we are more touched by the "too early" of their fatal decisions, and the impression of the drama is thus not tragic, but romantically sentimental.

Sentimentalism is overcome to a certain extent in *Die Pfarrose*. Here the main antagonism between unnaturalness, calculation and intrigue, on the one hand, and naturalness and humanity, on the other, is continued. The haughty pastor's wife seeks to marry her daughter to Fritz von Falkenstein, the owner of a castle, but at the same time she does not want her to miss the opportunity of an economically desirable marriage with a commoner. The avaricious pharmacist who shrewdly assists her in these manipulations tries to force Rose into an undesired marriage by making her the object of town gossip. She is, however, too natural and too independent to let herself be forced by external circumstances. To this extent, at least, Ludwig accepts the contemporary idea of the emancipation of women. Rose remains inwardly unconstrained by any gossip:

> Sollen wir deshalb keine Menschen sein, weil die Leute die Leute sind!
> (I. 8)

Ludwig's dramatic conception, however, shows decisive progress in motivation. The fate of the lovers is further motivated by the exaggerated passion of one of the two lovers, although this exaggeration is still the effect of intrigue and misunderstanding. Falkenstein's excessive male pride blinds him to the reality of Rose's love; he sees her only in the light of intrigue and gossip. Rose, almost at the brink of insanity, despairs of the value of this world and of the justice of God, who makes no distinction between the good and the wicked, and in her utter disappointment she ends her life. Again the irony of the "too early" and the "too late" mars the tragic outcome; the catastrophe occurs just before Falkenstein regains his self-control and judgment.

In spite of their esthetic defects, the last two dramas reflect a certain disillusionment with idealism and the fundamental goodness of man, but this disillusionment never assumes the proportions of the absolute tragic despair which we found in other dramatists of the period. The pessimistic end is always somewhat mitigated by a devout "in spite of all this," as, for example, in the final words of the parson:

> Weh dem, der unter Verleumdung und gemeinem Neid dein [Gottes] Ebenbild tragen will frei und wahr. Auf andern Sternen vielleicht wohnt das Glück der Wahrheit. Dieser Erde König ist der Schein. — Und dennoch, wunderbarer Geist . . . bist du die Liebe. (V. 10)

[141]

In *Fräulein von Scuderi*, Ludwig's disillusionment with regard to idealism is even greater, but his disappointment is accompanied by a more convincing positive solution of the problem. The theme is taken from E. T. A. Hoffmann's story of the same title. In Ludwig's drama, however, the Chambre Ardente evokes the revolt of his own contemporaries against aristocratic privileges and permits Ludwig to champion complete equality of the commoner; the class struggle is here taken up in a manner which reminds one of the *Communist Manifesto* of the year 1848.

Characteristically, Hoffmann's vague romantic explanation of Cardillac's demoniac love for golden jewelry is not motivated by prenatal influence only, but, more realistically, by social hatred of a class of parasites who live from unjustly acquired property and menace womanly honor by their lack of a serious occupation. Furthermore, Cardillac expresses the author's relation to the traditional values of idealism. In this respect he resembles figures like Grabbe's Herzog von Gothland and Büchner's Danton rather than the disillusioned characters of Ludwig's earlier dramas. His disillusionment, like theirs, turns to cynicism and nihilism. Human existence is for him a senseless void:

> Die offne Wunde an dem stummen Nichts,
> Und wir die Maden drin, und eine macht
> Die andre Made fürchten mit Vergeltung,
> Dem nebligen Popanz; so macht das Nichts
> Im Nichts das Nichts mit künftgem Nichts zu fürchten. (III,3),

Freedom, virtue, faith, love, peace—all these are but illusions. Destruction is the fundamental principle of all life:

> Die Vernichtung ernährt uns, wir ernähren die Vernichtung (III, 3),

and only the creator of this madness is responsible for the evil in this world, since he planted the seed of evil in man.

Das Fräulein von Scuderi, however, unlike the other dramas, does not end on a final note of despair. Absolute hopelessness is the fate only of the one character Cardillac who yields to his passion. Through him Ludwig tries to overcome his romantic idealism, for this is the type that is liable to absolute disillusionment.

> Ehe er [der Idealist] sich zwingen liesze, den Menschen, d.h. sich selbst überhaupt als eine Mittelgattung zu denken, macht er aus dem Engel, aus dem Menschen auszer ihm, den er trotz Mühens nicht zum unbedingten Engel machen kann, einen unbedingten Teufel. Allmählich musz er einen Engel

[142]

um den andern in seiner Phantasie — denn anders existiert er und existieren
die Dinge und Menschen ihm nicht — zu den absoluten Teufeln werfen.*

The other more realistic and balanced characters, like Fräulein von
Scuderi, Olivier, and Madelon, are also driven to the point of despair.
They are obliged to defend their sympathetic humaneness against
those institutions and ordinary persons which are emotionally para-
lyzed by the objective mechanism of traditional habits and customs.
Fräulein von Scuderi is hindered in her attempt to save the innocent
Olivier by the petty objection of her physician, Serons, that her life
would be endangered by the excitement of such a venture.

> Wenn man das Recht will mit rechtem Ernst
> Und nicht blosz auf eigne Ruhe denkt,
> Dann fühlen uns die Leute an den Puls. (IV, 2)

With these words she rejects the prudent advice of the physician and
risks the remaining energy of her old age in a courageous fight against
the hard-heartedness which would rather condemn the innocent than
take the trouble of furthering the good and of helping truth to victory.
Her fight leads to complete success: the Chambre Ardente is abolished by
royal decree, and the two lovers are united.

In *Fräulein von Scuderi* Ludwig has come to a positive philosophical
point of view. Although he closely follows E. T. A. Hoffmann's *Novelle*,
his literary expression is much more concrete and psychologically
much better motivated, in comparison with the typical and abstract
technique of his earlier plays. All of these plays, however, drew more
or less exclusively on the limited individual experience of the author.
Though they reflect the general intellectual situation of the period—
the decline of idealistic belief—they are, with the exception of the
motivation of Cardillac's character, somewhat detached from the specific
problems of the time. In *Der Erbförster* the problematic foundation
is consciously broadened, for here the individual problem is brought
into closer connection with the general problem of transition from an
organic patriarchal order to the mechanized organization of the later
nineteeth century. *Der Erbförster* is, in one sense, a character tragedy
of the same type as *Die Rechte des Herzens, Die Pfarrose,* and *Fräulein
von Scuderi;* for it is based on the conflict between exaggerated passion
and cold speculation, with the intention of establishing harmony between
natural and rational humanity.

*Otto Ludwigs gesammelte Schriften hsg. von Adolf Stern. 1891. Bd. VI, p. 11.

The most lifeless form of rationalism is represented by Möller, manager of the firm Stein and Son, which title Möller always uses in his endeavor to be impersonal. For him, nothing but the firm exists, and every human relationship has to be subordinated to business considerations. He is thus an uncompromising opponent of Robert's love-marriage, because it does not promise any economic advantage, and in order to prevent the marriage, he seeks to involve his employer, Stein, in a conflict with Erbförster Ulrich and so prevent any attempt at reconciliation. In business matters, the amiable Mr. Stein reflects the opinions of his manager; in fact, the less the ideas and principles for which he is fighting are his own, the more passionately does he defend them. In this respect he is a typical character of the transition period and is thus apt to substitute an unyielding attitude for his lack of conviction. The Erbförster, on the other hand, is at bottom a character of like good nature and gentleness; he is harsh and severe merely in order to save his authority, which he faithfully exercises as a duty imposed upon him by tradition. In contrast to Stein, he entertains firmly rooted convictions which are inborn in him and which he considers holy, and these convictions he therefore defends to the last stand. The violence of his character cannot be interpreted, as in Ludwig's earlier dramas, as a more or less occasional flash of temper required by the structure of the drama. It results more properly from his defense of a world view which is threatened by newer ideas. The Erbförster's stubbornness and fanaticism are the expression of despair in a man who sees the foundations of his mental being shattered, and who, through his despair, blindly contributes to his own physical destruction. His deepest tragedy is that he destroys his own organic principle of life in the attempt to save it.

The Erbförster is a romanticist defending a lost cause. The "uniformity of justice" which he defends is based on the organic and subjective conception of property and labor, whereas the "double standard" which he condemns and opposes in his friend Stein is the newer, mechanistic, rational, and objective form of justice. According to the older law, labor is a human accomplishment which in the last analysis cannot be bought with money, for the older form of labor was an expression of the personality, rather than a mechanical product. The Erbförster's profession is inherited from his father and his grandfather. It is therefore associated with deep-rooted emotional values, and entails the obligation toward his heritage to hold himself in readiness for the supreme sacrifice if necessary:

[144]

Ich hab' von Vater und Groszvater eine Ehre ererbt und bin sie meinen
Kindern und Kindeskindern schuldig; mein Vater hat vor mir die Stelle
gehabt und mein Groszvater vor meinem Vater; sie heiszen mich den Erbförster im ganzen Tal; ich wär der erste aus meinem Stamm, der abgesetzt
wäre . . . Herr, wenn Sie ohne Ihre Ehre leben können, so ist's gut für Sie —
oder vielmehr, so ist's schlecht von Ihnen. Aber sehen Sie, Herr Pastor, für
mich gibt's nur eine Wahl, entweder neben meinem Vater und Groszvater
unter die Tannen oder hinter die Kirchhofsmauer. (II, 8)

The product of labor itself participates in this emotional value.
Through the live interest which generations of men have taken in the
forest, it has become a kind of a living being itself and wants to be
treated as such. Stein and the group which he represents try to replace
the subjective and romantic conception of justice and labor with the
objective and rational conception of law and contracts. Part of the
subjective and organic justice is preserved in the civil service regulations, especially in the right of permanent tenure. Civil law, however,
knows only employment for a given term on the basis of the labor contract; the laborer sells the employer part of his time and energy for
a definite wage. He is therefore no longer interested in his work as such,
but the financial return for his labor; he mechanically obeys the orders
of his employer because he is without any responsibility. For this
reason, the Buchjäger can clear the forest and abandon it to the danger
of destruction, since his only interest in the object of his labor is superficial and materialistic.

The real bone of contention between the Erbförster and the factory
owner, Stein, is not the question of whether the forest should be cleared
or not cleared. This is but the realistic basis for the discussion of the
principles involved. The question really involves not only the author's
individual opposition to urban civilization, but also the entire conflict
of the Industrial Revolution in the middle of the nineteenth century.
Der Erbförster deals in a relatively concrete and realistic manner with
the same problem which Grillparzer discussed with greater reserve
and abstractness in the last act of *Libussa,* namely, the external and
inner danger of the man of the time who felt rooted in and protected by
an organically developed group, and who is shaken in his whole being
by rationalization and mechanization, by urbanization and the so-called
progress of civilization. Here is expressed the suffering of a man with
moral principles who sees that his values are being distorted and dis-
placed by lower values. Emotional attachment to the home and the
family, loyalty, and mutual trust—typical values of the organic com-

munity—give way to rational values such as cleverness, adaptability, and business efficiency. This change of attitude even invades the regulation of family affairs, so that marriage is degraded to a formal contract. Man loses his dignity as a personality and becomes the object of calculation—a replaceable part of a mechanism.

This interpretation of *Der Erbförster* helps to explain its much criticized form. The drama begins in a truly realistic manner: two obstinate characters are brought into conflict and their best intentions frustrated because each insists on maintaining his ground until it is too late for a reconciliation. This situation is not only characteristic of Ludwig, but also of the indecision of the conservative elements in a period of transition (as, for example, of Grillparzer). In a consistently realistic tragedy one would expect the fathers to persist in their opposite views and thus destroy their own happiness as well as that of their children. Such a development of the plot would also have fulfilled Ludwig's own esthetic demand that the atonement be essentially and causally connected with the guilt. Ludwig, however, in this instance turns away from realism to the technique of the fate-drama after the model of Werner, Müllner and of Grillparzer's *Die Ahnfrau.* He introduces all kinds of incidents to bring about the desired "too late" effect: the theft of a double-barrel gun with a yellow leather strap; the double confusion produced by the report to Stein that it was Robert who was killed and to the Erbförster that it was Andres; the Erbförster's hasty shooting by which he kills his own daughter, who protects her lover with her body. The gruesome romantic atmosphere of the last act tends in the same direction: the hunter's home in the forest with raging thunderstorms; the *heimliche Grund* which has been the scene of murders heretofore and which seems to demand more victims; premonitions and dreams; the false interpretation of a dream; and the mysterious behavior and disappearance of the forester.

This bowing to the supernatural can be explained, and to a certain extent, justified, only by the fact that Ludwig is, in spite of all his realism, strongly rooted in romanticism. The fatalistic end of the drama expresses the dejection of the man of this period who feels that the modern trend toward a technical civilization deprives him of his physical and spiritual stability and threatens the very roots of his whole organic existence.

Robert and Marie are characters who vacillate between the desire for organic existence and the tendency toward realism. In their conduct they realize the ideal of harmonious humanity which we observed in

Fräulein von Scuderi. However, even though they point the way to the harmony in which Ludwig seeks to solve the problem of his time, yet their tragic fate allows no more than the melancholy wish that the natural and organic form of life might be saved; it is no convincing argument for such a possibility. The character of the Erbförster himself serves to corroborate this impression, since the organic form of life has reached in him a stagnation point comparable to that of Meister Anton in Hebbel's *Maria Magdalene*. With all his sympathy he is an authoritarian and an absolutist, for whom the abstract principle means not only more than his own life, but also more than the happiness of his family; his inner feelings he hides behind a stern discipline and an obstinate self-righteousness, most obvious in his exclusive and insistent references to the most rigorous and least sympathetic moral prescriptions of the Old Testament.

The desire to preserve and revive the natural and organic community of man also permeates the tragedy *Die Makkabäer*. Schiller had dramatized in *Wilhelm Tell* the effect of the ideal on the several estates and groups of the people; he had shown the spirit of liberty to be a natural disposition of man, always ready to be awakened and guided to a higher end by intelligent leadership. Hebbel did not share this moral optimism; the moral idea is for him not a latent potentiality in man, but something which evolves in the course of human relations, which, first realized in great personalities, only gradually forces itself upon the masses as a necessary development. Ludwig lacks Schiller's absolute, idealistic confidence in the possibility of winning an entire people to fight for the ideal good, nor does he believe, with Hebbel, in the higher development of the idea in mankind. He wants to comprehend the people in all their diversity of character and motives, in all their positive and negative energies, and he leads them, despite all hindrances, to a goal which represents his harmonious ideal of human existence.

In Ludwig's previous dramas the characters could be classified into three categories: the opportunistic materialists, the idealists, and the modest and tractable realist-idealists, who are neither calculating in their relations to others nor ready to fight for an abstract principle, but who merely do their duty as human beings. We find a similar division of the Jews in this drama.

The Simeonites are opportunists without any religious or national convictions; they try to buy the favor and the clemency of the enemy by participating in their idolatrous ceremonies, but at the same time they expect to be considered as the saviours of their people. They are traitors who deliver up their own compatriots to the brutality of the heathen. To this group belongs Eleazar, the favorite son of the Maccabean, Lea, who falls prey to the flatteries of the enemy and deserts his faith; he remains, however, enough of a Maccabean to be shamed by the martyrdom of his brothers and to return to his people and to his God.

Contrasted with these opportunists are the idealists, who passionately fight and suffer for their ideals but who, according to Ludwig's moderate views, cannot achieve their aims. One of them is Lea, the mother, whose ideal aim is clouded in the beginning by her motherly pride and predilection for Eleazar. By arousing in this unworthy weakling the ambition to become king of Isreal and by sanctioning his relations with Antiochus, the general of the enemy, she unwittingly helps to defeat Judah and delay the triumph of the Jews and becomes an accomplice in the martyrdom of her own sons. Only as a witness of their tragic heroism does she find the humility and the modest humanity which here, as elsewhere, is Ludwig's ideal.

In the same way we have to interpret Judah's fate. It is not his passionate fight for national freedom which triumphs in the end. Although victorious in some twenty battles, he sees all his efforts frustrated by the rigorous legalism of Jojakim's adherents, who refuse to desecrate their Sabbath by pursuing the vanquished enemy. According to Ludwig's opinion, he must fail because his passionate will lifts him above the concrete basis for his action, the mass of his people; he must fail because he does not sufficiently heed the fact that the strongest individual is no stronger than the people he represents. "Herr, sende deinem Retter ein Volk" is his prayer, when he finally recognizes this fact. Therefore it is not he who finally triumphs in the fight against the Syrian oppressors, but the passive heroism of his brothers. The sight of their martyrdom demoralizes Antioch's army, a circumstance which is not very convincing from the point of view of psychological motivation, but which is, for this very reason, the more characteristic of Ludwig's conception of a moral world order. The ideal of moderation also explains the apparent double climax in the second and in the fifth acts. Judah's victory in the second act is not a victory in accordance with Ludwig's ideal, for it is only a momentary and personal triumph and not a lasting triumph of the entire people. A victory in the deeper sense of the word is won only when the entire attributes and energies of the people converge in one victorious leader, when the enemy recognizes this victory and of its own will renounces a repetition of the attack. It is the waning influence of his romantic conception of a people which causes Ludwig to represent the final victory as expressing the integrated will of the people: witness Judah and Lea who keep the national consciousness alive with their heroism; the pious and the just who command the respect of the opponent, by their unyielding and self-sacrificing obedience to the law; and Eleazar who joins his brothers in martyrdom and thereby discourages the Syrian army. Even the apostate Eleazar and the treacherous Simeonites, by their very treason, contribute to the victory, for it is the death of the extradited Maccabeans which brings about the final decision. The earlier plans for this drama placed considerable emphasis on Lea's hatred toward Judah's wife, the Simeonite Naemi, and their reconciliation; this is in accordance with the technique of Ludwig's minor dramas. This motif of hatred, though somewhat inorganically carried over from the earlier versions into the final one, is, nevertheless, in keeping with the main principle of Ludwig's writings, namely, to integrate the multiple quality of reality in the unity of the idea.

In *Die Makkabäer*, as in *Der Erbförster*, as far as his dramatic talents allow, Ludwig finally synthesizes his personal system of the values in human relations and his views concerning the conflicts of his time. In *Der Erbförster* he stressed more the general, social problems, whereas *Die Makkabäer* treats rather the two great internal political problems of Germany at the time of the Revolution, the unification of Germany and the'drawing up of the constitution. Ludwig's longing for a united Germany finds expression in the final organic coördination of all the energies of the Jews, and his hopes with respect to the constitution in Judah's voluntary renunciation of all hope of reigning and in his desire to *serve* his people and his God as a priest. Ludwig condemns any violent revolution, which he believes favors only the rule of the lower elements, but he hopes that the revolutionary demands will gradually be fulfilled. This point of view explains the fact that the final solution of the drama can be considered as a true expression of his artistic intention, although it is improbable in its psychological motivation.

In these last two dramas Ludwig solved the problems of his world view as far as possible in dramatic form. Those aspects still awaiting solution are treated in novelistic form, particularly in the story *Zwischen Himmel und Erde*, in which his personal tragedy finds perhaps its most perfect expression. It is the tragedy of an artist who suffers from an exaggerated obligation towards realistic detail and from his waning belief in the one great idea which had served to integrate the confusing mass of detail in an all-embracing, metaphysical unit. At the same time, this story is the most positive formulation of his belief in the moral signifi-

[149]

cance of the small, restricted circle of life, with its firmly established customs and traditions, in which the inner life finds calm and satisfaction through meaningful and well-regulated activity.

The personal tragedy is also apparent in Ludwig's last dramatic fragments, especially in *Der Engel von Augsburg* and its later version, *Agnes Bernauerin*. Ludwig fails in this attempt to give a more realistic interpretation to Hebbel's theme; the details degenerate into intrigues and episodes without being psychologically convincing. It is significant that this fragment does not reach beyond the point at which Ludwig's personal problem is essentially solved. Albrecht would like to abdicate from his throne and to seek his satisfaction in a less public life more in harmony with human nature; Agnes has conquered her vanity and ambition, and she too is ready to continue her life in the happiness of retirement. In its motivation the later version follows more closely that of Hebbel's drama than the earlier one and gives Agnes a nobler character from the very first scene on. Ludwig did not, however, finish more than one act; he rejected Hebbel's idea of a metaphysical guilt as guiltlessness, but he was not yet enough of a realist to derive a guiltless tragedy from merely realistic premises.

In his world view as well as in his artistic problems, Otto Ludwig belongs to the period of transition from romanticism to realism. His conceptions of life and life forms are essentially organic, and he sees in the decline of these ideas the principal danger for his time. Life is for him, above all, life with others, rootedness within a small circle. If he rejects the idealistic views in spite of his obligation to romanticism, it is because his conception of idealism is too abstract and because he fails to understand its possible application to life. His own work detaches itself only very slowly, and never completely, from its idealistic foundations. He begins with the romantic emphasis on the emotional values as contrasted with the rational calculation and superficiality which he considers to be the tendency of the time in general and of the literary movement of Young Germany in particular. At the same time, we notice a growing disillusionment on his part, for it is evident that he projects his own personal state of mind into the characters of his dramas. His disillusionment is manifested in the melancholy mood of the Polish nobleman, Paul Lubinski *(Die Rechte des Herzens)*, in the deadly despair of Rose *(Die Pfarrose)*, in the cynical denial of all ideal values in Cardillac *(Fräulein von Scuderi)* and it is encountered, finally, in the Erbförster's struggle for the right meaning of the words of the Gospel.

[150]

Simultaneously, Ludwig develops his positive belief in reasonableness, stability, and moderation. Hanns Frei's advice already points in this direction, and so does the attempted mediation of the Maltese knight *(Die Rechte des Herzens)*. This moderation gains greater significance in the characters of Fräulein von Scuderi, Olivier, and Madelon *(Fräulein von Scuderi)*, and of Robert and Marie *(Der Erbförster)*. In all of these dramas, however, the final effect is either implicitly or explicitly the demand for moderation and for a secure life in an organic community. This demand is rooted in an idealistic belief, but in the later, more temperate form of the Biedermeier period. It seeks its foundation not in an abstract principle, but in a concrete community. In his world-view, as well as in the products of Ludwig's artistic creation, unity is therefore conceived of not as the primary metaphysical fact, but as the result of multiple component elements. Ludwig is a "real-idealist," the greater part of whose work remained but a fragmentary attempt, for the decline of his confidence in the idealistic principles is compensated only in part by his ability to observe and to give artistic expression to the richness of reality.

CHAPTER XI

RICHARD WAGNER
(1813-1883)

OPINIONS concerning the literary value of Wagner's dramatic work
have to this day continued to differ as widely as did the judgments on
the worth of his music during the first decades after its composition.
The musical part of his music dramas, however, has finally received
universal recognition, but the value of the literary part is still a matter
of controversy. There is no doubt but that from the esthetic point of
view these dramas are definitely inferior to the products of any other
dramatic writer whose works are discussed in this book. Wagner's works
lack the perfection of form, the precision of expression, and the clarity
of structure which one may justly expect from a great dramatist. His
style vacillates between childish onomatopœia and gaudy rhetorical
phrases, between rational conciseness and lyrical vagueness. Yet, in
spite of all these esthetic deficiencies, his dramatic products deserve a
place in the history of German literature, for the reason that they are a
genuine artistic expression of the author's struggle with the problems
inherent in his personality and in his period, and even their deficiencies
are, at least in part, a result of his problematic situation. His struggle
has significance for our special study because its artistic expression as a
whole shows an organic progress towards a solution of the author's
problems, and thereby raises his writings from the class of ordinary
libretto to the rank of poetry. Since these dramas must be considered
as an integral musical-poetic unit, a merely literary analysis cannot
expect to do real justice to the author, for only in the combination of
word and tone are the dramatic characters endowed with emotional
life; only in the musical context do they reveal their foundation in the
romantic world of the cosmic oneness of all life, while, separated from
this context, they appear to have grown out of the materialistic tendencies
of the later nineteenth century.

Wagner's parents were not of distinctly contrasting types; both his
father and his mother alike were torn between desire for the intellectual
life and submission to the sobriety of the bourgeois middle class. His
father, who died in Wagner's early youth, had an esthetic interest in
the theater, but the indulgence of this interest was partly thwarted by

the prosaic duties of his position as a police official in the Leipzig city court. His mother's intellectual curiosity was restrained by her confinement within the circle of a large bourgeois household.

As a student Wagner only occasionally concentrated on his studies; on the other hand, he took a very active part in the sensual distractions of the emancipated youth within the Young-German movement. Yielding to his emotional impulse, he entered into an early marriage with Minna Planer, but he divorced her after several love affairs had disturbed their marital relation. He then experienced a deeper, more spiritual affection for Mathilde Wesendonck. This last relationship was finally superseded, however, by his devotion to Cosima Liszt, who became his second wife.

As an orchestra conductor, Wagner was engaged in continuous disputes with his theater managers by reason of his refusal to accept any compromise designed to satisfy the traditional and sensational tastes of the theatergoers. More than once the cost of publication of his works got him into such financial difficulties that he had to flee in order to escape his creditors. All these experiences served to increase his resentment toward the contemporary theater. Not until King Ludwig II of Bavaria had provided him with the means to realize his plans for a theater in Bayreuth, did he consider his fight for the sacred dignity of his theatrical art as ended.

On the whole, Wagner vacillates between voluptuousness and suffering, between surrender to his lower instincts and yearning for purity and inner peace, between a will for power and a desire for loving understanding, between luxuriousness and a simplicity which is able to sacrifice even the most primitive comforts of life. Mentally he is torn between optimistic enthusiasm and desperate depression. This extreme tension is the personal foundation of his art.

The character of his time helped to intensify his inner conflict, for it made him conscious of it and probably induced him to give his experience an artistic outlet. Wagner inherited from Late-Romanticism his belief in the idealistic order of the world and in the higher dignity and destiny of man. This belief provides the direction and the goal for his life and his works. It makes him an advocate of the ideas which led to the revolution of the year 1848, and after the political disappointment of that year it urged him to hope with increasing seriousness for the inner regeneration of mankind. On the other hand, he suffers like Grillparzer, Grabbe, Büchner, and Otto Ludwig from the superficiality, the materialism, and the disintegration of German culture which accom-

[153]

panied technical progress. He too, apprehended in the civilization of the nineteenth century a growing egotism and immorality, a brutality and bloodthirstiness. In the light of these developments, man seemed to him to be degenerating into a beast of prey *(Religion und Kunst)*. According to his opinion, man will soon realize that the machine cannot achieve anything, for the mastery of nature precludes a sympathetic relation to nature. Technical civilization is too petty; it is concerned only with the production of instruments, and it sacrifices man for this secondary purpose *(ibid.)*. In the rise of militarism during the second half of the nineteenth century he sees evidence that "God created the world in order that the devil may take it."

Wagner blames the materialistic trend of his time for the apathy with which his art is received. Yet, to see in his attitude mainly the reaction of a romantic idealist to the realistic trend of his time would be a misconception, for his character reflects too strongly the transition which his environment was undergoing from the idealistic to the realistic and materialistic point of view. Moreover, the peculiar form of his production — the combination of drama and music in the *Worttonkunstwerk* — however romantic the idea itself may be, is per se characteristic of this period of transition. The romanticists tried to dissolve the concreteness of conceptual art into a purely musical flow. By reason of its remoteness from concrete reality, Wagner, however, sees in the abstract idealistic music of the eighteenth century, and even more in the lyrical music of the romanticists, a degeneration of music. The spoken drama, on the other hand, he believes to be too superficial and too rational; lacks the unifying force of the emotional element and takes into account only the multiformity of a rationally perceived world. The ideal perfection of art, he claims, can be achieved only as *Worttonkunstwerk*, in which the music supplies the subconscious emotional setting for the consciously perceived word, a theory based on the romantic idea that emotion is an integral part of the universal will, from which rational consciousness detaches itself in the process of individuation. With this attempt to establish an integration of ideality and reality, of an emotionally unified "tone-world" and an individuated "light-world," Wagner participates in the general trend toward realism and naturalism. The orchestral accompaniment of the dramatic action supports and strengthens the psychological motivation and the individualization of character. What is lost in the verbal interpretation of the characters is more than restored by the subtleties of the instrumentation. Thus he paves the way for the refined characterization of Schnitzler's and Hofmannsthal's dramatic impressionism. In the same way, the use of the leitmotif increases the illusion of time by reënforcing and relating the impressions of preceding passages and by anticipating later stages of the dramatic action. In its motivating function, the music loses its melodious abstractness in favor of the dynamic and dramatic power which derives from the concrete stage event — from the endeavor to create the illusion of an esthetic reality.

Wagner's world view, as it is expressed in his dramatic and in his theoretical works, is closely related to that contained in Schopenhauer's philosophy and in Grillparzer's dramas. Its fundamental value is life; mere existence without the inherent ethical tendency which characterized Fichte's and Kleist's idea of the active ego. Life is, above all, nature conceived as a generative and formative energy:

> Alles Bestehende hängt von den Bedingungen ab, durch die es besteht: nichts, weder in der Natur noch im Leben, steht vereinzelt da; alles hat seine Begründung in einem unendlichen Zusammenhange mit allem. Jene treibende Kraft, die eigentliche Lebenskraft schlechthin, wie sie sich im Lebensbedürfnisse geltend macht, ist aber ihrer Natur nach eine unbewuszte, unwillkürliche, und eben wo sie dies ist — im Volke — ist sie auch die einzig wahre, entscheidende.*

Like Schelling's "Unconscious" and Schopenhauer's "Will," Wagner's vital energy is the primary function of life in all things, including human nature, while consciousness is only secondary. The idealistic order, according to which consciousness is the primary function, is, in Wagner's opinion, responsible for the failure of the revolutionary movement of 1848. Referring to this event, he continues in the passage just quoted:

> Im groszen Irrtume sind daher unsere Volksbelehrer, wenn sie wähnen, das Volk müsse erst wissen, was es wolle, d.h. in unserm Sinne wollen solle, ehe es auch fähig und berechtigt wäre, überhaupt zu wollen. Aus diesem Irrtume rühren alle unseligen Halbheiten, alles Unvermögen, alle schmachvolle Schwäche der letzten Weltbewegungen her.

Deprived of its ethical character, this vitalistic view leads him to accept the main idea of Schopenhauer's philosophy, which is substantiated by his own experience. Life is an impulse void of direction and aim, always striving from wish to wish, from fulfillment to fulfillment, never reaching the point of satisfaction, and therefore essentially dissatisfied. The psychological effect of this dissatisfaction is a desire to forget one's Self and to be redeemed from the restlessness of the will-to-live. This desire

*Das Kunstwerk der Zukunft. I, 4.

is strengthened by the experience that our unrestrained will is always inclined to violate the rights of others. The metaphysical oneness of all life, however, makes us partners in the suffering which our actions have caused in our fellow-sufferers; and our compassion corroborates the condemnation of life as a self-destructive impulse. In spite of the fact that it is founded upon disillusionment, Wagner's valuation of life is more positive and more optimistic than that of his master, Schopenhauer.

Wagner, unlike his contemporaries, condemns rather than praises the technical achievements of civilization, nor can he see anything but degeneration in mechanical progress. Just as Schelling attributes to his concept of the metaphysical Unconscious the ability in man to arrive at consciousness, so Wagner attributes this ability to Schopenhauer's will-to-live. Man, in turn, having gained this consciousness, is then able to repair the damage which the universal will has done in its blindness. The materialistic and egotistic degeneration of his age is a "school of suffering through which man must pass in order to be cured of his blindness, i. e., in order to feel compassion for the suffering of his fellow-men and to achieve their and his own salvation."

> Die Geschichte dieses Abfalles, wie wir sie in weitesten Umrissen uns vorführten, dürfte, wenn wir sie als die Schule des Leidens des Menschengeschlechtes betrachten, die durch sie gewonnene Lehre darin erkennen lassen, dasz wir einen aus dem blinden Walten des weltgestaltenden Willens herrührenden, der Erreichung seines unbewuszt angestrebten Zieles verderblichen Schaden mit Bewusztsein wieder zu verbessern, gleichsam das vom Sturme umgeworfene Haus wieder aufzurichten und gegen neue Zerstörung zu sichern angeleitet worden seien.

This moderate optimism is the combined result of Wagner's life experience, his artistic striving, and his intellectual contact with the philosophers of his time. As we found in the case of other authors, he did not simply accept the metaphysical views of the philosophers, but was drawn to them by an intellectual affinity resulting from a similar historical situation, so that their views merely helped him to achieve a conceptual clarification of his own world view. Schelling's idea of an evolution from the unconscious to the conscious, Feuerbach's anthropological concept of the central significance of man for the explanation of the universe, Schopenhauer's vitalism, his pessimism, and his idea of compassion—all contributed to the development of his thinking as well as of his musical-dramatic work, but without affecting their integrity and their organic growth.

*Religion und Kunst, III

Wagner's earliest dramatic attempts closely follow the romantic tradition in its degenerated form. *Die Hochzeit* is a gory mystery drama, which revels in the portrayal of sensuality and then inconsistently and insincerely leads the sinners to destruction in a conventional ending. The same dependence upon traditional plots is apparent in *Die Feen*. Like Chrétien de Troyes' and Hartmann von Aue's *Yvain*, Wagner's hero leaves the land of the fairies in order to defend his own country; but he forgets his fairy, is punished with insanity, and only after long and painful separation is he allowed to return. From the source upon which this early work is based Wagner accidentally carried over a type of structure which is typical of romantic philosophy in general, and which later becomes a conscious part of Wagner's own philosophy and art. The action proceeds in three stages: (1) man in harmony with and part of nature, (2) apostasy from the unity of nature through individuation, and (3) conscious restoration of the lost harmony with nature. If Wagner had been satisfied with the adoption of this pattern of thought, he would have been but one more of the many forgotten epigones of the romantic movement. It was only his reëxperiencing and rethinking of the problems of life and their significance that saved him from this fate and made him an artist of lasting fame.

The sensualism which in *Die Hochzeit* had been concealed under the veil of righteousness finds a much more frank expression in *Das Liebesverbot*, which is a characteristically Young German recasting of Shakespeare's *Measure for Measure*. A young man is condemned to death by a German governor of northern Italy because he has followed the freer customs of the South in his experience of pre-conjugal love, but he is saved when the rigorous judge himself is exposed as a hypocrite and a betrayer of women. Unimportant as this work may be in itself, for Wagner's development it marks the liberation of his artistic expression from the standards of traditional decency and the first assertion of his right to be himself. It is nothing more than the expression of an unrestrained will to live, scarcely balanced by concern for a moral regulation of life.

Such a regulative idea, however, appears in Wagner's next work, the grand-opera *Rienzi*. In spite of its dependence upon traditional forms, this work is Wagner's first characteristic creation. It reflects the author's striving for achievement and recognition and the disillusionment resulting from the inertia of the theater-goers and from the misery of an impecunious household. Like Grabbe, Büchner, and Hebbel in their early works, Wagner accuses the masses for their complete lack of understanding for real greatness, and for their absolute blindness even when their own welfare is at stake. Under Rienzi's leadership, the Romans exile the noblemen who have dishonored their daughters and menaced the peace and liberty of the city. But Rienzi makes the fatal mistake of trying to attain his political aims through intolerance and humanity; instead of killing his enemies, he treats them with generosity. This estranges his people from him, so that they can be roused against him by the same noblemen whom they had expelled with Rienzi's assistance. He falls victim to the same people whose liberty had been his only concern to the very last. But the just punishment for their egotistic and faithless desertion they meet through the hands of the same aristocrats whom they had called back in order to defeat Rienzi. The tragic impression is somewhat lessened by this justification of his attitude, but chiefly by the love and self-sacrifice of his sister Irene. The stupidity of the masses seems hopeless; even their own desires become unintelligible to them when they are translated from political phraseology into the plain language of facts. Apart from this pessimism concerning the relation between the genius and the people, there are some traits in this drama which may be interpreted as foreshadowing the future development of Wagner's ideas. The sensualism of his earlier work is sublimated into heroism; Rienzi loves his city as if she were his bride, and he sacrifices his life for this love. Irene's faithfulness is a first indication of the answer to Wagner's pessimism: compassion and absolute devotion.

The personal elements played such a large part in the libretto as well as in the music of *Rienzi* that Wagner was perhaps justified in seeing a misinterpretation of his artistic purpose even in appreciative criticism of his work. But in Paris, where he had gone with youthful high expectations, the artist met with complete failure and deepest humiliation. He saw shallow and empty operatic compositions enthusiastically applauded —if they were presented in a lavish setting—while he himself could scarcely make a living by arranging passages from favorite operas. He revolted against his destiny and against the artistic degeneration of his age. In his physical misery and spiritual despondency, the Irene-motive of *Rienzi*—the desire for rest and compassionate understanding—began to occupy his mind again. This, together with his homesickness for his German fatherland, became the theme of the musical ballad *Der fliegende Holländer*. It had first been conceived on the voyage from Riga to London, under the influence of a story by Heinrich Heine, but the depressing experiences of his sojourn at Paris were needed to bring the project to realization. Daland, the greedy Norwegian sea-captain who can hardly wait to sell his daughter, Senta, to the mysterious Dutchman whose ship is stranded near his home, personifies the superficial sensualism and the materialism to which Wagner ascribed his failure and misery. In the figure of the Flying Dutchman, who is condemned ceaselessly to roam the seas until he is at last saved by compassionate love, Wagner condenses all his most urgent wishes and longing: his desire for a salvation from the miserable life at Paris, his home-sickness, and, above all, the yearning for an understanding of his artistic struggle. But while Rienzi's tragedy was mitigated only by Irene's heroic companionship in sorrow and in death, in this play compassion is shown as capable of bringing about complete redemption. Devotion has the power of understanding and thus of saving one from the dejection of solitary striving. If devotion and self-sacrifice are genuine expressions of human nature, one may bear with the egotism and superficiality of the average man and hope for his moral resignation.

The main theme of *Rienzi* as well as of *Der fliegende Holländer* was the tension between the artist and his environment, the tragedy of misunderstanding and loneliness. The success of *Rienzi* and a call to conduct the Saxon court-orchestra at Dresden brought Wagner at least temporary relief from the direst of his cares. His antagonism toward the contemporary presentation of the arts continues unabated, but without the despair of former years and without the youthful complacency from which part of this criticism sprang. Formerly he had considered the artist as a being apart from all others, as the creative idealist tragically misunderstood by the uneducated and egotistic masses. Now he discovers in himself the same problematic tension between the egotistic and debasing desires of his lower instincts and the longing for the nobler pleasures in the realm of the ideal; he feels a "Verlangen nach dem Hinschwinden aus der Gegenwart, nach dem Ersterben in einem Element unendlicher, irdisch unvorhandener Liebe, wie es nur mit dem Tode erreichbar schien."*

This tension is expressed in *Tannhäuser*. It explains the scenic contrasts between the Venusberg and the Wartburg, between the cave and the castle, between the atmosphere of a melancholy autumn night and the joyful dawn of a spring morning. It explains the character contrast between the voluptuousness of Venus and the sublimeness of faith and chastity, as well as the musical contrast between the confusing ecstasy of the Venusberg and the melodic simplicity of the Pilgrim's Chorus. Tannhäuser himself, even in his greatest depravity, never yields completely to the sensual debauchery of Venus; he always remains faithful

Eine Mitteilung an meine Freunde

[159]

to the Faustian element in his character, which drives him to exhaust all the potentialities of human nature.

Wenn stets ein Gott genieszen kann,
bin ich dem Wechsel untertan . . .
aus Freuden sehn' ich mich nach Schmerzen. (1, 2)

Even in the arms of Venus he does not forget that a complete surrender to the pleasures of sensuality is identical with the sacrifice of the essential quality of human nature, the free creative will:

bei dir kann ich nur Sklave werden
nach Freiheit doch verlang' ich. (I, 2)

The departure from the Venusberg, however, does not restore his inner freedom; he leaves the embraces of his goddess in order to fight for her glory. In the Wartburg he answers Wolfram's and Walter's praise of the ideal of pure love with a confession of the sensual pleasures he experienced in the arms of Venus. Only the absoluteness of Elizabeth's faithfulness, which is abated neither by Tannhäuser's confession of his godless lust nor by his banishment, awakens in him the desire to suffer and to fight in the service of ideal love. That the pilgrimage of penitence to Rome cannot free him from the obsession of sensuality lies in the nature of asceticism as mere suppression of the instincts, without any attempt at sublimation. Thus, at the end of the pilgrimage, Tannhäuser's voluptuousness breaks forth with even greater force. He despairs of his salvation and is about to bury himself in the palace of Venus forever, when he learns that Elizabeth has sacrificed her life to save his soul. This highest and holiest fidelity redeems his nobler self from the tortures of his senses. In death he finds the fulfillment and the inner harmony of his self, which had been harassed by the superficial distractions of a materialistic world. The contrast between sensuality and asceticism, therefore, is not sufficient to describe Tannhäuser's development; as is evident in Wagner's earlier works, real fulfillment can be gained only beyond the boundaries of sensual distraction and of bodily existence.

The carrying over of the struggle between materialism and idealism into his inner self is the most important step in the evolution of Wagner's world view. Life is now seen in its polarity between a restless and ever dissatisfied will and the renunciation of this will in favor of a harmonious, contemplative existence. Despite the fact that there is in Tannhäuser's character a gradual development from the one pole to the other, that is, from the assertion to the renunciation of will, both of these elements are at all times an essential part of his character, though the relation between them is not always clear. The antithesis of these two elements calls for a synthesis, which is first attempted in *Lohengrin*. Wagner himself suggested this interpretation of *Lohengrin* when he compared the medieval legend, which was the source of his music drama, with the Greek myth of Zeus and Semele:

> Der Gott liebt ein menschliches Weib und naht ihr um dieser Liebe willen selbst in menschlicher Gestalt; die Liebende erfährt aber, dasz sie den Geliebten nicht nach seiner Wirklichkeit erkenne und verlangt nun, vom wahren Eifer der Liebe getrieben, der Gatte solle in der vollen sinnlichen Erscheinung seines Wesens sich ihr kundgeben. Zeus weisz, dasz sein wirklicher Anblick sie vernichten musz; er selbst leidet unter diesem Bewusztsein, unter dem Zwange, zu ihrem Verderben das Verlangen der Liebenden erfüllen zu müssen: er vollzieht sein eigenes Todesurteil, als der menschentödliche Glanz seiner göttlichen Erscheinung die Geliebte vernichtet.*

In this comparison the twofold tragedy of the *Lohengrin* drama is clearly indicated. It is, first, the tragedy of the genius who by his very striving and achievement is driven into solitude and dejection. But for the sake of his creation, he must be wholly himself. He must rise above the average and be, therefore, misunderstood if he is to fulfill his educative and cultural mission. For the same reason, however, he must experience of the sorrows of this world and learn to speak its language. He must desire to be understood, or at least to be received with sympathy and unreserved faith, since complete understanding is possible only through complete conformity with the average mind. The tragic alternative to being one's self in spite of the loneliness incident to superiority is that of losing one's self in a world of compromise and mediocrity.

Wagner gives in *Lohengrin* not only a deeper interpretation of the artist's problem, but also a fairer conception of the artist-lover. In the "Semele" tragedy he idealizes love and sympathetic understanding. Love and the will to understand are essentially one; but understanding presupposes congeniality; without congeniality, understanding is liable to violate the ideal through the natural desire to lower it to the level of the mediocre and the conventional. There is only one attitude which can prevent such tragedy: absolute devotion to the higher ideal and unwavering confidence in the impregnability of the ideal in an inimical world.

It is Wagner's own problem which is expressed in *Lohengrin*, the problem of the creative artist who has become conscious of his achievement, but who vainly longs for recognition and who, therefore, is in

Eine Mitteilung an meine Freunde

constant danger of succumbing to doubt concerning the value of his striving. This play also embodies Wagner's vision of a development of the arts to an unprecedented apex of expressiveness, on the one hand, and, on the other, the discouraging realization that their acceptance and influence depend upon such debasing factors as technical tradition and the unintelligence of the masses. Lohengrin leaves the solitary heights of the Gralsburg in order to protect Elsa von Brabant from the rapacity of Telramund. He proves his higher mission by the miracle of his appearance: in a moment when Elsa's fate seems to be doomed, he arrives in a boat drawn by a swan and defeats Telramund in a duel. Elsa's prayer is answered by the knight of the Holy Grail because she had absolute faith in the triumph of the ideal. Her dreamlike longing guided Lohengrin, and he found her because he himself was impelled by the desire to exchange his lofty isolation for sympathetic contact with man. What he seeks is the deepest human affection based on absolute faith in his personal value; it is not admiration and humble adoration that he needs, but human love which can save him from the loneliness to which he is condemned by his superior nature. This is the meaning of his warning to Elsa when she responds to his love:

> Nie sollst du mich befragen,
> noch Wissens Sorge tragen,
> woher ich kam der Fahrt,
> noch wie mein Nam' und Art! (I, 3)

Yet he cannot conceal his higher nature from her and from the world. Any superiority appears to the average man only as something unusual, as a deviation from the norm, which in his envy he can explain only as mean and abject depravity. So Elsa's faith is threatened and shaken by defamatory gossip: if Lohengrin is not an associate of Satan, why should he want to conceal his origin and name? If he loves her, she has a right to know his secrets, especially when silence endangers his life. She must ask the forbidden question in order to protect him, for the constant calumnies of her environment have undermined her confidence and belief that Lohengrin's superior nature is immune to the attacks of the world. Thus she forces Lohengrin back into his tragic solitude by the question which is a sign of unbelief and lack of understanding. His hope of realizing a sensual-spiritual unity is completely shattered. He experiences the tragedy of the creative genius in a world which is capable of accepting only what is sanctioned by age and tradition, in a world which, even with the best intentions, seeks to force the higher values down to the level of

[162]

mediocrity, instead of bowing in faithful gratitude to their mysteries. His is the tragedy of an age which has turned away from idealism to shallow materialism, the tragedy of all those whose efforts toward the realization of higher aims are constantly thwarted by the inertia of an unintelligent and therefore antagonistic environment.

In all his works, including *Lohengrin*, Wagner had presented his own personal and artistic problem; he had touched the problems of the time only so far as they affected his existence and his recognition as an artist. Through the translation of his personal experience into artistic form, he had revived the romantic belief that, detached from material interests, man would follow his natural inclinations and be capable of sympathetic understanding, of devotion, and of sacrifice. Senta, in *Der fliegende Holländer*, who, with the calmness of a somnambulist, gives her life for the redemption of the haunted sailor; Elizabeth, who by her faithfulness saves Tannhäuser from his sensual slavery; and Elsa, who, like Kleist's Käthchen von Heilbronn, sees in a dream her approaching savior and lover—these are the outstanding examples of such natural goodness. In characters like Daland, Ortrud, and Telramund, on the other hand, Wagner had illustrated the demoralizing effect of egotistic materialism. By contrasting these two groups and by demonstrating the tragic fate of superior personalities in a materialistic world, he had implicitly postulated the regeneration of humanity by reawakening its original sympathetic nature.

From the point of view of consistent development *(Werklogik)*, Wagner's next musico-dramatic product, *Der Ring des Nibelungen*,* attains the systematic synthesis of his ideas, as far as such a synthesis can be the concern of musical and dramatic art. He had planned to embody these ideas in the drama *Friedrich der Rotbart*, but dropped ihe plan because he was fraid that the mass of necessary historical detail might obscure his main idea of pure humanity. He then turned to the Nordic myth of the Nibelungs, in which he thought he had discovered the most appropriate subject for the artistic presentation of his ideal, the natural man who, with unbroken vitality and complete freedom from fear of suffering and death, fulfills the tasks assigned to him by the all-embracing cosmic principle of life. It was his belief that the old myths had saved for us the picture of man "in der natürlichsten, heitersten Fülle seiner sinnlich belebten Kundgebung," of man at a stage of development at which

---

*Rheingold 1852, *Die Walküre* 1852, *Siegfried* 1851, *Götterdämmerung* 1848-53; publication of the whole work 1853.

kein auszer ihm stehendes Verhältnis ihn irgendwie hemmte in seiner Bewegung, die aus dem innersten Quelle seiner Lebenslust jeder Begegnung gegenüber sich so bestimmt, dasz Irrtum und Verwirrung, aus dem wildesten Spiele der Leidenschaften genährt, rings um ihn bis zu seinem offenbaren Verderben sich häufen konnten, ohne dasz der Held einen Augenblick, selbst dem Tode gegenüber, den innern Quell in seinem wellenden Ergusse nach auszen gehemmt oder je etwas für berechtigt über sich und seine Bewegung gehalten hätte als eben die notwendige Ausströmung des rastlos quillenden innern Lebensbrunnens.*

This free and unrestrained man is for the Wagner of the *Ring* the beginning and the ideal aim of the evolutionary process, which develops in three stages: original integrated life, social disintegration by avarice and greed for power, and, finally, restoration of pure and uncorrupted humanity.

Rheingold, the first part of the *Ring des Nibelungen,* begins with a chief musical description of nature. The Rhine daughters play around the golden treasure, which for them is not material possession but the source of the splendor which brightens the home of the nymphs. Alberich, the Nibelung, approaches to steal the treasure which can be taken only by one who is willing to renounce all sympathy. Alberich pays this price, and by means of the ring fashioned of the Rhinegold he becomes the tyrannical ruler of the dwarfs of Niblheim, whom he forces to gather gold from the gold mines all over the earth. His brother Mime must forge the magic cap for him which allows him to assume any shape, and which is a symbol of the cowardice and hypocrisy brought about by the rule of gold. Thus, honest and responsible action is replaced by fraudulent veiling of real intentions, by opportunistic adjustment to circumstances for the sake of egotistic advantages. Even the gods are seized by greed for possession and power; they barter Freia, the youthful goddess of love, to the giants for the erection of their castle Valhalla. Their moral conscience has degenerated to such an extent that they can sacrifice a personal for a material value, and in so doing they must submit to the causality of evil, for only by a new act of injustice—the betrayal of Alberich—can they repair the injustice done to Freia. Such demoralization is the effect of the possession of gold, even before Alberich pronounces his curse upon the owner of the ring. The gods, who take it from him to satisfy the greed of the giants, draw upon themselves the curse of losing their superiority to the giants. They, in turn, do not profit by the possession of the gold and the ring. It is immediately the cause of the

Eine Mahnung an meine Freunde

most inhuman brutality, for Fafner murders his own brother, only to bury the hoard in a cave where he, in the shape of a dragon, guards the idle metal by sleeping on it. This again is a symbol of the utter senselessness of accumulating a material which in itself has no value whatsoever, and is, at the same time, a condemnation of the greed for materialistic possession in Wagner himself and in his age.

In *Die Walküre* the curse befalls Wotan, the highest god in Valhalla. His primitive nature, which found in love its unrestricted fulfillment, has been limited by a contract, a device which had become necessary as the only protection against lawlessness and encroachments upon the rights of others. As a protector of the contracts which are now concluded in his name he, the god, is forced to punish and destroy his dearest children, in whom his own former freedom continues to live. Siegmund, his love child, lives as an exile in a world of hatred and persecution. He meets his fate when he tries to protect a woman's most human right, that of choosing her own mate. Pursued by the kinsmen, who wanted to force her to accept an unloved husband, Siegmund escapes into the house of one of his pursuers, Hunding, who had abducted his own twin sister, Sieglinde, and forced her to a matrimonial contract. She is first seized with sympathy, then with love, for the unknown brother, a love which is simultaneously the highest freedom from moral restraint, because it is adulterous, and guilt, because it is incest. In this freedom of passion Siegmund carries on the heritage of his father Wotan, namely, the unrestrained will-to-live. In the love for his married sister he sins against the law which was forced upon Wotan by the moral degeneration of the world, the law of the sanctity of the matrimonial contract, which must be upheld, even if the contract was concluded against the will of one of the partners. Neither Wotan's sword—the symbol of original free will—nor Brünnhilde's assistance can rescue Siegmund. Wotan, as protector of the law, is forced to suppress every natural impulse to save Siegmund and is obliged to defend Hunding with the spear of right; he must reject his favorite daughter Brünnhilde because she has been moved by her sympathy to support the freest of all heroes against her father's unnatural and enslaved will. Sleeping under the protection of Loge's fire-wall, she waits for the hero whose absolute freedom and love alone can break through to awaken her. Tragically torn between freedom and duty, Wotan is unable to lead this world back to its original harmony. This redemption is left to man. Without the assistance of the gods, even, against their will, man must free himself from the curse of possession and power, from greed and the superficial system of contracts. There is still

[165]

hope, for Wotan's original nature was not destroyed in Siegmund's death. It lives on in Brünnhilde and in Siegfried, the son of Siegmund and Sieglinde, who in freest love dared to take upon themselves the heaviest guilt.

In *Siegfried,* the god who can free neither himself nor mankind from the curse of gold leaves the task of redemption to the man who was begotten in freedom. Siegfried is Wagner's ideal of natural man: a man without any burden of the past, without fear of the future, living completely for the tasks of the present moment; always active, independent, and full of genuine sympathy in his relations with his fellow-men; in fact, in such perfect harmony with nature that even the birds' language is revealed to him. Above all, he is free from the greed which dominates his foster-father Mime, who saved and trained him only so that he might win the hoard of the Nibelungs for him. Free from the inner discord of his father Wotan, he is able to forge the sword Notung anew and to break the spear of contracts in Wotan's hand. Free and fearless, he can kill the greedy hoarder Fafner, whom the gods themselves do not dare to approach. His passionate love, which is not weakened by any egotistic considerations, allows him to pass unharmed through Loge's fire-ring and win Brünnhilde. The curse would have failed to have power over him if he had not become the owner of the gold and thereby the object of envy, although he remains inwardly free from the guilt of attachment to material possession. But the mere fact that he is the owner of the hoard exposes him to the attacks of a greedy and selfish world, and this will be the cause of his destruction. Only Brünnhilde, who knows of the curse, could save him, by persuading Siegfried to return it to the Rhine-daughters, or in other words, to nature. In her emotional ecstasy, however, she stands so far above human considerations that she neglects to cause this obvious restoration and so seals Siegfried's and her own fate.

In *Götterdämmerung,* Siegfried—comparable in this respect with Lohengrin—has abandoned the higher realm of a naïve integrity of life and entered the "world," which is ruled by materialistic and selfish interests. He is less capable than Lohengrin of keeping himself free from the causality of materialistic degeneration. Exposed to the distracting influence of many diverging motives, he loses the naïvety of his unbroken will; in the symbolic language of the drama, he drinks the potion of forgetfulness which is handed to him by Hagen, the son of the Nibelung Alberich. Unwittingly and unwillingly he submits to the wishes of Hagen who covets possession of the hoard, and to Gunther, who wants to own Brünnhilde. Siegfried has forgotten his love for Wotan's daughter and yields, instead, to the charms of Gudrune, who will never be able to understand his deeper nature and value, and for her sake he commits the most ignominious treason against the highest and most sacred values: he betrays Brünnhilde, with the help of the magic cap and by bartering with Gunther over her most personal rights. Thereby he also drags Brünnhilde's divine nature down into the world, where she is torn between love and hatred, between faithfulness and falseness. She becomes another symbol of Wagner's struggle for the integrity of the arts in a materialistic and sensualistic world. In order to avenge the treason, she is compelled to make a pact with Hagen, who abuses her as the instrument of his greed for the hoard. Siegfried's treason against Brünnhilde thus engenders Brünnhilde's treason against Siegfried. But Hagen, the son of the evil powers, like all the possessors of the ring, is denied actual lordship over the world; for there is no power in the universe which can definitely destroy the higher essence of man—"pure humanity." This pure humanity rises triumphantly out of the catastrophe brought about by the tyranny of gold. Brünnhilde and Siegfried find in their death the purification of life and liberation from their attachment to this world of callous deceit, while the ring is taken back by the Rhine-daughters. The meaning of their liberation Wagner himself changed through various versions of the closing lines. In the revolutionary years around 1848, the glorification of death was a vision of political freedom which, in Wagner's opinion, was to be accompanied by a liberation of the creative artist. In the years during which his ideas were influenced and clarified by the study of Schopenhauer, this death meant the liberation from the ever dissatisfied urge of will:

Aus Wunschheim zieh ich fort,
Wahnheim flieh' ich auf immer;
des ew'gen Werdens
offne Tore
schliesz' ich hinter mir zu:

nach dem wunsch- und wahnlos
heiligsten Wahlland,
der Weltwandrung Ziel,
von Wiedergeburt erlöst,
zieht nun die Wissende hin.

The final musical redaction, however, follows an earlier plan, in the fulfillment of love:

helles Feuer
faszt mir das Herz:
ihn zu umschlingen,

umschlossen von ihm
in mächtigster Minne
vermählt ihm zu sein!

Death here becomes the expression of belief in the final victory of humanity freed from materialistic greed, an idea which corresponds to a later stage in the development of Wagner's thought, after he had overcome his pessimistic view of culture.

[167]

The Schopenhauer ending belongs to the period in which Wagner was working at the music-drama *Tristan und Isolde*. The dynamic activism of the *Ring des Nibelungen* had yielded to a more quietistic resignation under the depression caused by his banishment from Dresden and the hopelessness of finding any recognition for his work. All striving seemed to have lost its meaning in this utilitarian world. Schopenhauer's idea that suffering is the fate of man in the world of ever dissatisfied will, and that negation of this will must be made the highest moral principle, seemed to him only to confirm his own experience, when, in 1854, he read *Die Welt als Wille und Vorstellung*. He had always seen in egotism and avarice a menace to his ideal of pure humanity. Lohengrin, Siegfried, and Brünnhilde had been endangered in their existence and in their essence by contact with the materialistic spirit of the world and had been saved by returning to the solitude of contemplation, or to the realm of eternal harmony and rest. Lohengrin, however, remained essentially free from the moral entanglements of the world, whereas the *Ring* more consistently presented the dangers of a life in this world. The *Ring*, however, contains such a mass of confusing details and symbols that the basic ideas can be recognized only with difficulty: it still is an expression of the confusion in which the poet finds himself with regard to the realities of the world.

Compared with the *Ring des Nibelungen*, *Tristan und Isolde*, even in spite of its rigorously condensed form, further clarifies and gives a deeper emotional foundation to Wagner's world view. Emotion manifests itself linguistically in the transition from the national form of alliteration, with its emphasis upon the conceptual, to lyrically diffusive and musical language. This is evident in the reduction of the verbal expression to the essential minimum and in the perfect musical harmony between word and tone, which means, in turn, that Wagner succeeded in mastering the emotional content—the idea of pure humanity. Sympathetic devotion to one's fellowmen has become for him the absolutely certain basic principle of world redemption. In *Tannhäuser* this devotion was still evaluated either as pure and holy or as sinful and demoniac; in *Tristan und Isolde* it is the supreme value. This means that the conception of love, too, has developed from mere eroticism to the basic moral value of human sympathy, to which Wagner now attributes the power of liberating the world from egotistic and material considerations, and of piercing through the surface of the illusion to the essence—from *Wahn* to *Wesen*.

Worldly illusion and the desire for glory and honor were Tristan's motives when he persuaded his uncle Marke to marry and took it upon himself to find a bride for him. It is illusion and dependence upon the judgment of others which make Isolde think that she is obligated to avenge Morolt's death. Dominated by this illusion, both defy the sympathetic feeling which has destined them for one another. In this spirit, Isolde hands what she believes to be a deadly potion to Tristan. In response to their inner nature, both take the potion. Thus, what was meant to bring death is turned into an instrument of love; for in the face of death, anything that is superficial and inessential vanishes, and the essential quality of man, the sympathetic relation to his fellow men, is freed:

In deiner Hand	zeigte, was mir
den süszen Tod	die Sühne verhiesz:
als ich ihn erkannt,	da erdämmerte mild
den sie mir bot;	erhabner Macht
als mir die Ahnung	im Busen mir die Nacht;
hehr und gewisz	mein Tag war da vollbracht.

Through his ambition Tristan has made himself dependent upon the laws of the world, and neither he nor Isolde can cast off the effects of this surrender. Tristan cannot betray his loyalty and friendship for Marke and expose him to the mockery of his subjects; he must yield Isolde to the man whom she cannot love. The words "mir erkoren, mir verloren," which, as spoken words, stand out from the musical background, express the completely hopeless contrast between world-illusion and world-essence, *Weltwahn* and *Weltwesen*. Completely realizing this illusion, Tristan and Isolde try to consummate their innermost nature in love and thus to escape within this world the forces of the world. Night turns out to be the home of the eternal joy of love:

Ohne Wähnen	ohne Nennen,
sanftes Sehnen	ohne Trennen,
ohne Bangen	neu Erkennen,
süsz Verlangen	neu Entbrennen;
. . in ungemess'nen Räumen	endlos ewig
übersel'ges Träumen	ein-bewuszt:
nicht mehr Tristan,	heisz erglühter Brust
nicht Isolde;	höchste Liebes-Lust!

But the light of day leads Marke to the place of their love; day brings betrayal and the wounding of Tristan by the same Melot who had incited his avidity for glory and honor; day brings the separation of the lovers and the banishment of Tristan. In his fatherland he awakes once more to see the gloomy light of day; alone, far from his beloved, he realizes most deeply the tragedy of life in this world: it is endless longing and futile hope of fulfillment. Isolde arrives too late to save his life, nor does Marke's sympathetic renunciation avail. Isolde follows Tristan in his love-death, which is a symbol of redemption from the hopeless yearning of man in this world, a submersion in the eternal oneness of the universe:

Heller schallend
mich umwallend,
sind es Wellen
sanfter Lüfte?
Sind es Wogen
wonniger Düfte?
. . . soll ich . . .
untertauchen,
süsz in Düften
mich verhauchen?

In des Wonnenmeeres
wogendem Schwall,
in der Duft-Wellen
tönendem Schall,
in des Welt-Atems
wehendem All —
ertrinken —
versinken —
unbewuszt —
höchste Lust!

Tristan und Isolde relates closely to Wagner's own life and problems. It reflects Wagner's renunciation of his love for Mathilde Wesendonck, who had shown the deepest understanding for his work and in this way had, in the truest sense, merged her essence with his own. It also expresses his problem as an artist: the danger to which genuine art is exposed by the dependence for its effect on the fashion of the day and by the inner solitude which is thereby imposed on the creative artist. Finally, it shows his philosophic views: the world process is divided into three symbolic stages, similar to the three ethical stages of world development according to classical idealism or to the three metaphysical stages of the romantic theory. Just as Tristan and Isolde are destined for each other in their emotional and subconscious being, in spite of their antagonism, so men are originally and genuinely united in a natural organic whole. They are separated by the egotism of the materialistic will, the illusion of the world; they become individuals who forget about their inner relation and existential interdependence. It is the aim of the cosmic process to restore the existential integrity by overcoming the separation which is brought about by willing the inessential,—by yielding to the illusions of the world.

In this music-drama Wagner's philosophy establishes its closest contact with the systems of Schelling and Schopenhauer. With Schelling he shares the evolution of the conscious and individuated world out of the unconscious. As in Schopenhauer's system, Wagner's world is essentially "will" or striving, which can never be satisfied. The aim of the conscious will can therefore only be the night of eternal harmony, in which we are redeemed from all striving—the Nirvana. The ideas of glory and honor mislead the will into acting contrary to its inner desire for rest and harmony; the idea is a secondary form of life, an ever misleading function of the will. The compassion with which Kurvenal and finally Marke are seized, relieves the intolerable tension of life. This drama has the effect which Schopenhauer expects from a tragedy: it elevates us above the suffering of existence through contemplation of its inevitable necessity and through disclosure of the only possibility of its elimination, the renunciation of the will to live. The content and the poetic and musical form work together in this drama to bring about the visualization of this philosophic thought. The scenes of separation and danger are symbolically attributed to the day, those of love and temporal and eternal union to the night. The language shows a corresponding tension between logical pointedness, which retards the music, and an extremely musical flow of words, which obscures the logical structure of the language. The former may be illustrated by Isolde's words in the first act anticipating the final catastrophe: "Todgeweihtes Haupt, Todgeweihtes Herz," the latter by Isolde's closing aria (see p. 170). Thus, the verbal expression helps to create the tensive effect which ordinarily is left to the contrast of concrete conceptual language and aphonic emotional music. Since the action rises out of a purely musical prelude, passes through the more concrete *Worttondrama*, and resolves itself into music again in Isolde's death aria, the formal structure of this peculiar form of drama here becomes a symbol which emphasizes the material content as well as its metaphysical meaning.

In *Tristan und Isolde* Wagner exposes as far as possible within the confines of the music-drama, a world-view which he had formed around the central idea of pure humanity. His view left little hope for a realization of the ideal in actual life; the old antagonism between actual reality and the vision of the ideal, between the inertia of the masses and the championship of higher aims, remains; the antagonism was solved only by the metaphysical reference to the cosmic harmony of the Nirvana— the renunciation of the will to live in the individuation of the world.

Die Meistersinger von Nürnberg leads beyond this pessimistic quietism. Wagner, like many other authors whom fate granted the opportunity to "finish" their work, finds a synthesis of the two antagonistic attitudes towards the world, between life in interactive contact with the world and life striving to transcend the limitations of the world. What had been considered only as of negative value now gains positive significance. The phenomenal world with its confusing diversity, with its conflicts and illusions—"Lichtwelt" as Wagner calls it—enters into an existential relation to the "Klangwelt," the world of unifying feeling. Both worlds are manifestations of the same creative universal will *(Beethoven)*. The composer, or, according to Wagner, the *Wortton*-artist, has the same metaphysical function which Hebbel ascribes to the poet in the preface to *Maria Magdalene;* he interprets the spirit of the universe. He takes a dreamlike and unconscious part in the metaphysical being, and by his poetic creation he brings this metaphysical experience into the sphere of consciousness. The spirit of the universe manifests itself in the masses only in an unconscious and confused form, whereas in the consciousness of the artist it becomes an appeal to realize the ideal of pure humanity. Thus the formerly antagonistic poles become interdependent; the people are for the artist the source of his creative power, the artist is the leader toward the goal of realizing the people's most valuable potentialities.

This reconciliation with the fate of the artist's dependence upon the world is illustrated in the figure of Hans Sachs. The choice of this character in itself is related to this more concrete and integrated view: as a shoemaker he is rooted in the people, as a Meistersinger he is a creator of poetic and musical forms; his literary significance rests on the intimate relation of his poetry to the life of his time. The conflict which characterized the earlier version of the drama is expressed in the relationship between the Meistersingers and Walter Stolzing. The craftsmen, among them, especially Beckmesser, represent the artistic tradition against which Wagner had vainly tried to establish his art; pedantically they measure and count syllables and mark the mistakes, and with the mass of confusing rules and formulas they have lost their sense for real poetry entirely. Walter Stolzing, who embodies Wagner's own fate during his *Sturm-und-Drang* years, tries to keep away from the entanglements of reality and from artistic tradition. In the same unrealistic way in which he exaggerates the dangers threatening him as a lover and draws his sword at the appearance of the night-watchman, so he loses himself in poetic moods and dreams which he tries to describe in the broad flow of vague verses. His sentimental vagueness is restrained and adjusted to the realities of life with the help and by the example of Hans Sachs. Walter has to learn that pathetic reverie is just as far from the ideal of artistic achievement as the art of the Meistersinger with its traditional fetters, and that the emotional reaction towards nature

[172]

and human life has to be supplemented by formal self-discipline. As Hans Sachs raises himself above his passion for Eva in painful renunciation, so must art be more than a vague sentimental flow, it must be a restrained and regulated expression of emotional experience. That is the meaning of Hans Sachs' warning to Walter Stolzing:

> Verachtet mir die Meister nicht,
> und ehrt mir ihre Kunst!

To traditional art is attributed a definite and positive function in the history of German art:

> Dasz unsre Meister sie gepflegt,
> grad' recht nach ihrer Art,
> nach ihrem Sinne treu gehegt,
> das hat sie echt bewahrt . . . .
> Was deutsch und echt wüszt' keiner mehr,
> lebt's nicht in deutscher Meister Ehr'.

The attempt to do justice to the rules and demands of life and of art may lead to tragic situations, such as the one experienced by Hans Sachs in his relation to Eva; it may threaten to isolate the artist, as Walter Stolzing is isolated by the Meistersingers. But suffering is an integral part of life; it is inherent in the progress of life which necessarily passes from youth to age, from growth to decay and petrification; one has to accept these facts and to regard the obstacles as stimuli for further development. This struggle to find a meaning in the forces opposed to progress is, on the lower level, reflected in the cudgelling scene at the end of the second act which finds a sudden end when the night-watchman blows his horn. It is reflected in the entire poetic and musical form of the play: the tragedy is resolved in humor, which is by its very nature a resignation to the necessities of life and simultaneously an elevation above the grief caused by the opposition to one's will. It appears in the dramatic structure which culminates in the festival scene with the triumph of Walter's art disciplined by Hans Sachs' formal training. It is manifest in the march rhythm which reunites the diverging and chaotic tendencies of the masses in one powerful demonstration, in the musical domination of the chromatic by the diatonic form, and in the gradual detachment of the individual voice from the ensemble. This form is the expression of the fundamental theme, the inescapable existential integrity of the individual and his natural soil, the people.

In *Die Meistersinger* Wagner had overcome the pessimistic stage of

[173]

the *Tristan* period in a courageous assent to the world with its concreteness and its antinomies. *Parsifal,* on the other hand, in spite of its solemn remoteness from the world and its confusing diversity, is not a return to a stage previous to this comedy. It is true that Wagner ascribes the origin of his *Bühnenweihfestspiel* to a flight from the world, which in retrospect seemed to him to be ruled by the deceit and hypocrisy of organized and legalized murder and robbery, yet he sees in the contemplation even of such a world a prophecy of redemption.

> Wer kann ein Leben lang mit offenen Sinnen und freiem Herzen in diese Welt des durch Lug, Trug und Heuchelei organisierten und legalisierten Mordes und Raubes blicken, ohne zu Zeiten mit schaudervollem Ekel sich von ihr abwenden zu müssen? Wohin trifft dann sein Blick? Gar oft wohl in die Tiefe des Todes. Dem anders Berufenen und hierfür durch das Schicksal Abgesonderten erscheint dann aber wohl das wahrhaftigste Abbild der Welt selbst als Erlösung weissagende Mahnung ihrer innersten Seele. Über diesem wahrtraumhaften Abbilde die wirkliche Welt des Truges selbst vergessen zu dürfen, dünkt dann der Lohn für die leidenvolle Wahrhaftigkeit, mit welcher sie eben als jammervoll von ihm erkannt worden war.*

This world which he condemns is, as it was for Grillparzer in *Die Jüdin von Toledo,* the necessary stage of transition to the ideal of pure humanity. The experience of suffering from his volitive nature is the price man has to pay for his future liberation in a life which is to be free from suffering. Parsifal, like Siegfried and Tristan, passes through three stages; but now each one of these stages is indispensable for the attainment of the highest stage.

As a "pure fool," not burdened by any tradition and, therefore, without any knowledge of his origin, of his name, and of the harm caused by his sudden departure from the harmonious idyll in the forest and from his mother's care, Parsifal arrives at the castle of the Holy Grail. There he remains silent at the sight of King Amfortas' pains, not because convention forbids him to question, as in Wolfram von Eschenbach's epic poem, but because he is not capable of a compassion deep enough to have a healing force: he himself has not experienced the passion which has brought Amfortas to his present agony. This experience he finds in Klingsor's enchanted garden, where the flower girls vainly try to win him for their sensual play. Only when Kundry makes him feel the responsibility for his mother's death and tries to alleviate his sorrows by a sympathetic, yet passionate kiss, are those sensual desires aroused in him through which Klingsor tries to forestall the reign of

Das Bühnenweihfestspiel in Bayreuth

the humanitarian ideal as symbolized by the Grail. But the passion for Kundry is the same passion which caused Amfortas' agony. Thus, Parsifal feels, together with his own desire, the pains of his fellowman; the experience of compassion makes him conscious of his higher task, redemption from suffering through compassion. His compassionate brotherly kiss redeems Kundry, who has been condemned to a life ceaselessly torn between sensual seduction in the service of Klingsor and faithfulness to the ideals of the Holy Grail because she was not moved to compassion with Christ on his way to Calvary. Parsifal heals Amfortas, who has succumbed to temptation while fighting for the liberation of the Grail and who has remained a slave of his voluptuousness, suffering unbearable pains in his indecision between his sensuality and his longing for the ideal. Amfortas can be helped because he renounces his egotistic desire for death by unveiling the holy vessel. Parsifal also puts an end to the power of Klingsor, who has tried to win the kingdom of the Grail by seducing the knights, after having failed to win it by his own mortification. The Grail could only be won by him who was "durch Mitleid rein,"—or purified by compassion; but neither force nor the suppression of desires—which is not purity but concealed sensuality, and in Klingsor's case an egotistic perversion of nature—could have availed. The idea of redemption, which is at least implicitly present in all of Wagner's works, finds in *Parsifal* its highest sublimation and its final positive formulation. The ideal is no longer realized in the extinction of the individual in the harmony of the Universe, but in a society whose members are purified through the experience of suffering, who have consciously renounced an egotistic and degenerate will, and who have embraced the principles of sympathy and compassion towards all living beings as the foundation for the regeneration of mankind. Humanity has thus become the highest and truest form of religion and the artist, the high-priest of this religion. The theater became the temple where the redemption of man from his materialistic and egotistic inclinations is initiated, and the playhouse at Bayreuth was devoted to this task. This is Wagner's last reaction to the tendencies of the nineteenth century, under which he suffered the more, since he felt them to be an inescapable part of his own self.

Thus, Wagner's work, also, owes its existence to the tension between a declining idealism and a rising materialism. He wages in his essays as well as in his music dramas a desperate fight against the technical, political, and militaristic tendencies which he held largely responsble for the degeneration of artistic taste and understanding. He suffers not only as an artist from the indifference of an audience which he considers as spoiled by convention and sensationalism. The conflict between ideal will and sensual egotism is also Wagner's personal problem, so that his work can in part be interpreted as human and artistic self-liberation. Like other dramatists, he reveals his own conflict in both the positive and the negative characters of his dramas, in the characters representing the ideal postulate as well as in their antagonists. In the moral inferiority and the final defeat of the latter, we see Wagner's own victory over his sensual egotism and his freeing of himself from the fetters of the tendencies he condemns in himself and in his environment.

In the first plays, he schools his talent in imitations of conventional themes, imitations which reveal an interest in romantic ideas, but which are far from showing any proof of understanding these ideas. In *Liebesverbot* he revolts against conventional morality, encouraged by the emancipation movement of Young Germany. However, this erotic revolt is in *Rienzi* sublimated to ethical will in the dramatization of a hopeless struggle against the inertia and the materialism of the masses. The only comfort in this egotistic world is the devotion and understanding of a sympathetic being like Senta in *Der Fliegende Holländer*.

With *Tannhäuser* Wagner comes to the realization that the antagonism between the creative individual and the masses is accompanied by a corresponding inner conflict. A symbol of Wagner himself and of his period, Tannhäuser wavers between voluptuousness and a higher ideal aim, until the faithfulness of Elizabeth's love wins him for the essential values of human nature. Moreover, in this work the lesser values and disvalues are considered as negative, for they are not yet understood and interpreted in their functional significance for the process of life. The extreme polarity of this contrast, then, the fact that a decision between the masses and the creative genius, between sensuality and purity is unconditionally demanded urges Wagner to attempt to convert the exclusive antithesis into a conciliatory synthesis, such as can be found only in an integral conception of the problem of life.

In *Lohengrin* the creative genius leaves his lofty solitariness in order to display the richness of his personality in a close contact with active life. If by this attempt he is involved in the causality of the lower forms of existence, and thereby endangered in his essence, it is not only a tragedy for his superior being, but the lower world, too, participates in the tragic catastrophe.

The problematic nature of this lower world itself is recognized in *Der Ring des Nibelungen*, and thereby Wagner's world view approaches its systematic completion. Materialistic egotism is explained as a degeneration of human nature, originating in a greed for possession and power, and resulting in estrangement, diffidence, and substitution of trust by the dead letter of contracts, and finally, in murder and war. The aim of this development, however, is the absolutely free man who is capable of emancipating himself entirely from the egotism of the world and the love of possession in general. But Siegfried, who was chosen to achieve this redemption, was himself involved in the guilt of the world, and death alone can bring fulfillment. This idea reappears in *Tristan und Isolde* in a clarified form—the result of the study of Schopenhauer—and impresses by its metaphysical simplicity. The genuine and essentially sympathetic relation is obstructed by the will-to-live itself, inducing man to strive for glory, honor, and material ends, which, if attained, would only leave the will dissatisfied. Man can find peace only in the complete renunciation of his volition. The ideal of pure humanity, of immediate sympathy for man, can hardly be realized in this world.

In *Die Meistersinger* this pessimism is overcome, in that the actual world in its essential and spiritual totality is given a positive valuation. Even in the petrifaction of conventional life, even in materialistic confusion, there is contained a factor which is important for the progress of life; in its negative nature this is responsible for man's yearning for values, and thus provides creative man with impetus and strength to struggle for the regeneration of mankind. In *Parsifal*, finally, a temporary deference to the sensual and materialistic world becomes part of the evolutionary process of man; the road leads from naïve and unconscious harmony, through suffering in the world and consequent compassion for those who have yielded to the illusion of this world, to the sphere of the higher and conscious harmony of pure humanity.

> Der Verfall ist die Schule des Leidens, welche der Wille in seiner Blindheit sich auferlegte, um sehend zu werden.

In spite of the fact that his own life was affected by the materialistic tendencies of his time, and in spite of the indebtedness of his work to the mechanization of man and the disintegration of the culture of his century, Wagner never reconciled himself with these tendencies. The idealistic point of departure always remains effective in his thinking and in his creation as a longing for a regeneration of man through sympathetic understanding of the suffering caused by his surrender to the superficiality of materialism.

[177]

Chapter XII

HENRIK IBSEN

(1828-1906)

IF one chapter of this book on German dramatists of the nineteenth century is devoted to the Norwegian Ibsen, it is first because in the middle period of his production he continues in a realistic manner the dramatization of those social problems which Hebbel had still covered with a metaphysical veil; second, because Ibsen's dramatic work is more characteristic of the spiritual temper of the eighties than that of any of his German contemporaries; third, because he greatly influenced the further development of the German drama in the naturalistic period.

The Nordic landscape, with its cleft fjords and its small towns cut off for many months of the year from all connections by land with the outside world, is conducive, on the one hand, to a strong sense of the starkness of reality and a tenacious adherence to tradition and, on the other, to capricious meditation and aimlessly drifting imagination, which is liable to lose all contact with reality and substitute mere dreams for actual deeds. For nature demands of this people great sacrifices of physical energy, and at the same time condemns them to long periods of inactivity, during which the imagination is free to wander whither it will.

Only slowly and relatively late did Christianity reach these peripheral parts of the European cultural area, and less than in the central parts of Europe was it able to uproot Germanic and pagan traits of character and the remainders of old superstitions. The vital energies of the Vikings were repressed by a consciously acquired Christian morality, but these energies tend again and again to emerge in actions or in ideals which interfere with the conscious Christian will.

This experience and the resultant tension will repeat itself in a peripheral country when such a decisive change occurs in the social structure as the Industrial Revolution of the nineteenth century in the central part of Europe with its accompanying spiritual transformation. The imported ideas necessarily correspond only in part to the mental situation of the new country, since the rate of development is con siderably faster than that at the circumference, and since the mass of the people in the originating country is affected both more extensively and more intensively. The waves which reach the peripheral regions arrive there as mere intellectual theories, without a basic connection with an acute and actual problem. New ideas are, therefore, received with a greater reserve, and in a more rational and critical manner. They have a disquieting effect and fail at first because of the conservatism which is firmly founded in the nature of the country and in its geographical position. These ideas are of greater significance for the reason and the imagination than for practical conduct, so that the conflict between the alert individual, who is more immediately exposed to the cultural movement, and the power of tradition, both outside and inside of the individual, becomes even more acute. Thus, the progressive individual is forced into the defensive and into solitude even more than in the centers of the evolutionary movement; the greater the feeling of responsibility with which he tries to absorb the new ideas, the more is this true.

As with most of the other dramatists we discussed, the character contrast to which Ibsen was exposed in his home merged with the conflicting tendencies of his environment and of his time. It is the mother in this instance who represents the restraining and regulating element, while the father contributes the undisciplined strain. Ibsen's mother was a good-natured housewife whose activity was entirely devoted to her family duties, who kept her children under a hardly noticeable but strict discipline; she was a very modest woman, and in her old age retired within herself. Ibsen's father, however, was a daring speculator whose spirit was not broken until he had twice been forced into bankruptcy. A clever wit abetted him in his social relations, but his pointed criticisms estranged many people.

Henrik Ibsen inherited from his father a violent temper, a sharp and critical reason, and a restless mind. Perhaps he owed to him also that lack of emotional attachment which never allowed him to take root in any environment: he neglected all relations with his family because of religious differences; his attachment to the Norwegian theater at Christiania was intermittent, for he conducted it with the full devotion of his energies only at intervals; he left his home country because of his disappointment when the Norwegians failed to support the Danes in the war of 1864 and because, in its spiritual narrowness, Norway had become too small for him, yet neither Italy nor Germany ever really became a second home to him. To his mother he owed the introversion of his vital energies which is responsible for the artistic impulse. What Ibsen criticizes in his compatriots—namely, an imagination that outstrips reality to such an extent that the will for decisive action is thwarted—is his own heritage and his own sorrow, for he is unable to escape the conflict between his vitality and his inability to find for it any but an artistic mode of expression.

This tragic tension is all the more heightened by the materialistic tendencies of his time. Ibsen, too, is one of the epigones of the romantic faith in the moral power of the mind and the superior significance of the individual. The Danish critic Heiberg, an adherent of Hegel's philosophy, had confirmed Ibsen's belief in the moral progress of mankind, its rise from oppression and falsehood to freedom and truth. Thus, he sees in the revolutionary ideas of the year 1848 and in the national movement which swept over his native Norway not only a political or economic problem, but a moral obligation to seek the metaphysical self-realization of the universal spirit. He fights against all conventional falsehood and against self-deceiving ideological phrases. But he fights like one who sees the very foundation of his faith crumbling. With fanatic one-sidedness he formulates his moral postulates, and yet simultaneously he is the sceptic, questioning whether our human nature will be able to realize even a part of these postulates, or whether life is not rather based entirely on illusions.

Under the pressure of a time for which the production and the enjoyment of material goods meant more than creations of the mind, his moral optimism and rigorism change to a pessimism comparable to that of Schopenhauer and Eduard von Hartmann. He finds that the blind will of life, in the last analysis, is stronger than the mind and stronger than any moral considerations. Thus, he occupies himself with the question which had always been latent in him, whether life itself is not a basic value, and whether the hedonistic principle of John Stuart Mill, the principle of the greatest good for the greatest possible number, is, if not the higher, at least the more effective moral principle. The idealistic heritage, however, is so strong in him that he never could decide to accept a relativistic principle. In a deep-searching psychological analysis he reveals the complexity of moral consciousness, but he was never able to convince himself of a possible synthesis of his indomitable idealistic yearning and his natural human instinct. Darwin's theory of evolution also served to confirm his belief in the insuperability of inherited habits of action and thought which have their origin in the past and no longer serve a proper function, rather than to strengthen his hope for a future subjugation of the all-too-human

[180]

qualities of man, a hope such as Nietzsche had nourished and shaped in his fiction of the Superman.

Ibsen wrote his first drama in 1848, the year in which Central Europe saw the romantic hope for a constitutionally guaranteed liberty defeated, the year in which the governments definitely forced idealistic thought out of the public life and back into private life, and thus opened the way for the public rule of materialism. Disillusionment in the outcome of the great events of his time merged in Ibsen with a similar particularly Norwegian feeling: the consciousness of belonging to a nation which had once, in the distant past, led a heroic life but had now been reduced to insignificance. In addition, he nurtured a personal grudge against an environment which had no understanding for talent and inner worth, no sympathy for human misfortune, and which therefore refused him the social recognition he would have received but for his father's bankruptcy.

Thus Ibsen was in a mood of protest similar to that which animated Schiller when he wrote *Die Räuber*. Like Schiller, he selects as the hero of his first drama a social outcast, a man whom Cicero and Sallust had branded as traitor. But Schiller's Karl Moor is an idealistic visionary who turns to robbery in order to avenge the violation of the ideal of man; he is a symbol for the poet's conviction that the social order can be saved only by a radical renunciation of accepted norms. Schiller's drama is a first appeal for an idealistic reorganization of human society.

The hero of Ibsen's drama *Catiline* symbolizes the declining belief in the effectiveness of ideas. Catiline's character reflects the disease of the later nineteenth century; his national idealism is practically one with his egotistic materialism. He gets into debt by his extravagance; he resorts to bribery in order to turn the elections in his favor. He causes the suicide of one of his mistresses by his infidelity and the wantonness of his life. On the other hand, his conscience is still impressionable enough to impel him to submit to the vengeance of the dead woman's sister as an atonement for his guilt. It is similarly indicative of the undermining of idealistic conviction that the moral greatness of the Roman fathers, their righteousness, their love of freedom, and their republicanism, is praised in words, but neither illustrated in any character nor postulated in the depiction of its opposite, moral corruption, as was often done in defense of political freedom in the German Sturm-und-Drang period. Selfishness and ambition dominate the followers as well as the adversaries of Catiline. The only escape for the idealist, his only possibility of preserving his moral self-esteem in an egotistic world, is apparently complete retreat into an inglorious existence far from all politics, such as is demanded by Catiline's wife, Aurelia. But Catiline is not capable of accepting this solution: he is bound to this world by his ambition and by the guilt of his past. Even his death places him in a dilemma between fate and free will; he falls "halb von eigener, halb von fremder Hand," driven to his desperate deed by the revengeful sister of his betrayed lover, Furia, while his inner freedom is saved in death by the love of Aurelia. These two women embody the two principles which are fundamental for Ibsen's creation. Aurelia symbolizes moral freedom and self-preservation, which at this late stage of idealistic thought seems possible only as a retreat into the self. Furia, on the other hand, represents the nemesis of the will to participate in the affairs of the world, an attitude which involves a moral degradation and the recognition of the futility of life, and is capable of thus driving one to despair and self-destruction.

In this first drama, man is conceived of as a being who, in spite of his determination to be free and responsible in his actions, remains fundamentally dependent upon the levelling and degrading forces of his environment, if he attempts at all to be a man among men. Ibsen's subsequent dramas express less his own personal problems than his desire to add his contribution to the Norwegian national movement. By his national dramas he wants to free the Norwegian repertoire from its dependence upon the Danish and French theater. They are the result of a literary and esthetic interest, and consideration for the taste and the demand of his audience determine both the content and the form of these plays. As a Norwegian theater-critic and theater-director he takes part in the patriotic self-glorification of his countrymen, borrows from Icelandic sagas, and occasionally adapts Scribe's intrigue-technique to his Nordic material (*Lady Inger of Ostrat*); or he avoids a tragic ending in favor of a conventional Christian moral (*The Feast of Solhaug*); or he turns to the popular form of the fairy-tale (*Olaf Liljekrans*).

The author's manner of production reveals a continuous struggle between two opposing factors. Dramaturgical concerns constantly inhibit his poetic will to self-expression; purely incidental literary and esthetic problems hinder the expression of essential personal problems. As a dramaturgist he is constantly forced to present Danish and French plays and thereby to go against his plans to nationalize the

[182]

Norwegian theater; as a poet he is threatened by his dramaturgic interests, which compel him to consider the needs of the national stage; both as a dramaturgist and as a poet the attainment of his ideal is rendered difficult because of human limitations.

This tension between will and ability enters as a main theme into the dramas of Ibsen's romantic and national period. In *Lady Inger of Ostrat* the heroine has inherited from her father the leadership in the Norwegian fight for independence against the Danes, a task she could carry out only with the self-denying devotion of her whole personality. But her concern about the life of her natural son impels her to marry a Dane whom she does not love. Through this compromise she becomes guilty of the physical and moral destruction of her daughters, and finally allows herself to become so blinded by her ambition that she murders the same son for whom she has betrayed her national duty. Similarly, Margot, in *The Feast of Solhaug*, betrays the natural feelings which have caused her to become Gudmund's companion. Without any affection, she follows the wealthy landholder Bengt, a stupid, boasting dolt, in the expectation of being admitted to the noisy distractions of court life. She, too, demoralizes herself by yielding to superficial motives, and only chance saves her from murdering her own husband. While in these dramas Ibsen shows mainly the destructive moral consequences of faithlessness towards the inner self, in the fairy-play *Olaf Liljekrans* he illustrates the positive side of being completely one's self without any concern for personal disadvantage and danger. Alfhild and Olaf, who have drifted with esthetic aimlessness through life, attain a deeper realization of their selves in the assumption of moral responsibility for their actions.

With even greater emphasis this challenge is dramatized in the Brunhilde tragedy, *The Vikings of Helgeland*. The right and the duty to develop one's personality are here placed above all conventional rights and institutional safeguards of these rights. Like Siegfried, Sigurd violates Hjördis' most personal right, that over her own body, by winning her for his weaker friend Gunnar, for whose unprepossessing and inactive nature she has nothing but contempt. Sigurd's perfidy is not only treason against the loving woman, but also treason against his own nature and calling. The tender Dagny, whom he prefers to the congenial Hjördis, suffers only from his demand that she should strive for honor and follow him to his battles. Thus she keeps him from devoting his energies unreservedly to the duties of his calling. Hjördis, on the other hand, even after the unhappiness Sigurd has caused her by

[183]

his treachery, is still willing to deny her marriage vows, to abstain from all sensual satisfaction, merely to follow him, as a Valkyrie, to great deeds. His narrow Christian conscience, however, ties him to Dagny, for whom he has no love but only respect, while Hjördis grows to pagan stature in her passionate murder and suicide and becomes a dramatic symbol of the demand to be faithful to the laws of one's own nature. This problem is still concealed under cover of a traditional theme, but it distinctly prepares for Ibsen's social dramas, in which such problems are treated with absolute intelligibility and the conviction of one who for years has wrestled with them in his life as well as in his art.

Ibsen's next drama, *Love's Comedy*, brings a change in this direction, and thus proves that the national dramas, which seemed to be mainly an esthetic compromise with the tendencies of his environment, were part of his most personal struggle to find a calling, a fight against everything that might keep him on the level of mere momentary expediency. The fate of the ideal will in everyday life is illustrated in this comedy by the degeneration of love in the institutionalized forms of engagement and marriage. The couples in this drama began as idealistic dreamers. Finally, however, nothing remains but the appellations for ideal states which barely suffice to disguise disillusionment and make the barren truth endurable, while concealing it from others. With the presentation of disillusionment Ibsen has really become himself; he unveils, without any respect for the sensibilities of the well-adjusted bourgeois and without any conciliatory imagery, the ambiguity of all conventional relationships, and exposes thereby the spirit of the time in its antinomy of a declining romanticism and an unconfessed materialism.

Lind begins with the ideal aim of becoming a missionary and a pastor for emigrants, but the aunts of his fiancée easily succeed in persuading him to sacrifice his ideals for the more prosaic occupation of instructor in a girls' school. Early in his engagement he had even dared to write his love verses on official stationery, but now, in the eighth year of his engagement, he disavows these extravagances of his imagination for fear of losing his position. At rare intervals only does he yield to the temptations of amorous raving, namely, when his eternal fiancée sings her love song, "Ach, du lieber Augustin." His fiancée also has lost almost all of her loving nature except an old-maidish eroticism. Pastor Strohmann too, who once had been admired as a genius and who had eloped with his fiancée in a spirit of romantic adventure, has degenerated to the stage of a poor bread-earner, a farmer-pastor, a childish and thoughtless propagator of the human race; his constant praise of the family idyll in the traditional manner of the Biedermeier is the only shabby and threadbare justification he can give for his bovine stupidity.

In the relation between Falk and Schwanhild Ibsen seeks a more positive solution of the problem. Falk is at first nothing more than a superficial egotist, whose cheap mockeries hardly suffice to raise him above his environment, and whose affection for Schwanhild is no more refined than Pastor Strohmann's propagative instinct. Consistent with his theories, although not convincing in the psychological motivation, Falk abandons his desire for marriage; for he believes the indissoluble obligation of marriage would be a constant menace to any deeper relation. A poet, he can consent only to active and dynamic relationships; acceptance of an institutional relationship would be treason against human nature and even more against his poetic calling, which, according to Ibsen, presupposes an ever-active concern with the problems of life. By a prudent match with the elderly Goldstad, Schwanhild somewhat inconsistently and unnecessarily sacrifices her personal freedom in order to further Falk's ideal aim.

Such idealization of the sacrifice of a woman's life for a man's calling is untenably one-sided. It is characteristic of how slowly Ibsen's individual and personal experience developed into a universal moral demand. Correspondingly, the comedy form and a certain superficiality in the characterization must be taken as an indication that the author has not yet realized all the implications of his moral principle. Falk's sacrifice is at most only the renunciation of a short pleasure and not of the happiness of life; and his poetry is mere dilettantism and as such dependent upon the acclamation of the society which he wants to entertain. But the character of Schwanhild, with her determination and her willingness to sacrifice, suggests that her attitude is meant as a criticism of himself and an expression of his desire to find a deeper foundation of life.

This self-educating significance of *Love's Comedy* was greatly increased by the effect of its presentation on the stage, since not only was the idea of the play criticized, but the character of the author himself was attacked by his gossipy critics. Failure and disappointment raised the resultant conflict and scepticism, which he had sought to clarify in his dramatic works from *Catiline* on, to the tragic consciousness which alone can create a genuine and important poetic symbol. The poet has to pass through the stage of the deepest sorrows of doubt in order to find his real self. He whose work had been inspired by a patriotic movement needed the pressure of a bitter experience in order that the counteracting will of absolute self-assertion might be aroused in him. A deep personal crisis, with despair on the one side and belief in himself on the other, this is the experience through which Ibsen had to pass in order to attain to European significance. The attacks upon his personal integrity and his consequent suffering must be considered as a boon of fate, for they were necessary in order to raise his fame above that of Björnson, whom he envied for his influence on his compatriots. It was a boon, because it gave him inner contact with the most essential problem of his time: the crisis of the individual whose intellectual independence and moral will conflict with an environment rotten with superficial lust for power and other tendencies of mechanized civilization.

Bishop Nikolaus, in *The Pretenders*, is a degenerate character typical of this situation. Without any inner calling, without physical or moral justification, he conceals the hollowness of his desire for power without responsibility under the ideal mask of his pastoral office. Since he cannot assume wordly power, his only aim and the only content of his life is to spread discord and hatred among all those who might attain more power or more positive ends than he. So he becomes a mephistophelean caricature of the irresponsible materialist concealing his inhumanity under a disguise sanctioned by tradition.

Whereas Bishop Nikolaus represents only the negative side of the problem, Jarl Skule, "God's stepchild on earth," as his more fortunate adversary Haakon calls him, is torn between an undaunted lust for power and an equally invincible reverence for traditional rights, a fate which he shares with the poet and his contemporaries. He forfeits one chance after another of seizing the royal power, by waiting for a legitimate succession to the throne, always ready to bow to those who present a better claim, but always inhibited from proving his inner right and drawn to violence whenever the legal rights of his opponent seem doubtful to him. The doubt in himself and his inner value makes him blind to the proper task of the king, who should place the peace and the harmony of his people above all egotism and personal ambition. Therefore, he must be defeated by the creator of the "royal idea," Haakon, for whom the calling of a king is an absolute and impersonal ideal, not the right of kings but service to the people, a royal duty. But he, too, is surpassed in human value by those women who are capable of unlimited sacrifice, who rebel against the inhumanity

[186]

of the masculine calling, but who, on the other hand, are not conscious enough of the values they represent to oppose their ideal of charity to the hatred of men.

In the character of Haakon, the ethical will is still connected with the demand of national unity. Ibsen's expectations, however, are shaken by the attitude of his compatriots during the Danish war of 1864. Their failure to support the Scandinavian cause against the German and Austrian invaders was for him proof that their nationalism was but hollow oratory, and Ibsen could not free himself from the guilt of egotistic unresponsiveness. He, too, was able to give his will for unreserved sacrifice only an esthetic expression, without realizing it in active life. Disappointed he now leaves his home country in order to free himself from the demoralizing tendencies of his environment. In a letter written from Rome in 1865, he himself attributes this effect to his departure from Norway; only absence from his country, he says, could give him independence from the thoughtless uniformity, the empty self-glorification, the irresponsible inactivity of his countrymen:

> It was of decisive importance for me to gain sufficient distance from our own conditions in order to see the hollowness behind these self-created lies of our so-called public life and the pitifulness of all the empty talk which is never at a loss for words, when the point is to swagger about a "great cause," but which never has the will nor the power nor the obligation to do great deeds. How often does one not hear people talk about Norwegian level-headedness with deepest satisfaction, when they really do not mean anything but that luke-warm temperature of the blood which makes it impossible for an honest soul to commit folly in the grand style. The herd is well drilled, that cannot be denied; it has a uniformity exemplary in its kind; the same pace for every one.*

This struggle to be free from his heritage of continuous compromise is dramatically expressed in *Brand*.

> Room within the wide world's span,
> Self completely to fulfill, —
> That's a valid right of Man,
> And no more than that I will!
> To fulfill oneself! And yet
> With a heritage of debt?   (Act II)

A "heritage of debt" and an impending danger is the compromise attitude with which all ideal demands are accepted and applied to the issues of life:

*Letter to Magdalene Thorsen, December 3, 1865, translated from the German.

> A little pious in the pew,
> A little grave, — his father's way, —
> Over the cup a little gay, —
> It was his father's fashion too!
>
> . . . .
>
> Partial in good, partial in ill,
> Partial in great things and in small; —
> But here's the grief — that, worst or best,
> Each fragment of him wrecks the rest! (Act I)

Men are always motivated by considerations of material comfort and material care. Brand's mother suppresses her love for the poor son of a tenant-farmer and sells her body to an unloved man; her greed degenerates into avarice so that she cannot see the worthlessness of material possession even in the face of death, and would rather risk eternal condemnation than sacrifice her earthly goods. The peasant cannot control his cowardly fear of the avalanche even when the salvation of his dying daughter is at stake. The official representative of the church is not concerned about the individual soul; his aim is rather to use the influence of the church and its ritual to subdue a mass of people to the absolute authority of the state:

> Let each his own excrescence pare,
> Neither uplift him, nor protrude,
> But vanish in the multitude. (Act V)

Realization of the ideal of individual responsibility would be treason against the church and state.

Brand seeks to overcome this steady conflict between theoretical rejection of materialism and yet practical adherence to it by fighting for the absolute realization of the idea. He sacrifices his ambitious plans to be pastor of a large and influential community in order to devote himself completely to the small and poor community in a remote valley hidden even from the rays of the sun. He sacrifices his child and his wife and all the ambitions of his life, and through his example he imbues his parishioners with the spirit of sacrifice. But they are not capable of following him in the service of the highest impersonal God, who lives far from all earthly bonds in the infiniteness of nature. The phantom of a large catch of herring suffices to nullify the effects of his idealistic preaching and example. He is abused and stoned by those for whom he had sacrificed everything in order to free them from their selfish enjoyment of earthly pleasures and to guide them into a life of

[188]

higher spiritual values. In complete despair over the materialism of his age, without the consolation which Grillparzer's Libussa found in a similar vision, Brand meets a welcome death under an avalanche released by the arrow of the insane Gerd. His last question to his God is:

> God, I plunge into death's night, —
> Shall they wholly miss thy Light
> Who unto man's utmost might
> Will'd

whereupon he receives the mysterious answer:

> He is the God of Love. (Act V)

Brand's tragedy proves the cruel fate of his idealistic demand, "All or Nothing"; he is forsaken, mocked, persecuted, and finally redeemed by an insane woman; he is lost in a world which is opposed to any advance toward what is essentially human, and which is degenerating steadily into a materialistic civilization:

> Hearts that fall of brothers rends not,
> Nor their own to fury frets,
> Hammer-wielding, coining, filing;
> Light's last gleam forlornly flies . . . (Act V)

Only one consolation remains: God is Love. But who God is, and who is to benefit from His love, whether it is to affect only those radical searchers for truth like Brand, or whether it implies a sympathy with all human nature, which in its idealistic striving is bound by the conditions of life on this earth—these questions are not answered in this drama. *Brand* cannot be Ibsen's final answer; for an idealism which cannot keep men at the height to which they have attained by their striving, which destroys life instead of uplifting it, such an idealism elicits the question whether only the realized ideal has value, or whether man's dependence upon his physical nature is so strong that the least spark of a higher and striving nature is venerable and worthy of divine Love. Ibsen is already so remote from the times of an enthusiastic idealistic conviction that he himself cannot escape this human doubt. He can combat the demoralizing influence of the rising materialism which characterizes the latter part of the nineteenth century only by holding before himself and his audience the example of inexorable severity and an absolute ethical will. He must also show the moral insufficiency of man and his constant danger of corruption by material interests as the indispensable complement and justification for his absolute postulate.

Brand's ethical conduct was guided by the principle of a categorical "be thyself," which is defined by the Button-Moulder in *Peer Gynt* as self-mortification, as renunciation of all egotistic interests in favor of a sympathetic devotion to others. Opposed to this principle is Peer Gynt's hypothetical imperative of egotism, "Be sufficient to yourself," an attitude which is symbolized in the Boyg, who, with smoothness and opportunism, avoids all decisions which can be made only on the basis of a moral principle. Opportunism and moral principle are mutually exclusive, and, in this drama, Ibsen rejects any compromise because of its demoralizing effect on character and the relation between men; yet, the last word of this drama, as of *Brand*, is not moral rigorism but love, sympathy with the inborn weakness of man. Peer is not wanton by nature; circumstances and education are responsible for his lack of principles; a prodigal father spoiled him and a shallow mother deceived him about the real tasks of life. This situation not only reflects Ibsen's personal experience, but also the typical conflict of the Norwegian and the Central European during the second half of the nineteenth century: the conflict between pleasure-hunting Epicureanism and romanticism which had lost the force of its conviction. With this heritage, Peer degenerates in meaningless adventures and wanton sensuality instead of following Solveig who might have saved and developed his true character. The poet leads him along a symbolic way through the stormy desert, where he experiences how his soul is destroyed by the satisfaction of his lowest instincts, without, however, having the courage to enjoy the pleasure of voluptuousness without reserve. He emigrates to America, where he makes his fortune as a shipowner and a slave trader; but the more he devotes himself to his business, the more he loses his inner self. Miserable and shipwrecked, and yet too cowardly to die, he returns to his home country. It would be fitting that Peer, who was never genuinely good, and who at the same time never dared to be a real sinner, be melted in the ladle of the Button-Moulder and that he lose his identity, since he had never been himself, but always a slave of superficial things and considerations. Yet he is saved by *caritas* in the person of Solveig, whose love he betrayed, for he has lived on in her and she in him, although only in his subconscious mind; and this seemingly negligible human relation is sufficient to preserve his human character. It may be, as many have maintained, that Peer does not deserve salvation. The fact that Ibsen, however, grants him salvation and redemption,

[190]

proves how firmly he was convinced of the tragic burden placed upon man by his double nature, especially in a period of a material progress which favors the expression of his lower egotistic instincts.

In his first dramas, Ibsen dealt with the conditionality of human nature as a psychological phenomenon without any further theoretical reflection on the implications of such a view. Historical symbols were used not so much out of any necessity inherent in the problem, as they were inspired by the secondary intention of creating a national theater. In *Brand* and *Peer Gynt* the conception of man is clarified to such an extent that the absolute ethical demand could be regarded only as a regulative principle, while moral judgment was humanized in a sympathetic understanding of the relativity of all earthly endeavor.

Compared with the conclusions of *Brand* and *Peer Gynt*, the drama *The Emperor and the Galilean* presents an even deeper understanding of the human situation, for here the conditionality of existence is interpreted not only as a psychological, but also as an historical and metaphysical problem. Man is no longer conceived of as an individual in an abstract and unrelated existence, but as an individual belonging to a very definite historical period, which in turn determines the conduct of man according to its specific superindividual laws in such a way that man's assumed freedom is simultaneously a historical necessity.

Julian.	What is my mission?
The Voice.	To establish the empire.
Julian.	What empire?
The Voice.	The empire.
Julian.	And by what way?
The Voice.	By the way of freedom.
Julian.	Speak clearly! What is the way of freedom?
The Voice.	The way of necessity.

(*Caesar's Apostasy*, Act III)

Freedom and necessity, in this historico-metaphysical sense, govern the actions of the individual in whom actual tendencies of the historical moment are combined in such a way that the individual becomes the most important instrument for historical progress. This is the question which Ibsen, like Hebbel before him, asks himself with regard to the situation of his age: has our time reached the point at which we can be sure that we are moving to a higher cultural level?

Ibsen professed his belief in the principle of historical progress at a banquet in Stockholm in the year 1877: "On several occasions it has been said that I am a pessimist. And so I am, insofar as I do not believe in the eternal duration of human ideals. But I am an optimist, insofar as I believe in the possibility of propagating and developing ideals. Especially and more specifically, do I believe that the ideals of our time in their decline are moving toward that stage which I indicated in my drama *The Emperor and the Galilean* by the term 'the third empire.' " The third empire which Ibsen describes in this drama is a cultural stage similar to that which Heinrich Heine had longed for, a condition in which a synthesis of the ancient ideal of physical beauty and the Christian ideal of truth would be achieved, or, if we project the problem back into the nineteenth century, a synthesis of Young-German liberalistic emancipation of the flesh and of idealistic spiritualism. But the time is conceived as declining toward a lower level of morality and as not yet ripe for a higher synthesis: "The old beauty is no longer beautiful, and the new truth is no longer true" (Part I, Act II).

Julian Apostate, who represents the new ideal, expresses also the sorrowful disillusionment that the time for its realization has not yet arrived. He has neither the pagan robustness of conscience which allows his brother Gallos to commit Caesarian brutalities among the Christians of Antioch nor even that of Emperor Constantius, who is driven by his distrust into superstitious Christian fear and to the murder of his relatives. Julian's sensuality, his vanity, and his ambition are the heritage of his pagan origin. To his Christian education he owes a metaphysical interest which reveals to him the insufficiency of Christianity, the one-sidedness of the doctrine of the other world, the worldliness of the church and its adherents, and the general conflict between life and doctrine. He laments the loss of his pagan temper in the contact with Christianity. His natural sensuality has degenerated into mere estheticism, which is constantly disillusioned by the decadent and orgiastic form in which Greek beauty appears at his time. Julian's vanity fluctuates between festival displays "with roses in his hair" and the cynicism of wandering about in the disguise of a beggar. In his ambition, Caesarian madness and a Christian-like self-sacrifice for the idea of the Third Empire are combined. As he comes to recognize more and more the futility of his struggle for the realization of this idea, his actions degenerate more and more into a foolish caricature of a genuinely active existence. This degeneration is signalized by his writing of pamphlets, the content of which becomes increasingly inessential and childish. Furthermore, he loses his ability to judge men and circumstances according to their real value, so that he finally must admit his defeat by the Galilean. But the latter's victory is not a complete victory. Most of his followers are opportunists who adhere to the Christian faith only because it is the prevailing custom, and who therefore are always ready to apostasize, if this apostasy promises a material advantage. They persecute the heathen the more ardently, the more booty they can expect from them, and when the heathen have been defeated and plundered, they turn with the same fervor and intolerance against those of their Christian brethren who by chance belong to another sect. The essence of Christianity, too, has disappeared from life and is buried in books. Since it appeared later on the historical scene, it is a somewhat more living force than the earlier paganism; there are still Christians who would sacrifice their lives as martyrs for their conviction, and who, like Basilios and Macrina, practice love of their enemy as their religious duty.

The aim of Julian's unsuccessful striving is, therefore, justified; it is deprived of its original character only as something which is imminent and inescapable, and appears as a hypothetical aim: if we can expect any progress at all, it can only be in the direction which is indicated in Julian's desires and hopes. Julian's fate is the tragedy of man in a period of transition; the historical tendencies become conscious in him, but without reaching a real and decisive harmony. It is his tragedy that he realizes the necessity of future development before the energies of his environment have converged in the new aim. It is his tragedy that his superhuman will degenerated to inhumanity, that he sank from the sublime to the ridiculous, merely because the historical moment had not arrived. It is the tragedy of the nineteenth century, as Ibsen experienced it in himself.

Whereas Ibsen had shown in *The Emperor and the Galilean* the historical conditionality of human action and will, he begins to understand man in his social determination in the *League of Youth*. This intrigue-play, the structure of which follows the French pattern, is in the main an attempt of the poet to free himself from the two Norwegian parties—the liberals and the conservatives—which fought against him or claimed him as a supporter of their principles, whereas he considered both attitudes as equally dangerous. Therefore, he presents the conservatives as well as the League of Youth—which poses as a liberal organization—as equally guided by egotism and opportunism, although the representative of the liberals is more severely criticized: for his demagogic phrase-mongering, his appeal to the lower instincts, and his absolute lack of character. In spite of the typical and superficial treatment of

[193]

the theme, we find in this drama the beginning of Ibsen's later socio-analytical studies; for he ascribes to even this liberal demagogue the extenuating circumstances of low birth, the brutality of his parents, and a school eduation which was more concerned with the training of abilities than with the development of character. This drama, too, ends on a note of resignation and criticism. This, the poet implies, is a picture of our time, in which no one is really himself; everyone is actuated by non-essential interests. Yet this situation does not lead to catastrophe, because almost all people are just so, and, being so, they understand and get along with each other. Our time is sick, to be sure; ideas which once represented real values and convictions have become mere political shibboleths in the service of materialistic aims. But we are not yet ready for a transition to a higher stage. Thus *The League of Youth* comes to a conclusion similar to that of *The Emperor and the Galilean*, which, in fact, was finished somewhat later than the former.

In this latter drama, the historical situation—the present moment as projected into a distant past—is conceived as a tension between two strata of different age. Both are guided by ideas and ideals which have once been living issues; but both have lost their convincing power and their influence upon men, although in different degrees according to their age.

The depiction of man in his dependence upon the social forces which began with *The League of Youth* is related in *Pillars of Society* to the conception of man as a historically determined being. If this does not lead immediately to a deeper exposition of the problem, it may be attributed to the fact that Ibsen in this drama is still too much on the defensive against the influence of the social norms upon his inner self and that he, therefore, uses the drama as a vehicle for criticizing society, as he did in *League of Youth*. The characters are exaggerated and caricatured, their motivation is improbable, and the artistic objectivation of the problem is neglected in order to attack the hypocrisy of society and the decline of its Christian ideals. Thus, the Christian virtue of charity is shown as a traditional and merely perfunctory observance, deprived of its former meaning and vitality. It is replaced by moral complacency which finds its satisfaction in gossip about the immorality of others; by hard-hearted condemnation of one's fellowmen, though their motives and intentions be unknown; by an absolute segregation from the world insofar as it does not offer any material for such moral gossip. With its prejudices and its religious and moral self-deception, such a society has lost every genuine and immediate contact with men, and its attitude must evoke in any naturally sympathetic individual the desire to escape into a world where there are fewer "decent and moral" people, as Ibsen himself did. For the norms of this society encourage just that immorality which it pretends to combat. Consul Bernick feels compelled to conceal the consequences of his relation with Dina's mother; to throw suspicion on his brother, and to drive him abroad; to repudiate his beloved and to marry her unloved but wealthy sister; to endanger willfully and consciously the life of the crew and the passengers of an entire boat in order to save and to improve his moral standing in society and his economic position, which is dependent thereon. The order of values which is preached in this group is the exact reverse of that revealed in their actions. Material profit is the actual driving force, whereas the ideal values have degenerated into a barely concealing mask for the lower instincts and the inner emptiness from which this society suffers. True, the main "pillar of society," the potential criminal Bernick, is finally moved to a public confession through a series of badly motivated incidents such as the unexpected return of his former mistress, Lona Hessel, and of his brother Johann; the latter's love for Dina, who is believed to be his natural daughter; his own son's escape on the boat which, according to his plans, was to be wrecked on the high seas. Yet such a confession is but a pitifully theatrical disguise for the dramatic challenge of a society to be regenerated on the foundation of absolute truth. It is a demand which is less sensationally, but more convincingly presented in the reaction of the genuinely truthful characters, women like Lona, Martha, and Dina; it would have become even more effective without the forced evasion of a tragic ending. But a tragedy presupposes a deeper understanding of the human problem than Ibsen reached in this drama.

In *Pillars of Society*, the degeneration of ideals which had been a living force in the past, and its demoralizing effect on the present, appeared as a casual development in a remote small town which had resisted the progress of modern civilization. The drama still bears traces of the poet's anger over the treatment his works had received in his fatherland, and over the restraint which life in the petit-bourgeois atmosphere had imposed upon him and from which he could not inwardly emancipate himself.

In their attitude toward their fellow men the majority will always be determined by conventional and traditional standards, and only a selected few will be guided by their natural sympathies and the merit of the individual case. In *A Doll's House* Ibsen accepts this differen-

[195]

tiation of men as a normal social phenomenon. Ordinary man is a being like Helmer, a model husband and master of the family, who sees in his wife a somewhat inferior comrade. Her main function is to intersperse the monotony of his professional life with the joyful entertainment of her dancing, reciting, and singing. He is the pedantic householder who does not dare to contract any debts, even if the only chance of non-payment would be his sudden death caused by a tile falling from a roof. He is an official with the strictest sense of duty and a timid concern for his dignity, always afraid that this dignity might be endangered by the familiar *Du* of a subordinate or by the rumor that his wife might exert some influence on his professional decisions. He is so honest that he gives up his position as a lawyer because he would occasionally have to defend criminal cases. He is an enemy of untruth, which, if admitted at one place, might overthrow the entire bourgeois order. If Helmer is alarmed at Nora's thoughtless forgery and afraid of its legal and professional consequences, this is the only normal reaction from a man so well rooted in bourgeois society as he. From this standpoint, we are inclined to excuse his egotism when he first sees in Nora's confession of her well-meant forgery a menace to his personal interests, and when he generously pardons the "criminal"—after the danger for himself is over—and when he finally feels flattered that his playmate now needs his benign protection so much more. If he makes himself a bit ridiculous with his heroism, which fails miserably when confronted with the facts, that, too, is such a common occurence in everyday life that one can not condemn Helmer for it. Yet we are not supposed to sympathize with him, and we cannot, because the whole tenor of the play concentrates all our sympathy on Nora. If we feel naïvely with Nora, then it seems right to commit forgery for the sake of a beloved man. From her point of view, it was fully justified to violate the outward forms of law and society by fulfilling in a higher sense their inner spirit. Just as naïvely, she considers it right to keep the secret of the forgery from her husband in order to increase her value in his eyes, "when her beauty shall wane."

Furthermore, should Nora fail to win our sympathy, it would nevertheless not go out to Helmer. We should admire, in second place, another example of womanly heroism, Mrs. Linden. After the failure of a money-match, she uses all her energy to reïnstate her first lover, Krogstad, in the good graces of a world which despises him for his dishonest conduct.

In everyday life we should accept Helmer's conduct at its face value.

But with Ibsen, who compels us to examine it more searchingly, we reject Helmer's bourgeois living. We recognize with disgust that the fear which Helmer betrays in an unguarded moment is the basic motive of his actions: the fear of deviating from the norms which regulate the conduct of his class; the fear of losing his reputation; the fear of the law and of gossip; the fear of jeopardizing his external dignity by a confidential relation to one of his subordinates; the fear of undermining the system of bourgeois order in which his economic and moral existence is rooted. He lacks all genuine, independent feeling for values. According to his own words, he can more readily overlook Krogstad's deficiencies than tolerate the menace to his official dignity. His conduct is entirely regulated by his concern for the conventionalities which dominate the social group to which he belongs. Actually it is cowardice without any principles. Although Helmer's conduct assumes an appearance of vigor, since it is firmly guided by pedantically followed norms, yet in this rigidity it is but the lifeless caricature of the idealistic freedom in voluntary subordination under the moral law. Helmer's attitude is inner and external dependence on what others expect from him and on what they might say or think of him. It is dependence on the past, for these everyday norms have validity only because they have been followed for decades and centuries. What this average man lacks is the natural simplicity and the human sympathy which would enable him to experience the situation without any bias, the courage to judge a situation on its own merits, and the active moral feeling which is capable of laying down the principles of its decisions for itself. Ibsen finds this feeling to be more active in women than in men; for men, according to his opinion, are responsible for the amoral, if not immoral authoritarianism of a one-sided "man-made civilization." The overcoming of this situation by the natural feeling of women is his desire. But the belief in this regeneration is again tainted with the scepticism of a late idealism. Nora has won over Helmer, she has humiliated him, and she is going to leave him; but will she not return to him as a good bourgeois and a subservient playmate?

Even if Ibsen had not explicitly confirmed his opinion that "nobody can present in poetic form anything for which there is not, to a certain degree or at least at certain times, a model within himself,"* we should have to see in the conflict between Helmer and Nora the dramatization of his own problems, which assumed a more general meaning for him when he saw others struggling with the same conditions. The problem

*To the Norwegian Students, September 10, 1874.

of man's dependence on the ideas of the past receives a deeper and more impressive interpretation in this drama, since the conflict of the past with the living demands of the present is here projected into one single individual, instead of being impersonated in two different antagonists. Man's personality is thus recognized in its historical stratification, that is both past and present are formative elements of his conscience. In effect this stratification already occurs in Ibsen's early dramas when he created such broken characters as Cataline, Sigmund, Jarl Skule, and Julian. It was, however, always presented statically as an actual break, or at the most, as an increasing demoralization, but not dynamically and progressively as an ethical self-liberation from the heritage of the past which divides the individual conscience. This clear conception of the Self in its temporal stratification is dramatically presented in *Ghosts*. Darwin's explanation of the atavism in the structure of the human body may have contributed to the clarification of this psychological and moral problem, with which Ibsen himself was wrestling, the "conflict between word and deed, between will and task, in general between life and doctrine."*

Helene had submitted to the traditional marriage laws and had accepted from the family council the hand of the wealthy, but unloved and licentious chamberlain, Alvin. She had, upon the pious admonition of her lover and her friend, Pastor Manders, obeyed the laws of the church concerning the indissolubility of matrimony and had endured the martyrdom of this marriage until the death of her husband; she had borne a son to him and taken upon herself the sacrifice of being separated from this only child in order to protect him from the demoralizing example of his father. Even after the father's death, Helene had an orphanage built in honorable memory of his name in order to present toward the outside world the appearance of a happy union. She sacrificed her life for the sham values of a dead tradition and of a cowardly convention, following the standards which had been imposed on her by her family, by society, by the church and the state, but suppressing the natural, trustworthy impulse of her moral conscience. Only in the loneliness of her fundamentally immoral marriage with Alving did she free herself from the "ghosts," the residues of the "old dead belief"; the belief that marriage as such is a sacred institution, no matter whether the particular marriage contract was entered into out of love or out of materialistic considerations, under pressure on the part of conventional relatives; the belief in the authority of a church, which

Ibid.

[198]

for the sake of general respect for her moral system forces an immoral action upon the individual, and the representatives of which are more interested in the preservation of external appearances than in truth itself, which they claim to protect. In a brave fight she won the intellectual freedom which she hopes will allow her finally to live her own life. But the past lives on in her environment and in herself. Again and again it rises as a ghost out of the deeper strata of herself, or, coming from the outside, causes an emotional reaction in her which makes an independent decision of will impossible.

The dependence on convention and tradition was the first link in a causal chain which, with cruel tragic irony, resulted in catastrophe at a moment when she believed that she had won her inner freedom. It was her yielding to tradition which was responsible for her return to her diseased husband, for the birth of Oswald, and consequently for the latter's insanity. By inventing the myth of an exemplary father, she had driven her son to morbid self-reproach and thereby hastened the outbreak of his malady. The burning of the orphanage, erected to perpetuate this myth, gives Oswald the nervous shock which, together with the erotic excitement caused by Alving's natural daughter Regina, completes his fate. It is a last unbroken tie to her conventional past that places her before the most difficult decision, one which can be made only with complete inner freedom: since she has brought Oswald to this subhuman state, will she now be strong enough to free him by giving him poison, as she promised? But whether she is capable of keeping her promise or not, her tragedy remains the same, the tragedy of one who is fighting for her inner freedom and is made to realize what an extraordinary sacrifice in human happiness she has had to make to a dead, yet still overpowering past. Helene Alving deserves the happiness, the "sun" for which her son is reaching at the beginning of his dementia. Ibsen, however, cannot give her this happiness, for her tragedy is to be a challenge of liberation from "old and dead views, from piteous dread of light;" it must demand a new autonomous morality and the responsibility for the happiness of one's own life and that of coming generations. Such happiness, which has its foundation in autonomy and responsibility, is the ideal which arises from such a catastrophe. To urge this moral attitude upon man, is the sense of this tragedy. Those who never attain to moral autonomy are spared the tragic complication of life, but their existence will remain devoid of any deeper meaning. People of the type of pastor Manders cannot but have either a comical or a frightening effect upon a serious mind,

[199]

for their naiveté and their fear blind them to the evils they continually create. Nothing can be more contradictory in itself than Manders' position, which should involve the highest moral freedom, but which, by its official character, forces him to yield to popular criticism and thereby place himself in the service of immorality, by accepting the protectorate over Engstrand's sailors' hostel. He has never struggled for real freedom and he deserves his fate, which serves as a warning for those who fear the fight with the ghosts of the past.

This drama defends the ideal of responsible self-realization against a world submerged in opportunism and egotism, or, regarded from a literary point of view, romantic idealism against bourgeois realism. This explains the form of the drama: it explains the naturalistic description, based upon the theory of heredity, of the causes and the beginning of Oswald's disease; it explains the technical concentration of the action in the final moment just before the catastrophe; it explains the realistic technique of the dialogue with its continual revelations and surprises, the so-called analytical exposition, which gives the last premise for the understanding of the events towards the end of the drama. Most of these traits, which are characteristic of the nineteenth century, are taken over by the naturalists. This technique was, however, not chosen by Ibsen for its naturalism, but as a symbol for the effective presentation of the ideal. In spite of his concessions to naturalistic determinism, Ibsen continues the tradition of romantic idealism. In this respect, we may compare him with the romanticist E. T. A. Hoffmann whose stories combined a strong realism with a sometimes phantastic idealism; the emphasis, however, has decidedly shifted from the idealistic to the realistic and naturalistic side.

The content and the technique of the drama *An Enemy of the People* are more closely related to those of *Pillars of Society* than those of *Ghosts*. It was planned while Ibsen was engaged in the controversy over *A Doll's House* and was completed while the attacks on *Ghosts* were raging. Therefore, *An Enemy of the People* again reflects Ibsen's disappointment over a public which in its hypocritical indignation at open discussion of the "unmentionable" disease and the author's attitude towards incest-marriage and euthanasia failed to comprehend the moral postulates of the drama. Ibsen's bitterness appears especially in the manner in which the hero defends his thesis that the "compact majority" is always wrong, and in the complement to that statement, which immediately suggests itself, that the minority is always right.

In spite of all personal polemics, the idea of the "temporal" conception of man is further developed in this drama; but, as is often the case with Ibsen, its theoretical presentation is clearer than its dramatic visualization. Truth is a living entity, which by its very nature is in constant evolution:

> A normally-constituted truth lives — let us say — as a rule, seventeen or eighteen years; at the outside twenty; very seldom more. And truths so patriarchal as that are always shockingly emaciated.
> (Act IV)

Since the development of truth can be achieved only by the individual, and since truth in its advanced stage reaches the broad masses but very slowly, Ibsen arrives at a relation between the individual and the mass similar to Hebbel's:

> the few . . . who have made all the new, germinating truths their own . . . . . . stand, as it were, at the outposts, so far in the van that the compact majority has not yet reached them — and there they fight for truths that are too lately born into the world's consciousness to have won over the majority.
> (Ibid.)

While Hebbel finds this tragic aloofness of the higher individual from the masses only in periods of transition, Ibsen declares it to be the ever recurring and inescapable tragedy of mankind. In the case of both dramatists, the superior individual has the relative consolation of suffering as a martyr of a "new truth"; but the Hebbelian idealistic faith in human progress toward truth is tempered in the case of Ibsen by the cynical conviction that the hero's suffering is in vain, that he is so far ahead of his time that he will never be overtaken. For as soon as the new truths have become the possession of the majority, they have become so old that they are no longer true; they are "truths so stricken in years that they are sinking into decrepitude. When a truth is so old as that, it's in a fair way to become a lie."* Ibsen speaks of "truths," while Hebbel expresses himself more clearly when he speaks of moral attitudes; but the context in which this passage occurs in *An Enemy of the People*, especially when it is considered in the light of Ibsen's whole development, leaves no doubt but that "truth" means not so much intellectual knowledge as inner truthfulness, a vital reaction to an actual situation.

It is this reaction which differentiates the characters of this drama as it does those of other dramas. Most remote from this inner truthfulness is the burgomaster and his "compact majority." They expose the

Ibid.

visitors of the bathing resort to the dangers of a gastric fever rather than vote for the necessary sanitary measures, and hide their inhuman avarice behind the hypocritical phrases: submission of the individual to the common weal and to the authorities who protect the interests of the community (*Act I*). It is the same lack of truthfulness which is passed from one generation to the other at home and in school, by an education based on the principle that what is supported by public opinion may be taught and done, no matter how much opinion contradicts the inner conviction and the principle of humanity. Whoever fails to heed such opinion is an "enemy of the people."

Although Ibsen voices his views about the ruinous, levelling effect of liberalistic majority rule through the words and deeds of Dr. Stockmann, he nevertheless does not completely identify himself with him: "The doctor is a greater muddle-head than myself," he says in a letter of September 9, 1882. The doctor is somewhat too temperamental in his attacks, a little quarrelsome and conceited because he has participated in establishing the bathing resort and because he has achieved medical discoveries, which, however, threaten the existence of the resort. Above all, he possesses the diplomatic awkwardness of the idealists for whom knowing about an evil means immediately willing its abolition, and who therefore have always aroused the masses against themselves because of the radical form of their demands. Thus, Stockmann cannot escape the fate to which the idealists of Brand's type are exposed in a "temporally" stratified society; ostracism, the tragedy of which is only relieved by his decision to devote his life to the education of truthful men, a decision which is practically impossible of realization in the given environment and which can only be interpreted as a symbol of Ibsen's hope for the survival of an advance guard of truth.

Even more than in *Brand, A Doll's House* and *Ghosts*, truth is represented in *An Enemy of the People* by a character who himself is human and "temporal," that is, conditioned and limited by his peculiarities; a person who, in spite of his striving, is somewhat affected by the egotistic spirit of his time; whose idealism, on the other hand, is so one-sided that it blinds him to actual conditions and the possibility of improvement. He fails to see that life means development and necessarily presupposes, on the one hand, a minority which paves the way and establishes new rules for action, and which "is justified because it has an intimate pact with the future,"* and, on the other hand, a restraining mass thriving on the truths which trickle down in the course of time,

Letters, Jan. 3, 1882

and which therefore hardly ever permit an original and vital reaction to the actual situation. This is the tragic fact, the recognition of which means bitter resignation for a champion of the idealistic principle such as Ibsen. It is this resignation which is the theme of *The Wild Duck*.

If real truth—inner truthfulness—is possible only in a small, intellectually and emotionally superior group, and if the mass of the people lives according to norms derived from a superior minority, there remain only two possibilities; either to try to educate more and more members of the mass for the higher stratum—which is Dr. Stockmann's plan— or to consider this situation of the masses as normal. In the latter case, the illusion of truth is a necessary substitute for the real possession of it; to take this illusion away from the masses would mean destroying their complacent happiness in moving thoughtlessly and easily along well-trodden paths. Such respect for tradition sacrifices the absolute value of truth, and life, or rather the happiness of life, is established as the basic value. Truth then becomes only a relative value, dependent upon its ability to further and deepen life and thus contribute to the increase of human happiness. As a foundation of life, it has value only for those who can deepen their human relations through immediate experience unhampered by the inhibitions of any norm imposed from without, whereas it may have a disturbing and even ruinous effect upon the average man. If the mass of people is opposed to the progress of truth, this is to be condemned under the point of view of the progressive principle, but it must be tolerated and approved as that attitude which corresponds to the intellectual and emotional abilities of the masses and therefore contributes most to their happiness.

In *A Doll's House* and in *Ghosts*, truth and happiness still coincided; in *An Enemy of the People* this equation seems to have become of dubious value. In *The Wild Duck* the two principles are consciously separated. Hjalmar Ekdal and Gina are leading a married life which is built on a lie; Gina is the former mistress of old Werle, and Hedwig is perhaps a child of this relation. With Werle's support and Gina's will to be a good housewife, the couple live an untroubled and, in spite of their poverty, contented life. Gina does all the work in the house and the shop, and Hjalmar, a lazy and egotistic day-dreamer, ruminates over an invention which will never take any concrete shape, but which as an illusion, serves the purpose of keeping him alive. Old Ekdal indulges in his passion for bear-hunting in the imaginary forests of the attic room and is happy when he has killed a tame rabbit, while in her youthful dreams Hedwig escapes a reality which is threatening her with blind-

[203]

ness. Into this idyll Gregers Werle intrudes as the representative of absolute truth. He takes it upon himself to give this marriage a sounder foundation in truth, but he succeeds only in estranging Hjalmar and Gina for a few hours, after which they return to their old thoughtless side-by-side existence—the price of Hjalmar's reconciliation is a substantial breakfast. Gregers attempts to awaken Hjalmar to an idealistic act of forgiveness toward Gina's and his father's child, by asking Hedwig to sacrifice her friend and playmate, the wild duck; he only succeeds in driving Hedwig to commit suicide in despair over her foster-father's sudden aversion. In this social stratum, illusion means everything, truth leads to catastrophe, and worse still, is a source of amusement for old sinners like Werle and his housekeeper Mrs. Sörby, who base their marriage on piquant confessions of their sexual aberrations. The old cynic Relling is apparently right when he says: "Life might be rather nice, if we could only be rid of these creditors who besiege us with their ideal demand." That human nature is capable of being truthful in Ibsen's sense of the word, is shown in young Hedwig's willingness to sacrifice. But life tears man down from his flights into the realms of idealism; like the injured duck, man dives into the depths of the swamp and sinks his teeth into tangle and seaweed. He loses his ability to experience the truth and to transform it into life-promoting energies. The pessimism expressed here is again deprived of absolute hopelessness, if one considers that in this drama, too, men are classified according to their ability to experience truth, and according to the complementary ability to make their own experience of truth a deep and enlivening experience in others. In this drama, a doltish, mad fanatic for truth undertakes to educate a person who has lost all capability of natural reaction.

In *Rosmersholm*, Ibsen turns more to the other side of the problem, the "advance guards" of truth. Are they at least capable of regulating their lives according to the principle of inner freedom? The freedom is similar to that of Helen Alving in *Ghosts*; she reached a high degree of inner freedom and found a tragic end mainly because she had been dependent upon tradition and convention in the past and then had made a decision, the consequences of which resulted in catastrophe just as she was ready to throw off the last fetters. In *Rosmersholm*, the external consequences of a former deed are not entirely missing. Before committing suicide, Beate had confided her jealous suspicions to her brother, Principal Kroll, and to Rosmer's enemy, Mortensgaard, and these accusations are raised against Rosmer in the hour of the catastrophe. But they have not the effect of an external fate, they only hasten his inner decision. Fate in this drama is the inner fate of a character in whom the historical stratification of Christian tradition and a pagan self-assertion, which looks only to the future, cannot be reconciled.

As a member of an old family of officials and army officers, Rosmer was born into a strong tradition. His obligation to his environment is further strengthened by his profession as a minister, which ties him to a dogmatic faith and makes his moral conduct a more or less public affair. This tie is all the stronger since faith and morality are, according to current belief, inseparably related, so that breaking with the faith of the past is considered a sign of moral degeneration. This dependence upon tradition is fatal for Rosmer; not so much because the outside world exerts its pressure upon him, but rather because he remains, in spite of his intellectual liberation, even more than Helene Alving, emotionally determined by the ideas of the past. His over-sensitive Christian conscience condemns him as guilty of Beate's death, although it was her hysterical disposition which almost forced him to accept Rebekka's affection as a mental balance. His conduct was the more excusable, since his almost sexless character guaranteed a merely "spiritual marriage." A man with less dependence upon traditional judgments should be able to master an even more real guilt without any detriment to his moral dignity; he should be able to draw from the consciousness of guilt the energies for an even more valuable life. In the last analysis, it is only a lack of active vitality, failure to see his aim concretely, that causes him to consider a guiltless conscience the fundamental prerequisite for educating an aristocracy of character. However much Rosmer may wish that his death atone for guilt of the past, it seems instead rather a sign of weakness, doubt in his own ability to will and to act and free his self in his actions. Rosmer appears as a precursor of Thomas Mann's characters, who pay for their intellectual refinement with a weakened vitality; that Rosmer, as the son of a major, chooses the ministry as his vocation points in this direction, too.

Rebekka is absolutely right when she answers Rosmer's demand of a guiltless conscience with the question whether man cannot be ennobled by pure love (*Act IV*). As a native of Finmarken, she inherited something of the unbroken pagan vitality; as a natural child and a mistress of her father (who was not known to her as such), she is free from the irrationalities of moral tradition, and, egotistically following her instincts, and without any scruples, she takes advantage

[205]

of the tension in Rosmersholm and hastens the catastrophe of Beate's derangement. In spite of that, she enters as a moral force in Rosmer's life. She attempts to persuade him courageously to deny the past and devote himself to the future. In order to help him overcome his dependence upon the past, she confesses her guilt, even at the risk of losing Rosmer's confidence. She makes her confession in the presence of Kroll, Rosmer's brother-in-law, so as to restore his honor before the outside world. All these sacrifices are in vain. Her death is the tragic renunciation of a life which aimed at synthesizing Christian altruism and Nordic vitality. In this respect *Rosmersholm* resumes the theme of *The Emperor and the Galilean;* the conflict theme is not developed any further, but the roots of the conflict have now been placed in the individual himself:

> The theme of the play is that conflict which every seriously-minded individual has to fight out for himself in order to establish a harmony between his life's conduct and his knowledge. For the various mental functions are not developed simultaneously and evenly in one and the same individual. The urge for possession hastens onward from gain to gain. Moral conscience, however, is very conservative. It is deeply rooted in traditions and in the past. Out of this situation arises the individual conflict.*

Ibsen's vitality is not strong enough to allow him to conform to the forces of the present, for he does not see any possibility of preserving the moral values of the idealistic past in an order which has life as its fundamental value.

The Lady from the Sea does not bring a completely satisfying solution which would really free the inner self of the poet; but the resignation here demanded contains some positive element. While Rebekka West inherited the unbroken spirit of the North, Ellida's home is the sea, the symbol of life with continuous flow, without direction and without aim. This indefinite lure of life is impersonated in the stranger; he is the object of Ellida's subconscious yearning; he prevents her from taking root in the sombre atmosphere of the remote little town on the Fjord; he is responsible for her pathologically vague and phantastic dreams. Her unrest, however, has a much more substantial cause in her lack of external and inner rootedness in her new environment. Wangel and his children still live upon the memories of their late wife and mother; Bolette, the oldest daughter, takes care of the household; and Ellida has married Wangel more for the sake of being pro-

*Letter, February 13, 1887; translated from the German

vided for than out of love. Thus, the life she leads in this family serves only to deprive her of external freedom and is without content and directive goal. This explains the hypnotic power of the stranger who lures her away into an indefinite and, in one respect, unrestrained future. Only one thing can retain her, the assurance that she, free from all external coercion, will be given a chance to become an integral part of Wangel's family. This assurance she finds in Hilda's loving devotion and in Wangel's renunciation of his legal rights. Her decision is not made with the absolute freedom of will which idealistic ethics demands. Absolute autonomy has become an illusion for Ibsen; Ellida simply acts without coercion. Her inner attachment to these people, whose deepest sympathy breaks forth in the moment of her greatest desolation, is the cause as well as the aim of her decision to remain with them. Her vitality receives in "free" responsibility a definite direction and with that a higher meaning. She is cured of her inner disturbance, which was but a symptom of her suppressed vitality and of her lack of a worthwhile goal, for the attainment of which she might have exerted her natural energies.

According to Ibsen, the courageous and irreverent vitality of paganism was broken by Christianity; it continues to thrive in the subconscious and has found its only possible expression in the intellectual sphere. Our life, however, is regulated by the responsibilities imposed on us by the exigencies of communal life. The inner attachment of man to man, the concrete mission in a concrete and limited circle, is a harmonizing moral force. This is also the standard by which the secondary characters of the drama are measured. On the one hand, there is Hilda with her unbroken energy, her irresponsibility, and curiosity, and Lyngstrand with his esthetic dreaming and playing, despite the imminence of death. Contrasted with them in their attitude toward life are Bolette with her complete resignation to an illusionless future in a prosaic marriage of convenience, and Ballested's perfect acclimatization to the small town by virtue of his innumerable "professions." These characters present life in its different stages of adjustment between the two poles of natural, directionless freedom and complete stagnation in a situation determined by external conditions. These different modes of life are less severely criticized than in *The Wild Duck*. This follows logically from Ibsen's increasingly deterministic conception of the will. Ellida is not submitted to any moral judgment either in her yearning for the stranger, or in her marriage of convenience, or even in her final decision; she is rather considered as a patient of life, and, accordingly, Wangel the doctor replaces Rosmer the minister and reformer. *The Lady from the Sea* is the product of a philosopher in whom the passions of life are still active, but who, at the same time, has learned to observe them with quiet reserve; it is the drama of a man who finally resigned himself to the fate of being rooted neither in his own fatherland, nor abroad, nor even in the heart of any relative or friend.*

Rebekka West and Ellida found an inner form for the urge of their vitality in the will to live a valuable life for others. In the attachment to and the responsibility for others they found a limitation which at the same time was an enrichment and a deepening of their womanly character. The protagonist of *Hedda Gabler* belongs to the same category of characters; she, too, inherited an unbroken nature with a claim to unlimited freedom from any duty and responsibility. Like Ellida, Hedda is at the beginning of her married life constrained only by the external forms of convention, which neither allow her to follow her desires with natural unconcern nor to give herself entirely to a valuable human mission; so that her shallow soul is poisoned by inactivity. Already in her youth her nature was confined by an aristocratic environment, and these limitations were strict enough to break her natural courage and cause her to seek in the habits and the judgments of others the standards for her own actions. These rules, however, have left enough freedom to prevent a strong self-assertion of her original nature. Riding, dancing, socially uncompromising admiration by a superficial society, Lövborg's tales about his erotic adventures—none of these have exceeded the sphere of the playful and the esthetic; everything has been accessible to her without any personal risk and, at least to her imagination, without any restriction. Thus, her capability of sympathetic understanding has remained undeveloped; neither human beings nor the creations of the human mind are capable of attracting her deeper interest.

Her marriage with Jörgen Tesman was perhaps that action of her life to which she had given the least thought; her only motive was to be provided for. Hedda hardly knew her husband before the wedding-trip, and then she only learned to despise him for his boring and learned stupidity, for his philistine tactlessness, for his corpulence and his constant perspiring. She hates his child even before it is born, not only because it is the child of this husband, but above all because she is unwilling to take any responsibility and is incapable of doing so.

Letters, June 3, 1897

[208]

In spite of all her voluptuousness, she has become so cowardly that she does not dare to follow her desires in a serious love affair with Lövborg, whom she likes for his licentiousness. Hedda's natural instinct is only strong enough to make her jealous of Thea and of the book which Lövborg wrote under her influence, and to impel her to test her womanly power over Lövborg's enervated character by trying to alienate him from his companion and inspirer. But she succeeds only in driving him to despair and into an "unesthetic" death, whereas she was expecting him to die a "free and beautiful" death, her only ideal. This defeat and disappointment, the fear of a void, pedantic, and philistine life with Jörgen, her aversion to maternity, and finally the attempted extortions of Brack, who knows about her guilt in Lövborg's death and places before her the choice between submission to his desires and scandal— the combination of all these factors forces the pistol into her hand.

Her self-destruction is the only act of her life, which one might be inclined to call free and courageous. But her death is no idealistic heroic act like that of Emilia Galotti. It is an escape from a world which has offered nothing to attract and develop her inner nature or direct her energies to humanly valuable activities; from a world which, on the other hand, deprived her of the possibility and capability of following her nature without restraint. It is less the tragic fate of Hedda Gabler which moves us (some critics even see in this drama the coldest and the least personal of all of Ibsen's works), than the tragedy of a materialistic period, in which men are only superficially stirred, but not deeply attached to anything; a tragedy from which Ibsen himself must have suffered more than others, because it was increased by his tragic feeling of homelessness. In this respect *Hedda Gabler* is the precursor of *John Gabriel Borkman*. It is an almost desperately tragic truth that Ibsen has expressed in this drama: true humanity consists of deep and responsible sympathy with others, the application of all vital energies in the service of others; yet he discovers nothing but superficiality and external activity around him; it is a time when only the well-adjusted average persons like Jörgen and Thea (the latter being, for that reason, less valuable than Hedda) have a good chance to survive.

In his last four dramas, *The Master Builder*, *Little Eyolf*, *John Gabriel Borkman* and *When We Dead Awaken*, Ibsen further refines this psychological analysis. Mental abnormalities, such as infantilism, autoeroticism, narcissism, and the like, occupy our interest to such an extent that we are inclined to forget the dramatic theme proper.* They

*Cf. the detailed analysis in H. Weigand, *The Modern Ibsen.*

contribute hardly anything new to the solution of Ibsen's life problem. In these dramas, Ibsen looks back on his life and work and asks himself whether the road he has chosen has been the right one, whether it has brought him closer to his aim or whether it has led him farther away from it. In various symbols, he conceives of his work as an evolution in three stages. He began with an idealistic faith in the future; he believed man could regenerate himself through developing his inner self in the struggle against mechanized traditional conduct. The second stage, during which he turned to the criticism and analysis of society, appears to him in retrospect as an apostasy from this idealism. He has outgrown all religious and national tradition; but, by his attempt to improve the foundations of human life and raise men to a more conscious existence based upon responsibility towards themselves, he has also destroyed the happiness of those unable to free themselves from the forces of the past. Now he has entered the third stage, in which he looks back on his achievement and in which the desire to return to the idealism of his youth reawakens. Only the unbroken faith of youth can free him from the feeling of guilt, but there is no return; he may *want* to conquer the skepticism with which the observation of reality filled him, but he must necessarily fail.

That is the meaning of the two artist dramas, *The Master Builder* and *When We Dead Awaken*. Solness, the protagonist of the former, began by building churches for the service of God. Then he turned to the erection of human habitations and learned the painful truth that men do not want new houses, but feel more content and happier in the old ones which they have inherited from their ancestors. Will Solness, at least, be able to enter his new home at the end of his career? Will he be able to climb the tower which he has erected, will he fulfill the hopes of his youth in his own self? No. In him, too, lives the past, and he falls to his death because he has risen too high above the everyday world, to the lonely heights upon which only that man can stand who is capable of freeing himself entirely from worldly ties.

The sculptor Rubek in *When We Dead Awaken* renounces the satisfaction of his sensual desires and those of his ardent model, in order to create the ideal statue of Resurrection. Then he allows himself to be seduced by his fame into making portrait busts for the sake of material profit; he remains faithful to his former search for truth by portraying, beneath the surface of his sculptures, the true animal nature of his patrons, only visible to careful, analytical observation. At the end of his productive career, however, he realizes the futility of these distortions. The model of his idealistic statue, in the meantime, has languished in an insane asylum, and his sensual wife has deserted him for a robust huntsman. This drama parallels Ibsen's own development: only by his complete emancipation from the idealistic tradition, which he had hitherto tried to uphold (and which is symbolized in the drama by the model and the plans for the Resurrection group), was Ibsen's naturalistic technique raised to the higher dignity of a secessionist art movement.

Was not his whole dramatic art a crime against life? Was not the transcendence of reality in phantastic creation merely an escape from the responsibilities of life? Was not the decision to live in solitude, which alone made his creative work possible, a renunciation of the most valuable things of human life? Solness hardens himself against the unhappiness of his wife and the creative efforts of his assistants for fear of being surpassed by a younger generation. Allmers in *Little Eyolf*, who intends to write a book on human responsibility, fails in his life's task because he remains, in spite of his striving, fundamentally a petty, revengeful egotist who has to bow to Rita's practical and concrete feeling of responsibility. John Gabriel Borkman's idealism is, on the whole, only a *postfacto* superstructure over an egotistical past, in which he has robbed thousands of their small savings by his phantastic plans; his withdrawal from life into the dreams of a future, in which his idealism will be justified, is but a new violation of the value of life. Finally, Rubek sinned against life by devoting himself exclusively to the ideal; and he violated the ideal, in turn, when he yielded to life. In this dilemma Ibsen concentrates the whole tragedy of his life and of the life of his period. The ideal is no longer effective enough to allow the sacrifice of actual wishes and desires to appear as justified. Life in the form in which it is found within and around us is not deep and immediately human enough; the vital energies are broken, instead of being placed in the service of humane values; they are harnessed to petrified forms of behavior, instead of being developed into the radiant virtue of disseminating inner richness. The question of whether the younger generation will be capable of fulfilling this hope has apparently also to be answered with a disconsolate "No." Youth may have the will to create, as did young Ragnar in *The Master Builder*; but youth, as represented by Erhard, Fanny Wilton, and Frida in *John Gabriel Borkman*, and by Maja in *When We Dead Awaken*, is in its superficiality, its sensualism, and its lack of responsibility only less restrained in its egotism than the preceding generation. While the older generation was still able to maintain the appearance of dignity in the pretense of an idealistic attitude, youth only falls back to a more animalistic stage of existence.

Ibsen finds in idealism the starting point of his dramatic creation. He leaves no doubt that idealistic beliefs and enthusiasms were still effective during his middle period, although he laments in his last, retrospective works the apostasy from the ideals of his youth. Idealism dominates his production as a desire for a free, responsible development of personality. All that changes in his successive plays is, in the last analysis, only the intensity with which he believes in possible realization of the highest values. Even his first drama, *Catiline,* betrays a certain distrust of the power of man to be entirely himself. Active and reactive contact with human society binds and fetters men in spite of their ideal intentions and degrades them to the level of materialistic and egotistic dependence. There remains only the late idealistic retreat into a world free from all striving for external values and content in the seclusion of the self; but it is doubtful whether man is still capable of freeing himself from the bonds of a demoralized society. In the nationalistic dramas which follow, also it is the tragedy of man that his will is prevented by material considerations or by his ambition from doing what unrestricted human sympathy and a higher sense of values would urge him to do. This failure of man in his devotion to the ideal is treated from a more generalized social viewpoint in *Love's Comedy.* Here it is the levelling influence of habit, which can only be overcome by a special decision of will; but this decision is still here presented at least as possible. King Haakon in *The Pretenders* is animated by a will to carry his ideal to victory. In *Brand,* the idealistic attitude reaches a climax; simultaneously, scepticism in the determination of human nature to follow the ideal breaks forth again. The superhuman efforts of one individual succeed in inspiring a whole community with the will to sacrifice for the ideal; but the expectation of a moment of material happiness destroys a work which has been created in years of self-denial. The compromise attitude that denies egotism in theory, but accepts it in practice seems to be the highest level to which the majority can be lifted. Human nature always yields to pleasure and meaningless existence for the moment. If the moral demand has any meaning at all for the majority, it is only as a regulative principle which may keep the average level at a higher point. But then human nature is so feeble, that the moral judgment must yield to sympathetic understanding. That is the real meaning of *Brand* and *Peer Gynt.*

If Ibsen later rejects the work of his second period as apostasy from the ideal, his self-reproach can be understood only on the basis of a fundamentally idealistic point of view. Actually his self-reproach is not justified. For, in fact, though only by implication his suppressed idealism forced him even in the plays of the second period to present the ideal as a principle which should regulate the life of man, in spite of the opposite, materialistic trend of the time. This self-reproach, however, is not justified, so far as Ibsen's analysis of human weaknesses and their conditions was motivated by the same idealistic will to help by understanding. In this effort he is driven into the tragic situation of one who understands and recognizes the depressing and the retarding factors of moral evolution as well-nigh insurmountable. Julian in *The Emperor and the Galilean* is in his longing for the Third Reich tied to the historical moment. His efforts are necessarily doomed to failure, because the tendencies which he represents have not yet gained the necessary momentum.

Although *League of Youth* and *Pillars of Society* are rather polemic in character, they mark a noticeable progress in the historical conception of man. The religious and the idealistic principles which had been a living issue in a higher social stratum have now fallen into the hands of political demagogues and into a society which is demoralized in its egotism; principles have disintegrated to slogans,—now they only serve (as in a more limited way in *Love's Comedy*) to conceal the miserable moral condition of the average man. If Consul Bernick in *Pillars of Society* grows beyond his environment and his own past, that merely shows Ibsen's desire that man could possibly be converted. In a more positive and deeper way, the attempt of the individual to revolt against a morality which has petrified into empty words and gestures is undertaken in *A Doll's House*. The question as to how far the struggling individual is himself dependent upon the prejudice of a dead past, is not yet answered in this drama.

The temporal stratification of the factors determining the human will—that is the simultaneous operation of habits and judgments developed in the past and of judgments based on the merits of the present situation—is clearly exposed only in *Ghosts*. Tradition is here conceived of as a power emotionally rooted in man, a power which he may check with the assistance of his intellect, but which makes itself felt with its old strength in all important decisions. Man remains inwardly exposed to the menace of traditional valuations and is always threatened in his existence by the decisions made under the rule of tradition. This double determination by past and present, that is historical stratification, is recognized as an important social factor in *An Enemy of the People*. In this drama the domination of tradition is no longer seen as a transitional and conquerable condition, but as an irrevocable tragedy. The masses can act only according to principles which in the course of years and decades have sunk from the higher level, where responsibility and an inner disposition for the experience of values prevail; they remain, therefore, necessarily slaves of tradition and are never able to reach the inner freedom of the "advance guard."

If this situation is inescapable, it follows that the sluggish masses deserve our sympathy or at least our toleration; understanding for them is expressed in *Brand* and *Peer Gynt*, although not fully developed. It becomes the principal theme in *The Wild Duck* in which Ibsen admits in painful resignation, but with unrelenting consistency, that the lie upon which the life of the masses is founded is best suited and most satisfactory for them, and absolute "truth," the regulation of human relations on the basis of an immediate, sympathetic reaction to the actual situation, is harmful for them. It cannot be expected that the unintelligent masses should independently regulate their lives if even the "advance guard," possessing such noble qualities as Rosmer does, remains emotionally dependent upon the past and incapable of founding a new life, with higher responsibility, on the spirit of love. Thus, Ibsen arrives at the conclusion that the moral achievement of man is essentially confined to growing, as a responsible member, into a group and contributing to its inner growth and happiness (*The Lady from the Sea*). The tragic result of modern civilization, however, is that, on the one hand, the traditional and mechanical regulation of life has broken the energy of mature intellects, and, on the other hand, the vitality of the unbroken man can hardly find a cause worthy of devotion (*Hedda Gabler*), and thus is driven into a senseless life of superficiality, materialism, and sensualism.

Ibsen's last dramas are essentially a retrospect over a life and a work which began with idealistic hopes and was disillusioned by the general materialistic tendencies of the time. His work as a whole expresses a growing recognition that man is less a free individual than an integral part of a community. As such, he is either completely determined by the habits of the group to which he belongs or he tries to contribute to its advancement. Even the most undetermined character, however, carries his historical burden, from which he can hardly ever free himself completely, and thus even he will never be able to come to an absolute decision based only upon the value of the actual situation. It would be easier for the natural man whose vitality is not broken by tradition to give life a greater depth and meaning through the assumption of responsibility, as Rebekka does in *Rosmersholm* and Rita, in *Little Eyolf*. The failure to control vitality through some responsibility, as is apparent in the young people in *John Gabriel Borkman*, is but a liberation of animal nature and not an elevation of mankind, which was Ibsen's hope and aim. This also determines Ibsen's place in literary history with regard to his naturalistic followers. With his "historical" and existential conception of man, he marks the transition from idealistic indeterminism to a radical, deterministic naturalism, which denies that man can be held responsible for his actions. What distinguishes him from these younger poets is the fact that the idealistic faith of his youth remains a decisive factor in his practical and theoretical attitude toward life throughout, and that he only reluctantly relinquishes hope that life will and should be essentially enriched and deepened by making man free to respond sympathetically to the situations confronting him.